DAVE'S LAST LAUGH

June 5, 1991. David Letterman is devastated. The news he has been dreading is in every newspaper, on every television station: his friend Jay Leno has been chosen to succeed Johnny Carson on *The Tonight Show*.

The dream Dave had nurtured since he was a kid in Indiana is dead.

August 30, 1993. After a furious bidding war that ultimately brought him $14 million a year, the *Late Show with David Letterman* debuts on CBS. Even without "Stupid Pet Tricks" (which NBC has declared its "intellectual property"), it consistently beats *The Tonight Show* in the ratings.

The Late-Night Wars are over. And the guy with the gap-toothed grin is laughing all the way to the bank.

DAVID LETTERMAN:
ON STAGE AND OFF

ROSEMARIE LENNON

PINNACLE BOOKS
WINDSOR PUBLISHING CORP.

PINNACLE BOOKS are published by

Windsor Publishing Corp.
850 Third Avenue
New York, NY 10022

First Printing: June, 1994

Printed in the United States of America

To my parents, Lawrence and Frances Lennon,
for their unconditional love and unswerving support.

Acknowledgments

My thanks to Dick Belsky and Marion Collins for giving me the time off to write this book; to *Star* magazine for the generous use of their library (not to mention their copying machine); to Melissa Key, Carolyn Callahan, and Cathy Caruso for their help and encouragement; and to Christopher, for being divine throughout.

Contents

Prologue

June 5, 1991. David Letterman was furious. He was also frustrated, bewildered, and deeply hurt. The news he had been dreading was in every newspaper: Jay Leno would be taking over as host of *The Tonight Show* when Johnny Carson retired in May of the following year.

It hadn't come as a surprise to Dave—he had been informed of the decision the night before by the NBC network brass, who had flown in to New York from Los Angeles to break the news to Letterman. Dave had responded by asking to be let out of the two years remaining on his NBC contract and walking out of the meeting. He knew in his heart, though, that he had lost the fight for *The Tonight Show,* which had started earlier that year when rumors began spreading that Johnny was ready to step down. He had managed to maintain a small shred of hope. Until the formal announcement was made to the press, Letterman prayed that NBC would come to its senses and see that he was the natural successor to the *Tonight Show* spot, the rightful heir to the Johnny Carson legacy. Maybe his strong showing at the meeting would lead to an eleventh hour reversal of the decision he knew NBC had come to months earlier.

For Letterman, losing *The Tonight Show* represented the death of a dream he had nurtured since childhood.

The first time young David saw cool, debonair Carson

on television, Johnny was hosting an afternoon game show called *Who Do You Trust?*

"I was mesmerized," recalls Letterman. "It just seemed effortlessly funny to me."

Years later, when Dave would watch Carson holding court on *The Tonight Show,* he knew that's what he wanted to do, too. Someday, the shy, insecure teenager told himself, he would sit in the King of Late Night's chair. It was a lofty goal, to be sure, but one that David, from that day forward, spent his adult life working toward.

He had begun his preparation in college, majoring in radio and television at Ball State University in Muncie, Indiana. While still in school, he had landed a part-time job as a fill-in television announcer. Unlike most of his classmates, who goofed around until graduation day, Letterman had a broadcasting job at WLWI-TV in Indianapolis waiting for him when he graduated in 1969. He spent the next five years honing his broadcasting skills in a series of radio and television jobs in his hometown, Indianapolis.

By 1975, he felt he had taken his broadcasting career as far as he could in Indianapolis. So he packed up his life and headed to Los Angeles, determined to crack that broadcasting market. When friends suggested he try his hand at stand-up comedy, he overcame his fear of performing before a live audience and auditioned at the Comedy Store, then the premier comedy club in L.A., where most young comics got their start.

More important, it was the place the Carson scouts went to look for new comedic talent to bring on the show.

For three long years he labored at his craft, perfecting his comedy routine until it was flawless. In 1978, the call finally came: *The Tonight Show* wanted him.

Letterman was an instant hit with Carson, who knew a

star when he saw one. After just three appearances, Carson told his producers he wanted David Letterman to guest-host for him. It was the swiftest move from a stand-up spot to guest-hosting in the history of *The Tonight Show.*

Carson wasn't disappointed with his protégé. Letterman was so adept at hosting that he became Johnny's most frequent replacement, hosting the show twenty-nine times. Word quickly spread around the *Tonight Show* studio that Johnny had finally found his heir.

When Letterman went on to do his own late-night show in 1981, it only seemed to seal the deal. Who else would slip into the 11:30 P.M. spot when Johnny retired but the man who followed him at 12:30 A.M. so successfully?

He couldn't believe that the dream had slipped away. The most heartbreaking part of all was that he had come so very close.

Part One
The Early Years

Chapter One
A DREAM IS BORN

David Letterman was born on April 12, 1947, the middle child and only son of Joseph and Dorothy Letterman of Indianapolis, Indiana. Both his parents were children of miners who eventually became farmers.

David and his sisters, Janice—now a married mother of two in Indiana, and Gretchen—a married mother of one who writes editorials for Florida's *St. Petersburg Times*—enjoyed a comfortable, middle-class existence. Joe owned a flower shop and, mainly to pass her time, Dorothy worked as church secretary for the Second Presbyterian Church in Broad Ripple, Indiana. The family lived in a modest home on a lovely tree-lined street and attended church together every Sunday.

"It was right on the money for lower-middle-class mid-American family life," says Letterman.

Young David was fascinated with broadcasting at a very young age. When he received an Erector set as a young boy, a friend from childhood recalls, the first thing he did was build himself a microphone. He never sang into his fake microphone, like most kids would. He'd give speeches into it. Or tell jokes. Or make commercial announcements. Or introduce guests.

Dave wanted to be a broadcaster.

Sometimes he'd pretend to be Arthur Godfrey, one of his favorite television performers. He'd practice announcing his next guest, or tell stories and joke with the audience, just like Godfrey did.

Aside from his obsession with broadcasting, Dave was your average Midwestern boy. He loved playing sports. He was in Little League all through grade school and ran track in high school. He attended Sunday school every week and, though he wasn't terribly religious, became president of his church's youth group as a social outlet.

He was also industrious, getting up before dawn every day to deliver newspapers so he could have a little spending money. When he was old enough to get his working papers, he got a job packing bags at the Atlas Supermarket in Broad Ripple.

He made a lot of local housewives angry those first few days on the job, when he was arbitrarily shoving five-pound sacks of sugar on top of bags of potato chips. But as soon as an older, experienced cashier took him aside and explained the physics of packing groceries, he excelled at his job. To this day, he remembers her name: Mildred.

He spoke of the job lovingly to Pat Hackett of *Interview* magazine:

"All my friends worked there and we had a lot of fun and we got to steal as much beer as we could. I worked there for three years, sacking groceries and pricing cans and working in the butcher department and checking out groceries. Looking back, it was one of the best jobs I ever had."

To this day he loves packing his own purchases.

"There's something very satisfying about taking $100 worth of groceries and neatly and orderly assembling them into four well-balanced bags," Dave told the *Philadelphia Inquirer.*

"And then you take them to your car and you go home and you have the satisfaction of unpacking them. It's physically and aesthetically quite pleasing and relaxing. I know I sound like a complete fool here, but it's the truth."

David was an indefatigable child. Despite his sports and his job and his friends and school, he had energy left over and not enough outlets for it. Like many bright kids, he was smart but he hated to sit still long enough to study. Consequently he did not do very well in school. Dave's poor grades were the source of a lot of tension in the Letterman household, particularly because his sisters did so well with their studies.

His mother, Dorothy, was not just concerned that David wasn't applying himself in school. She was worried that this silly dream he had of becoming a broadcaster was standing in the way of Dave pursuing a sensible course of study, like engineering or accounting. Then there was the matter of the after-school job. Dorothy was pleased he had taken on the responsibility, but she knew darn well that he and his friends spent just as much time drinking beer as working.

Dorothy used to wonder out loud how he was going to succeed at anything if he didn't hit the books and raise his grades. Even easygoing Joe backed her on that one. The Lettermans just couldn't understand how this crazy kid who wanted to be on television and radio could be their child. Their daughters were so easy . . . so normal.

"My parents and I had huge fights over my grades, which were mostly C's and D's," he told the *New York Daily News* in a 1983 interview.

"My sisters were both good students and I was the disappointment. In my high school, there was a top 10 percent on the honor roll, a bottom 10 percent stealing cars, and a middle 80 percent—where I was—just going through the motions."

While Dorothy continued to badger her son about the way he was ruining his life, his father—whom he adored—secretly supported his son's ambitions. Joe Letterman was somewhat of a prankster himself, always telling bad jokes and generally acting silly around the house, much to the consternation of Dorothy, who was much more cerebral and serious.

Dorothy didn't know what to make of her only son, who was obviously bright but did poorly in school, was obviously personable but could count his friends on one hand. All she knew was that David was a constant source of disruption in the Letterman household.

"The house I grew up in was nuts because I was there," he told *TV Guide* last year.

"I was a maniac. From the time I was 6 until I was 16, there wasn't a peaceful minute. I was always picking fights, starting trouble. I don't think there was a single meal where my mother didn't have to say, 'All right, David. If you can't behave, take your plate and eat outside.' Maybe it was all that estrogen. One older sister, one younger—it was like, 'Hey! I'm fightin' for my life here!' But what I put those poor folks through!"

A neighbor told reporters Jim Nelson and Denny Johnson that when Dave was about eight years old, he and his little friends once banded together to build a tree house. That seemed innocent enough, until it was discovered that they were using it to position their mirrors and shine the sun into the windshields of oncoming motorists! Their high jinks almost caused a few serious car accidents.

Dave was very close to his father, who shared his nutty sense of humor. Joe tried to see the funny side of every situation, a trait Dave obviously inherited, judging from the way he can make a simple stroll down Broadway a hilarious segment on his show.

Joe secretly encouraged his son to pursue his dream, never mind what Dorothy said about him ending up in the poorhouse.

It's a source of much sadness to the *Late Show* host that his father died before David realized any of his dreams.

Joe passed away in 1974.

"He was goofy-funny," Dave recalls of his beloved dad. "Told a lot of corny jokes, did a lot of silly things, mostly calculated to keep the house in an uproar."

Dorothy was more reserved and didn't think Joe was doing their son any good by encouraging his silly antics instead of demanding better grades. And she scoffed at the notion that Dave would someday earn a living with his kidding.

But Dave knew differently. He may have been insecure in other areas, unpopular with the girls, not admired by most of the boys, but he knew at a very young age that he had a talent for comedy. The problem was convincing his solid, conventional parents that he could make a living at it. He was determined to study radio and broadcasting. Dorothy thought it was a foolish waste of time that would put him smack on the road to nowhere.

Luckily, David had faith in his abilities. His mother could cluck her tongue all she wanted at the idea of him becoming a broadcaster; he was going to do it. And he was going to succeed. He was going to make his easygoing father proud and make his doubting Thomas mother sit up and take notice.

From Dave's point of view, he had no choice but to go into broadcasting. It was the only thing he could do well. It may not have been the easiest field to crack, but, the way he saw it, there was nothing else he had a natural ability for.

"Early on I realized I had this one little tool," he says.

"I could make people laugh. The problem was, where? How? What am I going to do? Join the circus? In the meantime, my family is convinced I'm gonna go through life being a wiseass. I wasn't in the smart classes in high school, I couldn't do math. I couldn't learn German. So instead of college courses, I was getting put into things like general merchandising."

His four years at Broad Ripple High School don't hold the best memories for Dave. He was a bit of an outsider, longing to fit in with the groups considered cool, but never being accepted into any of them. So he hung around with a few other guys who didn't belong anywhere, either. They drank too much, smoked too much, earned money for their beer and pot at the local supermarket, and basically daydreamed their way through high school.

They also made a sport out of mocking their fellow classmates, the ones who thought themselves too good to include Dave and his friends in their crowd.

Those early, painful experiences of being left on the sidelines, just because he wasn't especially handsome or the football captain, left Dave with a lifelong distrust of the so-called beautiful people. He finds many celebrities shallow and pretentious and refuses to be swept into their world. Though he is on the A list himself these days, he eschews almost all Hollywood functions, preferring to hang out with the friends he's made among the *Late Night* staff.

Perhaps it's the snooty beauty queens at Broad Ripple

High who wouldn't give gap-toothed young Dave the time of day that Letterman is subconsciously thinking about when he feels the overwhelming need to knock a Hollywood starlet down a peg or two on his talk show.

David admits that he was always on the outside looking in as a teenager. And the way he dealt with it—the way most people react when they find themselves in a place they are not wanted—was to pretend he really didn't want to be there anyway.

"I had two or three friends," Dave recalls. "We made fun of anything we couldn't do. I was never with the really good-looking kids; and I was never with the really great athletes. But there was always a small pocket of people I hung out with, and all we did was make fun of the really good-looking people and make fun of the really smart kids and make fun of the great athletes."

Dave wasn't as big a loser as he tries to make himself out to be. What set him apart from his classmates at Broad Ripple High was that, unlike most of them, he had big dreams. He really wasn't as aimless and shiftless as he pretended to be as he stood on the sidelines mocking the kids from the Science Club. He just acted that way because that's how kids try to maintain their pride when they're rejected by the various school cliques.

Though he pretended to be too cool to be thinking about his future, he was thinking about it very much. He knew he wanted to be a broadcaster someday; he just hadn't yet figured out a way to make his dream a reality. Biology and algebra were not the way to go, so why bother? But he also knew that he was going to have to pin this thing down soon or he was going to end up stocking shelves and bagging groceries in Indiana for the rest of his life.

"There was a period in high school and maybe that's

when it comes for everybody, when you sort of had to figure out who you were," he told *Entertainment Weekly.*

"You think, 'Well, I'm not fitting in with this group, the really desirable blue-chip group, and I'm not fitting into that group.' And then you start to examine your own inventory and think, 'Is there anything I can do that is going to make me desirable or make me different?' "

What made Dave different, he had long ago realized, was his talent for comedy, his ability to see the absurdity in everyday occurrences, his penchant for performing. While his mother worried that he was wasting his time dreaming about a career that could never be when he should have been focusing on the studies at hand, Dave was actually as worried about his future as his mom was, and desperately trying to figure out what he was going to do with his life. Then it came to him.

He described his epiphany to *TV Guide.*

"Then one day I realized, 'I'm just as smart as my friends. But while they're studying calculus, I'm sittin' here reading a book about how to make a pleasing display of canned goods.' So I took a class in speech and just loved it. For the first time in my formal academic experience there was a subject that seemed to come easily to me, more easily than algebra or geometry or shop. I was not very bright, and may not be very bright in the rest of my life, but at that time it was clear to me that this was something to remember. That this was a valuable lesson.

"I thought, 'Wait a minute, how do you apply this?' And when I found out you could study broadcasting in college, I thought, 'Holy Cow! There you go! It's a miracle! What's next?' And what was next was figuring out how to get on the radio."

He also dreamed of being on television someday. Perhaps

because Joe and Dorothy severely limited the amount of time their three children could watch TV, Dave became obsessed with it.

Besides Carson, one of Dave's early influences was *The Arthur Godfrey Show.* He recounts his fascination with Godfrey to interviewer Steven Rea:

"The start of the show began with a shot of an empty headset. Big radio headphones dangling from a cord in front of a microphone, everything being as it would normally except that Arthur's head wasn't in the headphone. I liked the way the headphones and the microphone looked. And I thought, 'This stuff looks great.' It made a real impression on me."

By senior year in high school, Dave was no longer floundering. He had applied to and been accepted to nearby Ball State University, which had an excellent communications department. For the first time in his academic life, he was excited about school. He no longer felt he was just going through the motions, doing the minimum amount of work he could get away with to pass a subject he saw no use for in real life. Finally, he could channel some of that pent-up energy toward a real goal. His parents may have thought him daft, but he knew he had finally hit on something worth working for. He could hardly wait to begin college classes and get started. He'd finally be learning the mechanics behind the radio and television shows that had long fascinated him. And he'd finally have a legitimate outlet for his humor. He wanted to take writing courses so he could learn how to apply his humor to the written page. If he couldn't actually be on radio or television, though he was going to do everything to see that that happened, he could perhaps write scripts for his favorite comedy shows. All his life he had felt like a nobody, sleepwalking his way through his studies, wondering what the world could possibly have in store for him. Now he knew that there was a way to start tackling his dream. He could hardly wait to get started.

Chapter Two
CHASING THE DREAM

David Letterman was one of those lucky people who knew exactly what he wanted to do with his life from a very early age. It astounds him that not everyone is so clear-sighted about their career goals.

"You know, when I hear about a kid getting out of school and not knowing what he wants to do, I'm dumbfounded. What are you good at? Figure it out! If you want to fly to California you go to a travel agent and buy a ticket. And you get there."

Though David knew without a doubt what he wanted to do with his life, he was afraid to tell his parents. Joe and Dorothy didn't put much stock in what they considered to be frivolous activities, like watching television and going to the movies. They couldn't imagine their wisecracking son making such nonsense his life work.

"When I was a kid I never really went to movies. In my house, going to movies was pretty much equated with as big a waste of time as you could come by as a human."

They didn't think much of television, either.

Whenever his parents caught him lounging around watching TV, Dave recalls, they'd make him "go outside and do something real."

He adds, only half-kiddingly, that Joe and Dorothy regarded television as the "work of Satan."

Naturally, their young son loved to watch television, especially variety shows and comedies.

"When I got to an age where I could appreciate comedians it was guys like Jonathan Winters," Dave told *Time* magazine.

"He used to really make me laugh. I also liked the Steve Allen show. And after school I used to watch 'Who Do You Trust?' with Johnny Carson."

In spite of his parents' skepticism, Dave began chasing his broadcaster dream with gusto, enrolling in Ball State University as a communications major. He joined the Sigma Chi fraternity and enjoyed his share of college high jinks.

"It was fun, it was great social maturation for me—or thwarting of social maturation—but, you know, we'd just drink as much beer as we possibly could and sneak as many girls as we could into the fraternity house and we'd make fun of the people who lived in dorms and that was it," he told Pat Hackett of *Interview* magazine.

"For some people a fraternity does become a lifelong center of business contacts. They'll call you up in Phoenix and say, 'Well, I was a brother and so on, and what do you know about the Henderson account?' It's a big network for businessmen, but I never really fit into that. I mean, I didn't go to homecoming, and I didn't marry the Sweetheart of Sigma Chi."

Though Letterman attended college in the mid-sixties, he never got involved in the campus protests that were so prevalent back then.

Indeed, the only thing he ever protested, he says, was that the cafeteria cooks didn't wear hairnets. To this day, he stays out of politics.

"We were amazingly isolated," Dave told the *New York Sunday News Magazine.*

"I was only vaguely aware of the political turmoil of the time. The big thing was to get as drunk as possible as early in the day as possible so you would be conscious for the least amount of time. College enables young people to be stupider longer with minimal jeopardy. In fact, that was the shield of my fraternity in Latin: Stupider Longer."

Dave obviously has fond memories of his times at Ball State University; he's donated hundreds of thousands of dollars to the college since he graduated in 1969. But this time his boozing and fooling around were different. They weren't his whole life. He loved his radio and television classes, loved to hang around the campus radio station. Despite the high jinks that went on, Dave managed to keep his eye on the eight ball: breaking into broadcasting. David's parents needn't have worried about him. He may have been aimless in high school, but once in college he was a man with a mission. And Dave was ambitious. He wasn't content to sit back and wait until graduation. He wanted to get his career rolling as soon as possible, so he applied for broadcasting positions while he was still in college and landed a summer job as a replacement announcer at a local television station.

Like so many college students, Dave found himself drinking heavily during his university years. In fact, he had started to worry that he might have a drinking problem. Getting the broadcasting job gave him the motivation to quit. He was not going to let anything stand in the way of his brilliant career. So he got off the sauce and got down to business, arriving early at the station and staying late.

"Four years of drinking in the morning is enough for anybody, unless you're looking at it as a career. Instead, I got a job as a TV announcer in Indianapolis. I had to get there early to sign on, so that was the end of my all-day beer consumption."

Broadcasting didn't disappoint him. Letterman loved his television job, as he knew he would. He loved to wander around the station, asking questions, observing the crew, watching how things worked. He was fascinated by it all, and it just made him all the more convinced that he had chosen the right career.

What most amazed him about the job was that he didn't find it intimidating at all. Since he was just a college kid doing voice-overs and occasionally reading the news when someone was sick, there was little expected of him and little pressure on him. Naturally, the boy born to broadcast excelled. He even allowed himself to have a little fun with his assignments, slipping in an amusing comment here and there. No one seemed to mind. In fact, they were impressed with the tall, skinny college kid who was so full of zest for the job.

"It was a great time," he told *Time* magazine. "My first television job was while I was still in college, and I was hired against all odds by a station in Indianapolis. I started as a voice-over announcer doing station identifications. Then, gradually, through vacation schedules and attrition, I got to do morning news once; got to host a kids' show once; ended up doing everything you can. It was great fun because there was no pressure. I could pretty much do whatever I wanted, and nobody cared because I was always the fill-in guy. What you learn there is that television is the same at that level and at this level. In fact, here maybe a little lower."

During summer vacations, David worked as a booth announcer and weekend weatherman with the ABC-TV affiliate in Indianapolis. That's when he really started to test his comedic talents—and the limits of the station manager—by cracking such jokes during the weather as "We can expect hail the size of canned hams."

(No one knows where Dave's obsession with canned hams originates, but to this day it's a staple of his comedy. During the 1994 Winter Olympics, with his mother acting as his special correspondent, he directed Dorothy to present Gold Medalist downhill racer Tommy Moe with a canned ham at the finish line.)

When Dave was a senior at Ball State, he started to wonder how he could apply his comedy to a broadcasting career. Again, he didn't leave anything to chance. He started writing letters to every broadcast figure he could think of, beseeching them for career advice.

Gary Owens, most famous for his gig as the *Laugh-In* announcer, received a heartbreakingly earnest letter from the then unknown Letterman while Dave was still in college, asking Owens for help.

"I am a senior in college," the letter began.

"And I have spent the last three years in the field of commercial broadcasting, working and studying. While I enjoy, and find challenge in broadcasting, I have come to realize that is only because it gives me an opportunity to use material which I have written myself. I would enjoy a career in radio and television only if it would involve creative writing, more specifically, comedy. The problem is, however, that I don't know how to get a job as a writer."

Even though Dave was deadly serious, and wanted to be taken seriously, he couldn't resist adding some of his now trademark humor.

"I have had several occasions to perform my material successfully, but unfortunately I don't pay myself to write jokes. When I graduate in June, I have a job waiting in Indianapolis with the ABC television affiliate.

" 'Hot Diggity' you may be saying to yourself by now, but I would rather be a writer."

The letter ends with Letterman's plea for any career advice Gary Owens could offer. Owens wrote back, suggesting Letterman get himself a good agent.

"I could see the creative spark," says Owens.

His love life had also taken a serious turn. He had begun dating a pretty brunette named Michelle Cook. Michelle, a choral music major, was a statuesque beauty, six feet tall to Dave's six foot two. For a guy who had experienced nothing but rejection in his four years of high school, not even managing to scrounge a date for the senior prom, Michelle was a godsend.

Michelle wasn't just pretty and smart; she was supportive. She didn't scoff at his dream of becoming a famous broadcaster or scriptwriter someday; she cheered him on. Whenever he'd get discouraged, Michelle was there to boost him back up. They became inseparable and, while still in senior year, they went to a justice of the peace and eloped. Dave was just twenty-one.

They were poor, living in an apartment furnished with a neighbor's borrowed lawn furniture, but they were happy.

When they graduated in 1969, Dave took a job at the ABC station where he had worked during his school breaks. He was mainly responsible for the weather, but he took whatever jobs he could get his hands on to broaden his experience, even if they weren't terribly desirable. And he began sending out demo tapes of his work, hoping to be hired by a bigger affiliate.

"At various times I did kid shows, a late-night movie

show, anything that nobody else wanted to do," he told the *Chicago Tribune Magazine*.

It was good all-around experience, because it allowed Dave to get his feet wet in many areas of broadcasting and figure out which one he wanted to concentrate on. He knew early on, for example, that he did not want to be one of the talking heads who read the evening news.

"I had no desire to be an anchorman because in the early '70's the idea was that the TV news should be as slick and straight as possible. There was not much an anchorman could do besides read what was on the TelePrompTer."

Even though announcing storm patterns was not the sort of broadcast job Dave had in mind for himself in the beginning, he began to warm up to it, mainly because he found that he was able to slip in a little comedy along the way. For a while, he fashioned himself after a popular local weatherman who made it out of Indianapolis.

"I always thought I'd be the next John Coleman, the likable, funny weatherman who eventually got hired out of the market. And I never did. I'd send tapes out to stations in major cities, and rarely would I get a tape back, let alone an answer to my job application. So I began to goof around, which meant that sometimes we'd get huge complaints because Indianapolis is at the center of an agricultural area where a lot of people depend on the weather for their livelihood."

Sometimes his humor got him into trouble.

"I remember one night we reported that a tropical storm had just been raised to hurricane status. Well, I was amused by that phraseology and suggested that viewers send postcards to the storm, congratulating it on having made the step up to the major leagues. Of course, the next day it killed 8 million people and removed all of South Florida—

the most devastating hurricane in years. So I felt a little sorry about that."

On another occasion, he waited for the camera to pan to the weather map and announced, "The higher-ups have been at it again. As you can see they've removed the border between Ohio and Indiana, making it one big state."

He implored his audience not to stand for this.

"I just couldn't resist the temptation to just sort of goof around with the weather," says Dave.

Just imagine: If Dave had stuck with weather, he could have ended up being more of a nightmare to Bryant Gumbel than Willard Scott is.

"I guess it was immaturity more than anything else. It was kind of like goofing off in church—you do it to see what you could get away with."

In 1974, David had had enough of tracking weather patterns and began sending his resumé around. He landed a job on Indianapolis radio station WNTS for $16,000 a year. It was an all-talk radio station and Dave was assigned the afternoon drive-time show, a call-in show.

One would think that a radio talk show à la Howard Stern would be right up quick-witted Dave's alley, but it wasn't.

It was one job he says he never became comfortable with, though he tried to have fun with it the way he had played around with the weather.

Dave is not a man to suffer fools gladly, and he found it exasperating to have to take phone calls from total strangers, especially if he couldn't make fun of them. Worse, the callers mainly wanted to discuss politics, the one topic that opinionated Dave had little to say about.

"It was around the time of Watergate and most of our callers thought homosexuals and people from Jupiter were behind it all."

Perhaps if Dave could have cut loose like Howard Stern, he might have found himself in his element. But this was supposed to be a serious talk show, with Dave amiably conversing with listeners on a variety of topics. He found it just wasn't in his nature to feign interest where there was none.

"I hated it. I was miscast because you have to have somebody who is fairly knowledgeable, fairly glib, possessing a natural interest in a number of topics. That certainly is not me. I don't care about politics; I don't care about the world economy; I don't care about Martians cleaning our teeth."

So he took the same tack he did with his weatherman gig: He began to make jokes.

One day he told startled listeners that their treasured 230-foot Soldier's Monument had been sold to the island of Guam, who planned to paint it green in honor of the asparagus, their national vegetable.

That, to the station manager's chagrin, generated more than a few calls from worried listeners, who were then embarrassed and furious to learn that they had been duped.

It was at WNTS that Dave began having fun with celebrities, many of whom have remained his favorite targets/friends to this day.

Across town, *Dateline* host Jane Pauley, also a native of Indiana, was making a name for herself as an anchor at a local TV station. She was frequently Dave's victim when he tried to relieve the boredom of the job.

Pretty, kind Jane Pauley was a natural target for Dave's mischievous humor because she had such a wholesome, girl-next-door reputation in town.

When news and calls were slow one day, Dave decided to announce that Jane had gotten married. (She had not.) He urged his listeners to send the popular broadcaster cards and presents. Many did. Jane was mortified. Dave recalls those days for *The Chicago Tribune:*

"I was doing the kind of radio talk show where you get the guy from the Elbow Foundation or the woman who has 167 fig recipes and I just didn't care anymore. So I'd announce that Jane had been married and wait for her to call up seething."

Jane and David eventually became good friends, and remain close to this day. She's an occasional guest on his show.

"I always know I will not get the respect due my position when I go on *Late Night,*" Jane jokes.

In fact, Dave is so fond of Jane that he was furious when she was pushed aside by NBC in 1989 in favor of Deborah Norville. Dave had always had a prickly relationship with NBC executives, and that bonehead move, one that proved as disastrous to NBC's ratings as losing David Letterman would years later, did not endear themselves to him any further. Dave thought NBC treated Jane very shabbily when they rewarded her years of loyal service by pushing her to the side of the *Today* couch to make room for prettier, blonder, younger Deborah Norville.

David doesn't have many friends—in some ways he's still that high-school guy with three or four buddies who stand around making fun of everybody else—but when he makes friends, they're pals for life.

If you've ever watched Dave's easy banter with actress Teri Garr on *Late Night,* you won't be surprised to learn that one of Dave's first personality interviews was with Garr in 1974, when she was promoting her movie *Young Frankenstein.*

"He was exactly the same," she recalls.

"He said, 'So you live in Hollywood. What kind of car do you drive?' "

They had a terrific rapport, and Teri remains one of Dave's favorite guests. Though they don't socialize at all outside the show—Dave doesn't socialize with anyone much outside the show—Teri has appeared more times on his show than any other woman.

Despite the fun of occasionally needling Jane Pauley or alarming the good people of Indianapolis with some crazy announcement, Dave eventually got tired of his radio show.

Always a methodical planner, he decided to set his sights on television this time. His beginnings were modest, to be sure: His first full-time TV gig was hosting a 4-H Club TV show called *Clover Power*.

To this day, Dave isn't sure how to describe the program, which featured children and their agricultural school projects. Basically, it spotlighted kids who hoped to be future farmers of America.

"We made fun of little kids," is how Dave sums it up.

Not surprisingly, the talented young comic did not find that gig terribly fulfilling. Dave hadn't given up on his dream of incorporating humor into his broadcasting work, he just hadn't figured out a way to do it that wouldn't get him in hot water with the various station managers.

Perhaps, he thought, he should forget broadcasting altogether and concentrate on his other love, comedy writing. But what if he quit his job and never found broadcasting work again? Though he had achieved some success in Indianapolis—at the very least, he had worked steadily in his chosen career—he wasn't exactly setting the other affiliates on fire. New York, Los Angeles, and Chicago stations had yet to come calling. No one was exactly beating on his door to make him a major star in broadcasting circles. It began to depress and upset Dave, a man known to have more than his share of dark moods.

At night he'd go home and write scripts for *The Mary Tyler Moore Show,* knowing full well that they'd end up in someone's wastebasket, or what's known in the business as the circular file.

Michelle hated seeing how unhappy her husband was so one night she sat him down and told him she had a solution: If the major players weren't coming to young Dave Letterman of Indianapolis, they would go to them. They'd move to where the action was for a talented, funny, young man. They'd move to Hollywood.

Michelle told Dave she supported him one hundred percent in his dream to become a comedy writer. Actually, she was more than supportive. She was willing to make it happen for him. It was Michelle who convinced Dave that if he really wanted to make it big they had to take a chance. They had to quit their jobs, sell everything, pull up stakes, and move to Los Angeles. Dave hesitated; Michelle insisted. He had the talent to make it. She knew it and he knew it. And while he was writing comedy scripts for *The Mary Tyler Moore Show* or whatever it was he wanted to do, Michelle would support them. After all, she had a more conventional career—she was a clothes buyer—and she could get a job anywhere, certainly in a city as large as Los Angeles. When Dave still hesitated, Michelle simply announced that they were moving and started packing up their belongings. Dave finally saw the logic in moving.

"I was too unhappy with myself to stay in Indianapolis," says Dave. "If you're secure with yourself, then regardless of where you are, you're happy and you lead a productive life, and have kids and go to Rotary meetings and you have, you know, just a great life. But if you're insecure like me and millions of other young airheads, you move to Los Angeles and entertain drunks in bars. Or try to."

Telling his mother (his dad had died in 1974) he was going to Los Angeles wasn't easy. To put a more conventional spin on his dream of becoming a radio or TV star, Dave told her he was going to Hollywood to pursue work as a writer.

"It was easier to explain to the family than—'What? You're going to be a circus performer? What? What's he doing?' "

Dorothy was still skeptical, but at least Dave had a loving wife to help him. If Michelle wanted to support him while he pursued his foolish fantasies, well, he was a grown man, after all. He had just turned twenty-eight.

Dave never fails to credit Michelle with encouraging him to quit his job, pack his bags, and go for broke in Hollywood.

She was enthusiastic. He was certain they were headed for disaster.

"She started running around and packing the dishes and telling me this time we were really gonna do it. She was very supportive. I knew I was going to fail."

Chapter Three
HOORAY FOR HOLLYWOOD

Michelle and Dave arrived in L.A. excited and scared. They were somewhat relieved when Michelle got a job as an assistant buyer for the May Company. She told Dave to relax (as much as a hyperactive individual like Letterman can ever relax); she wanted him to just stay home and pursue his writing. Over and over she'd remind him: You have the talent and I know you're going to succeed. You just have to get down to it and do it.

Dave, an old-fashioned kind of guy, was appreciative but not terribly comfortable with not being the breadwinner. Or at least a breadwinner.

"It was the first time in my adult life I didn't have a real job," he recalls.

Still, he knew that if he didn't want to spend the rest of his days taking calls from bored housewives and nutcases on two-bit radio stations in the Midwest, he had to listen to Michelle. At least now they were where the action was. If he was going to be a comedy writer, he had to be in the place where deals were sealed, scripts were sold, contacts were made.

"I went to Los Angeles because I had done everything in local broadcasting that I could and I still wasn't getting hired out of the market," he later told the *St. Louis Post-Dispatch*.

"I'd watch network TV and think, 'Jeez, I'm at least that funny,' so I wrote a bunch of scripts and went to L.A."

When Dave arrived in Los Angeles, the last thing he had on his mind was becoming a stand-up comedian. He had no desire to make a fool of himself in front of a room full of people by attempting to perform his own material. He wanted to write witty lines for other people. Sure, he had had his share of fun at the weather station and with the talk radio program, but that was a whole lot different from performing to a group of people who are there with the full expectation that you are going to make them laugh—who have *paid* to have someone make them laugh. And, as everyone knows, comedy club audiences are the toughest audiences around. It's the hardest thing in the world to make people laugh. And people are not inclined to laugh politely at a paid performer the way they do when their boss or a close friend makes a feeble attempt to tell a bad joke.

The thought of walking on stage and telling jokes was enough to make Dave break out into a cold sweat. After all, he was the kid who stood on the sidelines and amused his friends by making fun of other people. No way was he going to put himself in the position of being mocked. He had no desire to be the one on display, being judged, the way he used to snicker at other people. The very idea terrified him, as it would most people. Studies have shown that speaking in front of an audience is the number one fear, worse than the fear of dying. Standing in front of people and trying to make them laugh puts that situation on a whole other stratospheric level of terror.

But Dave was ambitious and he was willing to do whatever it was he had to to make his dreams come true. He slowly came to realize that he was going to have to get over this stand-up anxiety of his if he were going to succeed.

After many months of trying, his comedy scripts remained unsold—not because they weren't good but because of the unbelievable competition in Hollywood. Hell, most of them probably hadn't even been read by the people he had mailed them to. At least, that's what friends told him. They weren't just humoring him either. They recognized that Dave was a funny guy; he could write funny things. And the fastest way to make a name for yourself if you're funny—you could write scripts later—was to perform your own material at the comedy clubs dotting Los Angeles. Everybody knew that *The Tonight Show* routinely sent scouts around to find new talent. If you were good—and David was—a spot on *The Tonight Show* could make your career. Then doors would be open to Dave that just weren't unlocking for an unknown from Indiana.

Dave recalled for *Playboy* how surprised he was to find himself doing stand-up.

"I told everyone, including myself, that I was going to L.A. to become a television scriptwriter. I thought that would be my best entry point into the business. . . . I'd take my scripts around and they'd toss them into a warehouse, and every Thursday, the guy with the forklift would go by, pick up all the scripts and bury them near the river."

It was his failure at scriptwriting, ironically, that ultimately launched his career as a comedian.

"When I couldn't sell the scripts, I started doing stand-up comedy because it was a way of demonstrating that you had what you thought was a sense of humor," he later explained to *The Chicago Tribune*.

"I'd never performed as a stand-up comedian before,

partly because there's just no place to do that in Indianapolis. Oh, you can do it in your home, but it gets very little response."

So Dave finally took the advice of other struggling young comedy writers he had met and went to the Comedy Store, the premier comedy club in L.A.

It was every bit as disheartening and difficult as he had imagined.

Just getting the opportunity to perform, for a nominal fee, was next-to-impossible. First he had to pass a series of auditions for the managers of the club, to prove that he wouldn't put an entire audience to sleep or, worse, have them heckling him mercilessly.

Much to his relief, he passed those private auditions. That's when the terror really set in. Now he'd have to walk up on stage and do his routine in front of hundreds of eyes boring into him. His palms were sweaty and his heart was beating as he took the stage. He doesn't remember much after that. He had practiced his routine so much that he basically just ambled through the words, with little or no inflection. It wasn't great, but it wasn't awful either. What it needed was a lot of work.

The bad news was that his first time as a stand-up comic didn't make Hollywood sit up and take notice. The good news was that it showed promise and he, much to his amazement, was invited back.

"The first time I found it very painful to get up in front of those people. I remember thinking, 'Jeez, I've come 2,500 miles and gotten onstage in this dimly lit bar in front of these mutants and I'm telling jokes.' "

Dave gave interviewer Steven Rea a painful portrait of just how excruciating stand-up comedy can be—especially to someone as insecure as Dave.

"When you go out there and you have something that you think is funny, it's such a personal little presentation. It's you trying to make a roomful of people laugh or a whole country of people laugh, and if they don't laugh, it's just like you've been embarrassed in your third-grade class and your teacher has reprimanded you. It's the worst sinking feeling in the world, it's the deepest embarrassment you can endure. Here you are showing off, and nobody thinks you're funny."

Not surprisingly for a man who still beats himself up daily over his talk show, Dave says his virgin stand-up voyage was a disaster.

"I got up and said from rote some stuff I had written that day. To dead silence."

He was demoralized, but he didn't quit. Instead, he continued hanging around the club, learning from other, more successful comics. The comedian that most influenced him in those early days was, ironically, Jay Leno, the man who, fifteen years later, would become his arch rival for the *Tonight Show* job. Jay was, at that time, considered the top comedian performing at the Comedy Store.

Dave told *Newsweek:* "I saw Jay and thought, 'Awww, I see, that's how it's supposed to be done. It wasn't two guys go into a bar, and it wasn't bathroom jokes. It was all smart, shrewd observations, and it could be anything—politics, television, education. The dynamic of it was, you and I both understand that this is stupid. We're Jay's hip friends.' "

Dave soon became one of Jay's hip friends and learned a lot from Jay's style. Jay was really just doing what Dave did when he ad-libbed on his weather station, i.e., joking about something in everyday life that he found amusing or absurd.

The difference was that Jay's jokes were well thought-out

and planned. When Jay noticed something funny as he walked down the street, or watched a stupid television commercial, or read a politician's statement he thought ludicrous, he immediately wrote down his thoughts, then tailored those jottings into a joke. Then he'd practice the delivery, playing around with timing, experimenting with the inflections, until he delivered it in a way that got the biggest laugh.

Dave really had the same kind of mindset. He, too, found amusement and absurdity in everything around him. No one was faster with a comeback quip. What Dave needed to do was harness his ad-libs and refine them into jokes.

Dave set out to learn from Jay's style and soon found his own, which he calls observational humor.

"I'm an observational comic," he told *The Chicago Tribune*.

"I try to serve my own sense of humor, and if other people like it, fine. What I look for are the setups in life, and then I fill in the punch lines.

"Like one of my favorite jokes came right out of the *National Enquirer,* which every week gives you a million setups. I'm standing there buying cantaloupes and there's this headline in the *Enquirer* that says, 'How to Lose Weight Without Diet or Exercise.' So I think to myself, 'That leaves disease.' I've been doing that word for word for years, and it never fails to get laughs.

"Or there was the time I was driving my pickup truck and I heard a guy on the radio screaming, 'Now you can buy breakfast at McDonald's!' And I thought, 'Boy, there's a dream come true.' They're not so much jokes as they are sarcastic comments, expressions of an attitude."

Dave, who hadn't been as awful his first night as he says or he wouldn't have been invited back—competition, after all, was stiff—began working at the Comedy Store on a regular basis.

Free, thanks to Michelle, to fill all his hours pursuing his art, he spent his days reworking, rewriting, and revamping his act, and his nights refining it on stage.

He worked tirelessly until he had put together a routine that even he, his greatest critic, began to think was pretty good.

More important, other people started to take notice. It was at the Comedy Store that Dave was noticed by comedian Jimmie Walker. Jimmie, who later starred in the series *Good Times,* gave Dave his first comedy job: He hired the new kid to write material for him.

"He wanted me to write jokes with a black point of view," recalls Dave.

"Which was interesting because he was the first black person I had ever seen."

Then Dave got his next big break. He was taken on by agent Jack Rollins, a major player in Hollywood whose talent firm handled such comic luminaries as Robin Williams, Billy Crystal, and Woody Allen.

But being signed by one of the best agencies in the comedy business was nothing compared to the thrill David felt when Part One of his childhood fantasy came true: He was approached by *Tonight Show* scouts looking for fresh, new comics to appear on Johnny Carson.

This, after all, was what he had worked for—what every comedian works for. A spot on *The Tonight Show* represented every comedian's big chance. It was not without its risks, however. It was a make-or-break deal: If you were good enough on Johnny to be invited back, you were pretty much assured that your career would skyrocket. If you blew it, you'd just as likely fade into oblivion.

But for Dave, the opportunity to be on Carson represented more than a chance to become a big shot comedian. It was the first step toward fulfilling that seemingly impossible childhood dream: to one day *be* Johnny Carson, to become the host of *The Tonight Show.* Being approached by the Carson people that first time remains one of the biggest thrills of Letterman's life, even though they told him they were interested in him, but just not yet. That might have discouraged, or even angered, a lesser man, but Letterman was mature enough and humble (or perhaps insecure?) enough to respect their opinion. He was grateful that they were willing to wait; he didn't want to go on *The Tonight Show* a minute before he was ready to knock Johnny dead. He was thrilled just to know that he had gotten their attention.

"In 1977 the Carson people came to me and said, 'You're not ready.' I said, 'OK, that's fine.' I was just thrilled they'd been watching me. And the last thing you want to do is go on and not be ready. So I kept working and building my act, and the next year, they called for me."

Sadly, at the same time his professional life was picking up speed, his marriage was going down the drain. Looking back, Dave admits that the breakup was mostly his fault. Though part of it could be blamed on circumstances—Michelle worked days, Dave worked nights—and they somehow let their relationship slip away, Dave acknowledges that it was more than that.

For one thing, Dave had simply married too young. After a dateless four years of high school, Dave was understandably thrilled when the statuesque beauty at Ball State was interested in him. They began dating and Dave never looked back: They were married while still in senior year. Dave basically married his first girlfriend. During the years they spent in Indianapolis he was content. And he was certainly grateful for Michelle's unfailing encouragement and support those first lean years in Los Angeles. Without her, he probably would have become discouraged after the first rejected comedy script, packed up his bags, and went back to the radio station in Indianapolis with his tail between his legs.

But things soon changed when Dave began performing at the Comedy Store. The guy who never fit in anywhere in high school began receiving accolades at the comedy club. He found a whole new set of friends amongst his fellow struggling comedians who hung around the club, drinking and buoying each other's spirits. He loved the camaraderie of the comedy club, and spent more and more time there. He also loved the female attention he was receiving for the first time in his life.

What happened to David and Michelle is what happens to a lot of couples who marry young: Dave simply outgrew Michelle. The man who had scarcely been outside Indiana—he hadn't even left home to go to college—realized there was a whole life out there that he hadn't explored. He wanted to experience it fully. And that meant he wanted to experience it alone.

There wasn't another woman involved; rather, there were a series of flirtations that made Dave realize that he had settled down too young. Dave had gotten into the performing business because he loved it, because it was what he felt he was born to do. Whereas a lot of young musicians admit that they first picked up a guitar because they knew it was the fastest way to becoming popular with the girls, Dave had no such thoughts when he began performing at the Comedy Store. He had no idea that comedians, like every other field of entertainment, had groupies. Every night there were pretty young girls watching the show, hanging out at the bar hoping to meet the comedians, making lascivious suggestions. It was the freewheeling, pre-AIDS seventies, after all. The Pill was available, the War was over, and everyone was looking for a good time.

The gap-toothed geek who couldn't get a date in high school suddenly found himself in the welcome position of having pretty Southern California girls throwing themselves at him just because he was the hip new comic at the trendy Comedy Store. He began coming home later and later, sometimes not at all.

Michelle, understandably, was beginning to wonder what was in this for her. Here she was, working all day to support a husband she never saw anymore, who was clearly drinking in his newfound popularity.

Still, Michelle was willing to hang in there. She had loved Dave since college and she loved him still. She took her wedding vows seriously and wanted to make her marriage work. After all, they had been together for eleven years, married for nine. She pleaded with Dave to come home more. His response shocked her: He wanted a divorce.

Years later, Dave explains what went wrong.

"Michelle was working at the department store, so at night she would come home and I would go out. We started not seeing each other week in and week out. And that was the reason for the divorce, ultimately. We just didn't know who we were."

But it was more than a simple drifting apart, Dave admits.

"I behaved badly," he confessed.

The man who loathes the shallowness of some of the Hollywood types he has on his show, men who annually trade in their mate for a younger, prettier version, is mortified when he looks back on those early years in Los Angeles. He describes his behavior in those heady days as "embarrassing and superficial."

"I ruined the marriage. It was just me being a dork: Hey, young girls! It took a long time for me to reconcile the guilt. For what I put her through, I felt like I should burn in hell for the rest of my life."

Michelle was brokenhearted, but she knew how single-minded Dave could be. If he wanted a divorce, then that was that. There was no talking him out of it. Besides, she had her pride. She filed for divorce and didn't ask for alimony. Dave kept his 1973 Chevy truck, silverware, and china. Dave got custody of their dog Bob, who later became known to millions of *Late Night* viewers.

Dave never saw Michelle again, even though she remained in California.

"It seems odd to me now. I was married for a long time, like nine years. My life is so different now from what it was then that it does seem strange that there was this other person with whom I was very close for all that time who now plays no part in my life."

Michelle went on to remarry. She now lives in Sacramento with her husband, Alan Siegel, with whom she owns a real estate company.

Dave was relieved when word got back to him that Michelle had remarried. He said he fervently hoped her new husband would "flush the horrible memory for her."

Michelle has never uttered a bad word about Dave, publicly at least.

One person who remains bitter, however, is Michelle's father, Bill.

"David broke Michelle's heart," Bill told the *National Enquirer* in an interview last year.

"He came home one day, packed his bags, left her, and

never looked back. Michelle was devastated—and she never got a dime from him."

After the marital split, Dave enjoyed a brief period of playing the field. He was bound and determined not to settle down again in any heavy romance.

But it wasn't long before he was seriously involved with another woman. Like Michelle, she was a woman who believed in Dave's talent and knew he could make it to the big time. Unlike Michelle, it was a woman who could truly share Dave's dream, since she harbored the same hopes for herself.

Her name was Merrill Markoe.

Part Two
The Booming Eighties

Chapter Four
THE ROAD TO *LATE NIGHT*

When Dave met Merrill at the Comedy Store, she was a bored University of Southern California art professor who, like Dave, had decided to try her hand at comedy writing and stand-up.

They met at the Comedy Store, where both were perfecting their acts. Because Dave, deep down, wasn't a shallow person, he had soon tired of giggly young girls who hung out at the comedy clubs hoping to get it on with a semifamous comedian. In Merrill, he found a friend first, then a lover. Merrill was someone who shared his world fully— the terror you feel when your name is called by the master of ceremonies and it's time to go on stage; the panic of momentarily forgetting what the send-up for your next joke was supposed to be; the exhilaration of leaping off stage to thunderous applause; the devastation of performing in front of a crowd who responds to your jokes with dull stares.

There was another reason Dave hit it off with Merrill, more so than with any of the other comedians performing at the Comedy Store at that time. Merrill shared his sense of humor. They found the same things hilarious, saw the absurdity in the same people, events, and situations.

With Merrill, Dave wasn't the only entertainer in the relationship. Merrill could match Dave joke for joke, gag for gag. Since both were interested in penning scripts for quality sitcoms (Dave had spent many days in Indianapolis writing unsolicited scripts for *The Mary Tyler Moore Show*), they began spending their days collaborating on scripts. They found that they made a devastating writing team. Though they still weren't selling much of anything, they were receiving good feedback on their work.

Soon things began happening for them. Merrill, who had decided to give up stand-up and concentrate on her scriptwriting, got a job writing situation-comedy pilots. She also landed a writing job on a show in development called *Mary* which was to be a variety show for Mary Tyler Moore, her first venture after calling it quits with her very popular series, *The Mary Tyler Moore Show.*

Dave was offered a spot on a short-lived comedy show called *Peeping Times,* which was supposed to be a satire of *60 Minutes.* It wasn't exactly the big time for Dave, but, as he had with all his other stop-and-start jobs in Indianapolis, he resolved to give it his best shot. Dave had had other embarrassing gigs, after all. He'd interviewed children about their manure projects on *Clover Power,* for heaven's sake. So Dave felt equipped to handle whatever *Peeping Times* threw his way.

Until they asked him to do something he found utterly reprehensible.

Letterman later recalled his first run-in with the plastic mentality of L.A. in an interview with *The Chicago Tribune:*

"The week before we started shooting I got a call from a secretary who says, 'We've been trying to get hold of your agent, but we can't reach him so we're just going to tell you—you've got to get your teeth fixed.'

"I run to the mirror thinking, 'teeth?' and honest to God

I notice for the first time that I have these huge spaces between my teeth. I fought it, but finally they said you can get inserts. Which was fine except that when I wore them I couldn't speak properly—every 'p' just exploded into the mike.

"So I'm not going to get my teeth fixed, or my nose either. And I'm also not going to get rid of my pickup truck because it's gotten to the point where it irritates people. You roll up to some places in Beverly Hills where they've got valet parking and they go: 'Oh, Christ, I ain't parking that. Guido, you park it.' "

When *Peeping Times* ended shortly thereafter, Dave got a job on Mary Tyler Moore's doomed 1978 variety show, *Mary,* where Merrill was laboring as a writer.

Dave was supposed to be the comic foil to straitlaced Mary. He loved Mary, but hated the show which, he said, kept dressing him up in silly costumes and trying to get him to sing and dance—not exactly his forte.

"The show was only on the air three weeks but it was a good experience because I got to work all summer with Mary, who is real neat."

It was especially thrilling to meet Mary after having penned so many unsolicited scripts for her hit sitcom when he was a struggling writer living in Indiana.

Dave later told interviewer Richard Zoglin of *Time* magazine that working on *Mary* was "the best experience and the worst experience I had had. I was living in one room on Sunset Boulevard, driving a '73 pickup truck. I'd get in my truck and drive to work every day—which was Television City. In Hollywood! And one of my coworkers was Mary Tyler Moore! It was great, the American show-biz dream come true. It was also difficult because in each show there was a big dance number, and every Tuesday the wardrobe people would come around and fit you for, like, a Peter Pan suit to wear in the number. I always described it as: What's wrong with this picture? Well, Letterman has no business being there with Mary Tyler Moore, that's what's wrong with this picture."

When the show was canceled, Dave was disappointed not to be working with Mary, but relieved that his part in the debacle was completed. At least this time he had a home to go to.

He was back at the Comedy Store the next night, continuing to hone his craft. In the interim, he landed some comedy writing jobs, like writing a few sketches for a Paul Lynde comedy special. He also did his stand-up routine on *The Gong Show*.

Finally, the people at *The Tonight Show* started noticing him again. The Carson scouts, who had told Dave a year earlier that they liked what they saw and would keep an eye on him, contacted Dave with the words he'd been waiting all his life to hear: "We want you on *The Tonight Show*."

The Carson people assured him he was ready, and even insecure old David had to agree. The big night came and Dave realized that all the anxiety he had experienced at the Comedy Store was nothing compared to the downright terror he felt sitting in the Green Room. He was confident in the sense that he had practiced his routine so long and so hard that he had it down cold. No matter how nervous he got, it was too indelibly imprinted in his brain for him to slip up.

Not only that, he knew the material was good. He had been working steadily at the Comedy Store for over a year and he knew from experience which were his most winning jokes, the ones that never failed him, the ones that got a big laugh time and time again. His routine was filled with those jokes. There wasn't a mediocre one in the bunch. It was going to be fine.

The date was November 26, 1978. A very nervous David Letterman took the stage and, despite his butterflies, performed his routine flawlessly. He was concentrating so hard on getting through his act, on getting the timing and inflection right on each joke so that each was delivered to perfection, that he didn't even notice the man to his right who was howling more loudly than all the rest. That man was Johnny Carson.

Johnny rarely invites a comic to sit with him after their routine. The comedians are usually unknowns who get their five minutes of fame and are expected to take their bows and leave. Only well-known, established comics with whom Johnny has developed a rapport are invited to exchange a few words with him after their set.

But Johnny was so impressed with Dave that he invited the young man to come sit beside him. It was the highest honor a comic on his first *Tonight Show* outing could receive. Because it meant just one thing: Johnny Carson felt he had a star-in-the-making on his hands.

The best part was, David didn't freeze up when asked to sit next to the great man. Flushed with what, for David, was an unusual amount of self-confidence after the perfect routine he had just executed, Letterman found himself in the surprising position of being wholly relaxed as he sat down and began bantering with his childhood hero.

"It was the most fun I ever had," says Dave.

"There I was holding my own with Johnny Carson. I knew then I could hit big league pitching."

The Carson people knew it, too. They immediately invited him to come back on the show. The next few performances proved equally impressive. So, after just three appearances on *The Tonight Show*, the Carson executives asked Letterman if he'd like a shot at guest-hosting for Johnny. David was flabbergasted. It was a record rise to King Carson's seat.

"It happened real quickly," says Letterman.

"During the middle of the third show, the *Tonight Show* producer came over and said, 'Have your people call me about hosting.' That was a real numbing experience, having that go through my mind while I was still sitting there pretending to be part of the show."

By 1980, the NBC brass had begun to take notice of the gap-toothed new sensation appearing regularly on *The Tonight Show*. There was talk of giving Dave a show of his own. They came up with a concept for a talk show called *Leave It To Dave* but canned the project before it ever got out of the planning stages. Instead, NBC decided David should have a go at a midmorning variety program.

David had by this time begun to live with Merrill. When Merrill had given up on doing her own stand-up, she had given David a lot of her jokes.

Now it was Dave's turn to return the favor: He promptly hired Merrill as his head writer. NBC guaranteed Letterman a six-month run of the ninety-minute morning show and he went to work.

Despite NBC's promise, *The David Letterman Show* survived only nineteen weeks.

Years later, Hal Gurnee, director of Letterman's *Late Show*, explained why to *Newsweek*:

"NBC wanted a service show. They wanted Dave to do cooking demonstrations. And he resisted. He wanted to do a comedy show."

At first, Dave tried to give NBC at least part of what they wanted and results were disastrous, not because Dave had lost his comical touch, but because NBC was forcing him to do a show that did not jive with his comedic talents. The network had some sort of half-baked notion that a variety show—with singing, dancing, the works—would fly in the midmorning hours when most competing networks were running game shows.

Dave knew the show was in trouble early on.

"We were looking at the audience leaving and I heard him say: 'Boy, thank God I'm not doing brain surgery,'" recalls Hal Gurnee.

The show was so bad that housewives began calling up the network, demanding the reinstatement of the game show that had been bumped in favor of Dave's show.

A funny thing happened on the way to disaster, however. When Dave and Merrill got the news after just a few weeks on the air that their show was being axed in four months, they felt revitalized. Instead of sleepwalking through the weeks remaining on their contract, they decided to have some fun on the show, to do the show they really wanted to do before the network insisted that they throw together a kitschy variety program.

They began infusing the morning show with the fresh, irreverent material and wacky remotes (that is, the segments that are shot outside the studio, like Dave wandering around the NBC cafeteria with a camera crew behind him) that later became the trademark of *Late Night* and now are the anchor of the *Late Show.*

Merrill came up with "Stupid Pet Tricks" in honor of Dave's dog Bob and the dog they had acquired together, Stan.

Once Dave and Merrill ignored NBC's directives and did the show they wanted to do, they began to develop a following. Even their director got into the act. One day he sent a herd of sheep to their studio. The sheep started to go nuts and Dave found his niche.

"Ladies and gentlemen, what you are witnessing here is a good idea gone awry," he told the audience as the sheep ran around him.

"Yes, a fun-filled surprise turning into an incredible screwup."

Dave had found his voice. Since there was no need to be afraid of the network brass, and no longer a fear of cancellation hanging over their heads (they'd already been canceled!), Dave started to have some fun.

He flew in a Missouri farmer named Floyd Stiles and invited everyone to celebrate "Floyd Stiles Day." He ran a "Have *The David Letterman Show* in Your Own Home" contest. He popped in to the NBC cafeteria on Valentine's Day to find out how people were celebrating. He and Merrill took to the streets looking for humor.

"On the morning show, Dave always wanted to go outside the studio," Merrill told *Playboy.*

"And it started out pretty easy. We had a big backlog of stuff that went by either geography or theme. We'd go to Chinatown and tie everything together that I could write a joke into or else we'd take a tour. One time we went to everything that had the sign 'World's Best Coffee.'"

The show was obviously a precursor of *Late Night,* yet it failed to build enough of an audience to stay on the air. Merrill thinks their time slot—and the fact that NBC gave them less than six months to find their audience—doomed them to failure.

"Dave's sensibility is, and was, 'You and me know he's nuts.' Dave and the audience are united in the knowledge that they're in on the joke. And he's been able to do that ever since I saw him.

"But the morning show was a delusion in the sense that we felt you could just do whatever comedy you wanted, any time of day or night. And when the show started to fail, Dave was going crazy. It was not a happy time."

Dave and Merrill had hit on the formula that would later make his late nights so successful.

People paid attention. The show began to build an admittedly small but fiercely loyal audience. The kind of committed, involved audience that advertisers love so much.

Though it was too late to save the show from cancellation, it caught the critics' eyes, too. So after the show was canceled (with Letterman winning an Emmy for hosting and Merrill picking up one for writing), the NBC honchos wisely gave Dave a one-year holding contract worth $625,000. What it did was prevent him from being snatched up by another network while NBC scrambled to find him a show.

Less than a year later, NBC found their opening. Tom Snyder's *Tomorrow* show, in the sleepy 12:30 A.M. spot, was about to be canceled. Did Dave want to resurrect his mid-morning show as a late-night fest, "Stupid Pet Tricks" and all? He did indeed, though, as always, Dave was less than optimistic about his chances for success. Once again, the boy from Indiana was on the move, this time to New York.

"I thought, 'Well, let's just try not to embarrass ourselves unnecessarily.' "

And so, on February 1, 1982, *Late Night with David Letterman* was born.

The first outing of *Late Night with David Letterman* immediately made people sit up and take notice.

It began with a warning to viewers that the next sixty minutes might shock and repel them. Then Dave was introduced by the Rainbow Grill Peacock Girls, a tacky group of showgirls minimally dressed in feathers.

Dave opened his monologue with the shocking news that one of NBC's top executives had just been arrested in a Grand Central Station bathroom "because his pride was showing."

Then he invited the audience on a behind-the-scenes tour of the studio, explaining along the way the delicacy of the operations, the complexity of the production facilities they were about to see.

Naturally, when he gently opened the door to the control room, the viewer was treated to the sight of a group of NBC employees boozing it up and dressed, inexplicably, in Bavarian costumes.

The Green Room was similarly strange; it revealed not anxious guests waiting to be called on stage but a variety of flowering plants that Dave explained were "some of the very few vegetables here at NBC not in programming."

It was time to bring out the first celebrity guest, Bill Murray, who had apparently consumed quite a bit of tequila before his performance. Luckily for all concerned, his alcohol-induced, impromptu aerobics lesson to the tune of "Let's Get Physical" somehow worked with the overall wacky feel of the show.

Next, Letterman rolled one of his now-trademark remote pieces, where he roams around New York City finding people to perplex, prod, and generally annoy.

On this day, he and his camera crew took to the streets in a segment called "Shame and the City." The brainchild of Merrill Markoe, it involved Letterman finding misspellings and grammatical mistakes on signs in the city. Dave and his crew then brought the shameful mistakes to the attention of the embarrassed proprietor and insisted they be corrected without further ado.

The show was an instant success, doubling the viewers that Snyder had been pulling in and—more importantly to the advertisers—attracting the very desirable eighteen to thirty-four age group.

Dave, as always, was skeptical of his instant popularity, which he was quite sure would be fleeting.

"Privately, I think that I'm not really somebody who has a network television show," he confided at the time.

"Celebrities are other people—Johnny Carson and Sylvester Stallone. I'm just a kid trying to make a living is the way I feel. Here I am, waiting for the fat kid to put unleaded gas in my car and I'm asking him if I can do it because he's having trouble resetting the pump, and I think, 'I'm not really that person on television.' "

Dave's modesty and pessimism aside, the NBC honchos were crowing about their late-night winner, which had much improved Tom Snyder's dismal ratings.

"This is the number one college show in the country," the director of East Coast programming told reporters.

"It's a cult already. People talk and say, 'Didja see what they did last night on Letterman?' I mean, they really love him!"

Chapter Five

SIGNATURE STUNTS

One reason *Late Night* shone so brightly, even at the ungodly hour of 12:30 A.M., was the hilarious stunts dreamed up and executed by Letterman, onetime head writer Merrill Markoe, and *Late Night's* brilliant young team of comedy writers.

Where else but on Letterman's cutting-edge show could one see someone—Dave, that is—don a Velcro suit and hurl himself against a Velcro wall? Or zip himself into a jumpsuit made of Alka-Seltzer and dive into a tank of water? Or put on a suit made of sponges and climb into a water tank? Or wear a suit made of Nacho chips and lower himself into a vat of yogurt dip? Or put on a coat of Rice Krispies and dip himself into milk? (The Alka-Seltzer bit was a trifle dangerous. When it was being tested by the prop people, it released so much carbon dioxide that it caused then head writer Steve O'Donnell to pass out.)

Better still were Letterman's taped segments. Who could forget strange-looking, squeaky-voiced Larry "Bud" Melman, aka actor Calvert DeForest, standing at Port Authority offering bewildered bus passengers a hot towel upon their arrival in New York?

People loved to see their perpetually smirking talk-show

host wandering around the streets of New York, badgering pedestrians into letting him see what was in their purses because he was "Mr. Curious."

Or popping into a shop called Just Shades and asking where he can buy a lightbulb.

Another time Merrill dreamed up a remote called "In Search of Jimmy," where Dave wandered in and out of Manhattan stores called Jimmy's Deli and Jimmy's Pizza and Jimmy's Hardware trying to find out "just what this Jimmy looks like."

Letterman also makes excellent use of "Viewer Mail" for gags. When he received a letter from a local woman who had insulted his sneakers, Dave took his camera crew to her home unannounced. No one was home, so Dave mowed her lawn while he waited for her. Eventually her brother arrived and let the *Late Night* gang into her bedroom, where Dave went through her record collection and passed judgment on the shoes in her closet. When he found out from her brother that she was working at the jewelry counter at Sears and wouldn't be home for several hours, the crew headed over there to find her. He convinced a shopper to fill in for her so she could take him to the shoe department and find him a proper pair of running shoes. To show his gratitude for setting him straight on sneakers, Dave bought her lunch at Nathan's.

Even better were the childish pranks Dave played. Like dropping a watermelon from a skyscraper window just to see the resultant mess. Or running over that annoying Energizer Bunny with a bulldozer to stop it once and for all. Or crushing a can of Spam in an industrial vise. Or flattening a franks 'n beans dinner under a hydraulic press. Or smashing a Smurf under a steamroller.

Perhaps more amazingly, Dave got his guests to do crazy

things. Mariel Hemingway has cleaned fish on his show; Tom Selleck has stuck his head into a tub of water to do his motorboat impression. Jane Pauley agreed to be interviewed in a dental chair. Sonny & Cher, who had one of the most acrimonious divorces in show-biz history, agreed to reunite on the show and sing their hit song "I Got You Babe." He got then Cosby kid Lisa Bonet to stuff thirty-four grapes into her mouth. He interviewed sportscaster Marv Albert as Albert took a bubble bath. He got newscaster Connie Chung, whom he's long had an open crush on, to go out on a shopping trip with him so he could suggest some new clothes for her husband, Maury Povich, whom Dave insists on calling "Murray."

One of Dave's finest moments was when he got old buddy Teri Garr, one of his favorite guests, to take a shower in his office. It all began when the air-conditioning broke down at the studio and Dave insisted it was too hot to do a show. So he brought his guests—Teri Garr and comedian Richard Lewis—out into the hallway and sat them down on a couch while he bounced around the studio in his sweatpants, generally annoying staffers and reading jokes he would have considered had he been doing a "real show" that night.

Richard Lewis's mother happened to be along with him and found herself on the couch with Richard and Teri as Dave would pop back now and again to talk with them.

At one point, a bewildered Mrs. Lewis asked Dave: "Am I an audience or a real person?"

Finally, Dave decided it was so hot that Teri Garr should cool off by taking a shower in his office (on camera, of course). Teri kept resisting, Dave kept insisting, and finally she stripped off her clothes and jumped in. She did have one major moment of panic when the camera crew seemed intent on moving in past the frosted shower door.

"Oh, no! No! I can't! I don't have my underpants on!" Teri wailed.

"Just turn on the water," yelled Dave.

"I hate you," said Teri. "Why am I doing this?"

He likes wacky civilian guests even better than celebrities. He once let supermodel Cindy Crawford stew in the Green Room while he chatted up a guy in the audience whose name delighted him: Herb Clumpy, III. Dave spent so much time talking to Clumpy that Cindy never did make it on the show that night. Dave wasn't terribly apologetic to the disappointed audience: He told them he'd bring Cindy on the following week . . . "or maybe never."

He and his staff spend many hours each week scouring out-of-town newspapers and news wire services for crazy stories and crazy people they can make use of on the show. Dave has interviewed a farmer from New Hampshire who refuses to turn back his clocks, and a woman who runs a Nut Museum. He tripped up an elderly spelling champion by asking her to spell the name "Buttafuoco." He introduced a man who keeps congealed food in his dresser drawer (as a hobby), and a woman who keeps snowballs from different years.

Other highlights include the time Dave, who prides himself on his ability to pack groceries as ably today as he did as a sixteen-year-old checkout clerk at the Atlas Supermarket in Indianapolis, invited the boy who won the national sacking competition on the show and challenged him to a sacking race. (Letterman lost.)

Letterman is at his finest at improvisational humor, especially when he used to roam around the other NBC studios looking for trouble.

He once took his camera crew into the offices of NBC executives and rummaged through their desks, showing off the contents to his viewers.

The real reason CBS was willing to spend $14 million buying and renovating the Ed Sullivan Theatre for Dave's new *Late Show* is probably to prevent him and his camera crew from descending on humorless newsmen like Dan Rather.

In any event, Dave barging in on neighboring NBC shows was one of the best parts of *Late Night*.

One great moment came when the *Late Night* staff heard that former President Jimmy Carter was across the hall at another NBC show plugging his book. They quickly dispatched a producer to ask Carter if Dave could dash over and interview him. Carter agreed; Dave panicked.

"What will I do?" Dave asked his writers.

"Sure, it sounds like fun. But I don't exactly see where the fun comes in. What is my angle? What's the joke?"

Ten minutes before air time, Letterman had it: He'd drag a shy young studio technician named Al Frisch along with him, telling Carter that Frisch simply had to meet the former president. Letterman got frisked (at his insistence), Frisch looked properly mortified, Carter was charming, the skit was sensational.

Dave has always had the ability to take the most mundane occurrences and make them funny. He often finds his material in Everyman's problems, little pesky annoyances of everyday life that we all experience.

Like supermarkets. Dave loves to do his own grocery shopping, but, like all of us, he has his run-ins with lazy and/or incompetent checkout clerks. One night, he spent most of his pre-guest chat telling Paul Shaffer about the infuriating experience he had had the night before with a supermarket clerk who couldn't get his can of beans to register on the price scan. Naturally, there was no price stamped on the can. Finally, she turned to Dave and asked, "Well, do you know how much they are?"

"How would I know how much they are!" a by-now thoroughly exasperated Dave yelled back. "I don't work here."

He got a lot of mileage out of the story on the air the next day, an occurrence we can all relate to. In fact, he made such a fuss about it that the store manager later called Dave to apologize.

Once he built an entire show around his frustration in getting the cable man to come to his home in Connecticut and hook him up. He knew that one would be great. Who, after all, doesn't hate the cable television companies? They're never available at your convenience, instead making you, the customer, hang around your house all day waiting for them to (maybe) arrive.

In the early eighties, Dave's troubles with his cable company became a running gag on the show. Finally, a faux-exasperated Dave confided to his viewers that he was just going to have to stay home and wait for that gash-darned cable man to come. So a camera crew followed Dave around his Connecticut home while back in New York the show went on as usual, band and studio audience in place.

Dave likes to occasionally do his show from a location other than his Manhattan studio. While other talk-show hosts fly their crews to interesting locations like Hawaii for their special on-location shows, Dave drags everyone into his office.

Announcing that he was "too tired" to do the show one night, he just had his guests brought into his office, sat them down on the couch, and interviewed them there.

Not surprisingly, *Late Night* soon got a well-deserved reputation for the most innovative programming around.

On one show, the voices of Letterman, bandleader Paul Shaffer, Chris Elliott, Raquel Welch, and Sandra Bernhard were all removed from the tape and dubbed by British actors.

For another show, the picture slowly rotated 360 degrees; on another occasion, the crew flopped the television image so the show appeared in a mirror image.

And who could forget Monkey Cam, where viewers watched the show from a camera strapped onto Zippy the Chimp's back, or Thrill Cam, where the camera raced around the studio like it was attached to a roller coaster. There was even Guest Cam; First Guest Bill Murray got that honor.

Like a hyperactive eight-year-old who had been given his own talk show, Letterman conducted elevator races, dog-sled races, pizza-delivery contests, and oyster-eating competitions.

The beauty of the Letterman show is that you're not watching a well-rehearsed script. It's amazing that shows like *Saturday Night Live* can have such tiresome scripts when the writers have a whole week to work on them and the performers an entire week to refine them. As David proved in his very first talk show, when the sheep were running around the studio and he was at his brilliant best, he is on the top of his game when he's playing off a situation. For the most part, David's writers don't write scripts for Dave to follow; they merely think of situations in which they can place Dave that will lend itself to humor. With Letterman, that can be almost anywhere. He is simply the master of ad-libbing.

When it comes to taking the barest outline of a skit and

running with it, to hilarious results, Letterman's finest moment came when the writers suggested that he act as sort of a welcoming wagon for the folks at General Electric, who had just bought RCA and NBC. Letterman decided he'd take a basket of fruit over to his new bosses as a gesture of goodwill.

In light of what everyone now knows is Letterman's deep and abiding dislike of General Electric, the results were priceless. When good-natured, smiling Dave and his camera crew ambled on over to GE headquarters with their ridiculous basket of fruit, the building security guard treated Dave like a terrorist with a hand grenade.

First viewers heard the guard demand, via an outdoor speaker, that Dave and his camera crew, "Clear the front of the GE Building."

In the confusion, Dave managed to slip into the lobby anyway, where he was rudely rebuffed when he offered his hand to the security chief.

"Just want to drop off the basket of fruit," said Dave amiably, clearly loving every minute.

"I'm gonna ask you to turn the cameras off."

"Gesture of goodwill," rejoined Letterman.

"Cut the cameras, please!" bellowed the guard, who proceeded to stalk over to the camera and cover it with his hand.

Just one of Dave's many triumphant moments, and a foreshadowing of the battle with NBC to come, in which he would also emerge the victor.

Dave also likes to play off people that he plucks straight from the streets of Manhattan. Once he sent his cameraman outside to pick a guy at random and offer to buy him a new suit. A little while later, they came back to the studio where the man proudly showed off his baby blue suit. He then asked Dave if he could sing a few bars of "Tonight" from *West Side Story*. Apparently, singing that song on television had always been his dream.

Dave often takes to the street himself in search of humor. On one show, he went to a cheap burger joint that boasted celebrity regulars by hanging their pictures in the window. Dave was fascinated by this and asked the owner to tell the home audience what Erik Estrada and Donny Most had eaten upon their visit to his fine establishment.

"Stupid Pet Tricks," Merrill's brainchild, became one of the most popular staples of the show. Week after week people paraded their pets on the air so viewers could watch things like the dog that fetched soda from a vending machine (and drank it!), the cat who sat quietly on her owner's head while the latter twirled a baton and sang, the collie that played basketball, the cocker spaniel that skateboarded, or the hula dancing Shetland pony.

Sometimes the pet turned a trick too risqué to show in full on the air. One audition tape, called Mr. Bun, showed a Dutch rabbit attempting sex with a fuzzy slipper that resembled a bunny. Late hour or not, the tape was edited for family viewing.

The stupid pet tricks that didn't make it on the air are almost as fascinating as the ones who did.

"People call and say, 'My cat, when it's thrown, will stick to a window screen,' " said "Stupid Pet Trick" coordinator Sue Hall in a 1986 interview in which she explained her screening procedures.

"Well, any cat will stick to a screen."

Hall has lots of tales from her odd job: like the chicken who was supposed to play dead but actually dropped dead before air time. Or the hamster who auditioned for the show wearing a red fireman's hat and sliding down a fireman's pole. He didn't make the cut because he looked so terrified at the audition. (The *Late Night* staffers were very sensitive to animal cruelty.)

Hall learned a lot working the stupid pet trick beat. She once placed a newspaper advertisement asking the provocative question, "Have you taught your pet to do something odd?" Apparently, "odd" meant sexual to many people. The word was changed to "unusual" and the owners cleaned up their acts.

Though Dave and Merrill never subjected their own pooches to the spotlight, Letterman acknowledges that Bob (who died a few years ago) and Stan did have their talents.

"Bob and I sounded the same when we ate potato chips. That was Bob's trick. And Stan's trick is that if you read him a list of television comediennes, he'll only get excited when you reach the name 'Lucille Ball.' The key word there is, of course, 'ball.' He loves to play ball."

As benign as "Stupid Pet Tricks" sounds, Dave once got into trouble during a segment—to the tune of a $1 million lawsuit. Maryjane B. Kasian of Boston brought her dog Benji on to demonstrate how he could walk on his hind legs. As Dave watched Benji perform his trick, he quipped: "I know the woman has performed unethical and intricate spinal surgery on the dog and that's illegal and she'll end up doing time."

Maryjane was not amused, saying Letterman had damaged her and Benji's career.

"Stupid Human Tricks" was another *Late Night* favorite, though those got even more disgusting than sexual animal antics.

"The worst thing is when people call in with things they can do with their noses," says Hall.

"One man called to say he could snort spaghetti up his

nose and pull the strand from his mouth; another claimed that he could snort a raw oyster in one nostril and blow it out the other."

Late Night's all-time favorite stupid human trick—one that has appeared live on several of *Late Night*'s anniversary specials, is the man who can stop a speeding rotary fan with his tongue.

He said it made him an instant celebrity in his hometown, with women asking him what other tricks he could perform with his tongue.

Unfortunately, Dave had to leave "Stupid Pet Tricks" and "Stupid Human Tricks" behind when he left NBC, who claimed them, ironically, as their "intellectual property."

NBC also claimed bald-headed Larry "Bud" Melman as a character, so Dave just brings him on now under his real name, Calvert DeForest. (Yes, Calvert is actually an actor. He was so convincing as bumbling Bud Melman that most people believed he was a civilian whom Dave had turned into a celebrity.)

Dave had done it before, after all. Now that he's moved to CBS, Letterman fans miss Meg Parsont, a woman who works at Simon & Schuster, book publishers with offices across the street from *Late Night*'s old headquarters at NBC. Dave spotted Meg at her window from his office window one day. He found out who she was and decided to give her a call on the air that night. She was so down-to-earth and delightful to talk with that she became somewhat of a regular. Dave would call her on occasion just to chat, or sometimes he'd get her to help him out on a gag. Once he called and asked her to drop beach balls from her thirteenth-story window. All in all, she's appeared on the show thirty-three times.

"We want you to throw beach balls out the window, but for the life of me, I can't remember why," he once told her.

Meg complied, while one of the *Late Night* crew members (stage manager Biff Henderson) tried to catch them below in a metal washbasin.

He rang Meg right after he announced that he had accepted an offer from CBS.

"We're going to CBS pretty soon, Meg, so I don't know if I'm going to get a chance to talk to you before we blow outta this dump. Meg, will you be able to come with us or not?"

"I think I have to keep my job here," Meg replied.

"I don't want to catch you with the new guy," Dave admonished.

"I've really grown fond of Meg," Dave told *New York Times* writer Bill Carter.

"Meg is such a solid human being. She really proves one thing we tried to show with this show: that the average person could be great on television."

Another civilian-turned-celebrity that viewers may remember from the mid-eighties was Arnie Barnes. At the time, Barnes was a nineteen-year-old meat shaper from Omaha, Nebraska, whom Dave called up randomly one day because he wanted Arnie's help on the *Late Night* "Rumor Mill." The idea was to get people in the Midwest to spread the rumor that Tom Brokaw had secretly married Peter Jennings in Mexico.

Dave so enjoyed talking with the monosyllabic Barnes, who'd answer questions like, "So what did you do last week?" with a sleepy "Got drunk" that he made him *Late Night*'s unofficial Midwest correspondent.

Barnes accepted Dave's invitation to become his Midwest

correspondent but was never quite sure what his duties were.

"I really don't know what I'm supposed to do," he told a *Chicago Sun-Times* interviewer. "I guess just keep an eye on things."

Actually, Dave got to like talking to sleepy, droll Barnes so much that he got him in the *Late Night* act quite frequently. Once he had Barnes describe himself on the air, as he would to a police artist, so *Late Night* could create a police sketch of him.

Being from the Midwest himself, Dave loves middle-America gags. He once had as his sole guests the sixteen residents that make up the tiny town of Bolan, Iowa.

Another time he called a librarian who was asking her hometown to give up television for a month.

"This woman has got to be stopped," said Letterman, picking up the phone to dial.

"Look at the shows you'll be missing the first week alone," he told the woman.

"There's the season premiere of *Riptide,* an encore presentation of *Foul-ups, Bleeps and Blunders,* and an all-new segment of *Punky Brewster."*

He picked a number from a Wichita, Kansas, phone book and asked the man who answered, Maurice Shanks, if he wanted to bet on the World Series. If the San Francisco Giants won, Letterman got one night with Darline Shanks, Maurice's wife of fifty years. If the Oakland A's won, Maurice won a case of scotch and an electric shoeshiner. Maurice won. The couple was flown into New York to collect their prizes and had the honor of being met at the airport by Larry "Bud" Melman.

Many of those calls are not as random as people might think. Dave admits that, if his staff sees an interesting item in an out-of-town newspaper and decides it might make a good on-air bit, they will call the person first and ask if they'd like to be on the show. If the person agrees, they call a few hours before show time and make sure it's still okay. Then, about ten minutes before the call, they'll phone again to make sure the person keeps the line clear.

"Otherwise the whole show would be dialing and arguing with operators," says Dave.

Though Dave embraces his own spontaneity, he doesn't always appreciate it in others.

Actor Crispin Glover once came on and scared the daylights out of Dave by suddenly swinging his platform-shoe-shod foot up in the air, nearly knocking Dave in the head. Not surprisingly, young Mr. Glover was gone after the next commercial break.

Letterman also looked a bit flustered when Sandra Bernhard practically took over his show one evening. Bernhard is one of Dave's favorite guests because she is lively and able to hold her own. (There's nothing Dave abhors more than a guest who won't pull his own weight, one who comes on and expects Letterman to do all the talking and asking.)

Bernhard was feeling especially frisky on this particular day. She strode over to Dave, kissed him on the mouth, then called out to her former buddy Madonna (they no longer speak, something about Madonna stealing Sandra's girlfriend). Madonna, dressed identically to Sandra, bounded onto the stage and the two outspoken women virtually took control of the show.

Not knowing what else to do, Dave finally sat back in his chair and—what else—lit a cigar.

Chapter Six

BREAKING UP IS HARD TO DO

Though *Late Night* was going like gangbusters, Dave's relationship was once again suffering. And this time it wasn't groupies getting in the way; it was Dave's old bugaboo, insecurity.

The specter of his first career fiasco—his midmorning show being canceled after just four months—continued to haunt him. So even though *Late Night* was by all accounts a success, Dave was terrified. In fact, the more successful the show became, the more frightened Dave was of blowing the whole deal by becoming too complacent. More and more, Dave came to feel that if he let down his guard for just a moment, all would be lost.

His worrisome, pessimistic attitude would be tough on any mate, but it was especially excruciating for Merrill, who both lived and worked with her lover. As Dave got more panicky about the quality of the show, he rejected more and more comedy suggestions. And since Merrill was his head writer, she bore the main brunt of his rejections. Much as Merrill tried to quiet his demons, hovering nearby at work, whispering encouragement in his ear during rehearsals, clenching his hand before show time, writing more and more material, nothing was ever enough. It would have been bearable if Dave could have left David Letterman the Talk-Show Host behind when he exited the office and become just regular old Dave at home. But it simply wasn't in his nature to relax. If anything, he was worse when he was at leisure.

Merrill spoke of the problem in an interview with the *Daily News*.

"David is more of a worrier when he's at home than when he's at the show. He's a lot more worried than he looks and a lot less easygoing than you think. He takes the fact that his sandwich comes late at the restaurant as hard as he takes anything."

Merrill was growing tired of Dave's incessant worrying. She had her own frustrations—like the fact that she had put her own career aspirations on hold to help Dave realize his dream. In the beginning, she was as excited about the show as he was. They were doing what they loved best— creating something together—and it didn't matter that they were living, breathing, and eating the show twenty-four hours a day. That's what you had to do to launch a successful show and build a loyal audience. You have to knock them dead each and every night so that old viewers will remain faithful and new viewers will get hooked. She understood that. And it had been fine for the first few years, when they were so busy dreaming up new concepts for the show that they really didn't have to think about their relationship or what both of them ultimately wanted out of life.

But now the show was established. Dave was still nervous that it could all end tomorrow, but that was Dave. He'd never change. What really bothered Merrill was that she was taking all this grief from him about a show that she was feeling less and less connected to. It wasn't that Dave was trying to steal the limelight. That wasn't his style at all. In fact, Dave hated to be in the spotlight other than that one hour a day that he was doing his show. In the rare times Dave granted interviews, he was always quick to point out Merrill's extensive contributions, to mention his brilliant team of writers, to give credit where credit was due.

But, at the end of the day, it was still Dave's show. He was the star, the on-camera personality. It was simply the nature of the beast. And Merrill was getting tired of working day in and day out, seven days a week, on a show that was increasingly Dave's dream, not their dream. It was *Late Night With David Letterman,* after all, not *The Dave and Merrill Show.*

But mostly she hated the fighting. To have to battle with David over *Late Night* decisions all day long at the office and then go home and rehash the show some more was just becoming too much. Especially because ratings were so good, and she was becoming tired of David's pessimistic, we're-on-top-now-so-there's-nowhere-to-go-but-down attitude. She knew he couldn't help it—cynicism was a part of his nature—but it was beginning to wear her down. She was not, by nature, a negative thinker. But Dave's constant predictions of doom were starting to turn her into one.

It's not that Dave was totally insensitive to Merrill's wants and needs. He truly tried to leave work at the office. They'd even come to agreements that they would limit the time they spent talking about work. He just couldn't do it.

People who know Dave—as well as anyone can know a basic loner like Letterman—say that he can't really be happy outside of work. Dave is the quintessential workaholic.

"I'm just the happiest, the best I ever feel, is from five-thirty to six-thirty," says Letterman, referring to the hour during which his show is taped.

There was another problem with Dave's compulsion to live *Late Night* day in and day out. It wasn't leaving Merrill any time to pursue other projects. *Late Night* might have represented the pinnacle of Dave's dreams—with the exception of *The Tonight Show,* of course—but it wasn't the end of the career road for Merrill. She still had dreams of writing television comedy scripts, maybe a screenplay.

Much as she wanted to have time to work on her own projects, however, Merrill was still willing to put them aside to stay with Dave. But, like Michelle before her, sacrificing for Dave never seemed enough.

Their relationship continued to decline. Ironically, the more Merrill tried to please Dave by shrugging off his rejection of her comedy proposals, going back to the drawing board, and coming up with more, the more tense things grew between them. Dave later explained it to *The Late Shift* author Bill Carter:

"Merrill is very disorganized about everything but getting ideas on paper. But the process that leads to that is just like an explosion. In her mind it's quite clear. And it was the beginning of the end of our relationship because I just felt like I was being poked with a sharp stick every day."

It hadn't always been like that. In fact, it was Dave and Merrill's comic synchronicity that brought them together in the first place. When Merrill first laid eyes on the lanky young comic from Indiana, she was smitten. Not only did she think he was the second best comedian working at the Comedy Store (Jay Leno was her favorite), she found him extremely attractive. After asking club regulars to tell her what they knew about the new guy in town, she discovered that they shared the same agent. Perfect! She had her opening line. She introduced herself and found she liked him even more off stage.

Dave, too, immediately found a soul mate in Merrill. She was one of the few people he'd met who shared his offbeat sense of humor. They began dating and, even though Dave had resolved not to get involved in another heavy romance so soon after his divorce, they soon began living together. As two struggling comics, it just made the most sense.

Since Merrill was more into comedy writing than performing, she was soon giving Dave material.

"When I first fell in love with Dave, I was busy writing him jokes," she told *Rolling Stone* magazine.

"It was like the things girls do for their boyfriends. You know, 'Well, here. Take all these. Here are my best jokes.' "

Merrill wasn't the prettiest girl in the club, but she certainly was the funniest.

And since Dave didn't go in for the Playboy bunny type—he much prefers a confident woman who doesn't wear makeup to a vain date who's peering into a compact every ten minutes—he was immediately taken with her.

Merrill was thrilled that Letterman, who was fast becoming the most popular comic at the Comedy Store, was interested in her. Merrill shared Dave's low self-esteem and, like Dave, was always worried about looking foolish. She saw how Dave had been temporarily distracted by the young beauties who buzzed around him after his divorce and feared she wouldn't be able to compete. Though Merrill is an attractive woman, with big brown eyes, a good figure, and lovely thick brown hair, she doesn't feel she was blessed in the beauty department.

"I've always had an obsession with how I can't pull glamour off at any level," Markoe once told *People* magazine.

"I can't pull off anything without tripping at the wrong

spot or finding that I have a big piece of marinara sauce stuck to the corner of my face. I mean, I've never had dinner with anyone where they didn't eventually wipe my face for me or pick bread out of my eyebrows."

Dave didn't care that Merrill wasn't gorgeous; he loved talking shop with her, bouncing ideas off her, sharing his dreams of the future. And he readily admits that he charmed her into giving him her best jokes.

"We had a real good rapport," Dave said in the same interview.

"She was an excellent source of material for me. I never wrote anything for her though. I have a kind of philosophy that has helped me skyrocket to the top—keep the good stuff for yourself."

Though Dave, just out of his marriage, had no intention of getting seriously involved with anyone, he and Merrill were soon inseparable.

"She's as nuts as I am," was how Dave once described Merrill.

"She would not say that. She would say that, of the two of us, she's more easygoing. But she's as high-strung and peculiar as I am. But I love her. I must add that, after calling her peculiar."

Their relationship was sorely tested early on, when both went to work on Dave's doomed midmorning talk show. Merrill, a roll-with-the-punches sort, took it in stride when the show was canceled after just four months. Dave, whose entire self-esteem was wrapped up in the show, couldn't be consoled.

"I made life pretty miserable for her," Dave said of those dark months after the cancellation.

"I thought that was my one shot."

The relationship weathered the storm, and soon Dave and

Merrill were back in business when NBC handed Dave Tom Snyder's 12:30 A.M. time slot in November 1981. Dave promptly hired Merrill as head writer.

The duo gleefully packed up their Los Angeles home—which, being workaholics, they had never really gotten around to decorating anyway—grabbed their beloved dogs, Stan and Bob, and headed for the Big Apple.

Those first few years in New York were heady ones. *Late Night* was Dave and Merrill's baby and they spent twenty-four hours a day, seven days a week, nurturing it. When even insecure Dave had to admit he had a hit on his hands, they went househunting and bought a modest home in New Canaan, Connecticut, with a big backyard for Stan and Bob.

The more popular David Letterman and his *Late Night* became, however, the more disenchanted Merrill became with being the little woman behind the scenes.

Dave understood, but what could he do about it, really?

"I always feel a little guilty," Dave told *GQ* magazine "because I'm the one who gets to go out there and for a few minutes I'm the focus of all the attention of those people. It's not the assistant director, associate producer. It's not the head writer. It's me. And I'm telling you, even if that's synthetic, the feeling of the response of those people just makes you . . . it's like being injected with a huge dose of morphine and you just think, 'Oh, man.' It really gets your attention. It can be a very emotional thing."

Merrill wasn't really looking for the high of being in the spotlight—she's just as private as Dave. But dreaming up new skits and jokes for Dave eventually became dissatisfying. Dave himself was getting tired of sparring day in and day out with the woman he went home with at night.

"It was a totally unmanageable situation," Dave said in a *People* magazine interview after Merrill stepped down as head writer in 1982, a step she hoped would both free her up to do other things and salvage their relationship.

"It was great that I trusted her comedy instincts. On the other hand, I felt like it was a 24-hour-a-day professional relationship. We both grew weary of that. Things are actually better now for everyone because I have no sexual interest in our present head writer, Steve O' Donnell, whatsoever."

"It was better to let somebody else fight the minute-to-minute battles," concurred Merrill.

For a few years, things were better. Dave and Merrill certainly had some hilarious times together, like when this determinedly unfashionable couple attended the Emmy Awards in 1986 because Dave had begrudgingly agreed to host the affair. Merrill assumed they were going to take a limo to the proceedings like everyone else; Dave said it was pretentious and suggested they drive themselves to the ceremony.

Merrill recounts the incident in her book *What the Dogs Have Taught Me:*

"Driving ourselves seemed like a fine idea to me, right up until the time we joined the unmoving crunch of gridlocked limousines that had converged on the Pasadena Civic Auditorium like salmon headed upstream . . . well, I guess to attend some kind of big salmon media event. The increasing frustration of moving only a vehicle's length per green light was starting to make my sometimes fiery-tempered escort kind of fiery-tempered. Which is why, as soon as he had an opportunity to make any turn that led out of this morass, he did so, even though that meant we were traveling away from our destination.

"This eventually led us to abandon our valet parking pass and park the car in a department store lot some six or eight blocks away. Next came a brisk walk through two very expansive department stores, followed by a very unpleasant high-speed footrace down many long blocks of city streets in over-a-hundred-degree heat. My escort maintained a constant fifteen-foot distance in front of me, glancing back only occasionally and gesturing significantly at his watch. I hobbled gloomily behind in my wool-blend tuxedo and nylons. The good times continued after we were seated. From that moment straight through the last song-and-dance extravaganza involving extras dressed up as cartoon characters, my escort subjected me to a continuous harangue as he grew more and more panicky about the safety of his car in a department store lot.

" 'You're sure you don't think they're going to lock up the place before we get out of here?' he kept asking. 'You think it's okay, right?' "

Sadly, the bad times were starting to outweigh the good times again. Quitting as head writer had eased up the tension for a time, but Merrill was still feeling stifled. She still had visions of writing sitcoms and screenplays in L.A., a dream that was impossible if she remained in New York and devoted all of her personal and professional energies to Dave's dream. Just because she was no longer head writer didn't mean she wasn't working just as hard at her job on *Late Night.* And living with Dave meant the focus of their household was the show, not her career. Being only human, Merrill was beginning to resent using all her talents to further Dave's career while hers came to a halt. Especially when Dave did nothing but complain about the quality of the show and fret that they weren't doing enough to keep it on top.

Actress Teri Garr, who knows both Dave and Merrill, told *GQ* magazine that she sympathized with Merrill.

"She's very talented and it's very hard when one person makes it so big and the other doesn't. There's so much luck involved. It's so arbitrary."

Meanwhile, another problem had arisen. Though they had had their share of problems like any other couple, Merrill loved Dave fiercely and wanted to marry him. During the first few years of their relationship, Merrill didn't really care about getting married, didn't even think about it all that much. When she first met Dave, he had just gone through a painful divorce, not the best time to badger a man for a wedding. Then, when things started to happen for them, career-wise, both were too consumed to even think about something as unimportant as a walk down the aisle. The commitment was there; who needed the piece of paper. Dave had publicly declared his love for Merrill in interviews, saying that, were he to marry again, Merrill would be the one. So there was really no reason to press the issue.

Things began to change—for Merrill, at least—a few years into *Late Night*. Though Dave was still grumbling and fretting over the show on a daily basis—that was just Dave's way—the show was a solid hit and things felt more relaxed. Merrill decided that she did want the commitment of marriage. Maybe even a family. Dave wasn't particularly opposed to the idea of kids, though he wasn't exactly embracing it either. Merrill started pressuring Dave about getting married. Dave, as he'd always done when problems arose in his personal life, simply withdrew. Merrill would bring up marriage, Dave would change the subject. The more she nagged, the more he dug in his heels. They were fighting more than ever, both at work and at home. Dave wanted to talk about nothing but the show; Merrill wanted to talk about anything but the show. It was a standoff.

Finally, in 1987, ten years after she and Dave had met, Merrill decided that she had to do something drastic to get Dave's attention. She didn't want to end the relationship; she wanted to save it. She knew Dave loved her, but if the relationship continued on the course it was on now, it was headed for disaster. Perhaps the only way to save it was to leave, put some distance between them. Make Dave wake up and realize that he didn't want to live without her. So she quit her job on *Late Night* altogether, packed her bags, and moved back to L.A. She wasn't leaving Dave; in fact, she hoped—naively perhaps—that the distance would help the relationship.

"It was very hard for me to leave," she told *People* magazine in 1988, when she and Dave were still engaged in a bi-coastal relationship.

"The show felt like a child that Dave and I had given birth to. But it got to a point where I wanted to do a lot more and couldn't without being in complete conflict with Dave. You get tired of one person always getting the final yes or no, which I'd always let him do."

The long-distance relationship worked for a time, especially when the Writers' Strike of 1988 allowed Letterman to relax in Merrill's Malibu house for a lengthy visit.

By the end of the year, however, the couple had called it quits for good.

It appeared that Dave was still trying to understand the nature of the breakup himself when he described it to *GQ* magazine a few years later.

"Without Merrill, none of this probably would have happened," he said, referring to *Late Night*'s success.

"She was an integral part of the evolution of this show. And, well, then it just became impossible and from that things came apart."

Sadly, in a replay of his breakup with his wife Michelle, he and Merrill haven't spoken since the split.

"Except I break into his house every few years," Merrill joked to the *Daily News,* referring to Dave's well-publicized stalker.

"I didn't think he would take it so bad."

Dave felt bad about losing Merrill and knew he would miss her, but he had come to believe that the relationship had run its course. Just as he speaks highly of former wife Michelle Cook to this day, he has nothing but good things to say about Merrill and their decade together. At times, he seems a bit wistful that things didn't work out differently.

In an interview last year with *Rolling Stone* magazine, Dave talked about Merrill:

"One night I think maybe Merrill and I will get back together on the show and do a couple of songs. I'm still very fond of her and she's one of these people to whom I owe a great debt. Sadly, I haven't talked to her in years. This is so silly, but in the time that has elapsed, Merrill's mother died, and I never knew about it. Two more years go by, and her dog Stan dies. So I sent her a note of condolence over the death of Stan—completely ignorant of the fact that her mother had passed. I somberly wrote, 'I now take pen in hand . . .' and she must have thought, 'Yeah, but what about my mother? She's been dead for a year and a half and you never said a thing!' But with Stan, word came to us that he'd somehow eaten an entire ham. Oh, God. And it just killed him. Too much ham."

While Dave has moved on to a new love, *Saturday Night Live* production manager Regina Lasko, Merrill is writing about the perils of still dating at forty.

"I don't know what people do on dates," says Merrill in her book *What the Dogs Have Taught Me.*

"I've been baffled by it for two decades. It's like a secret code. My definition of a perfect date is one in which, when I look back on my golden memories, I can honestly say, 'No weapons were fired, no lawsuits were filed, and everyone had pretty good hygiene.' "

This bright, talented, witty woman's career life continues to move forward, however. Merrill can be seen this summer on the new NBC replacement series *Nation*. She'll be playing a reporter on the program, which is a takeoff of newsmagazine shows.

It's obvious that, five years after the breakup, Merrill still feels a lot of pain over the way things ended.

Merrill told *Time* magazine last year that she hasn't watched Dave's show since the breakup and has vowed never to work on another late-night show again.

"I have no interest in helping any other white man in a suit do an inventive show. Let them all find their own damn inventive shows."

Chapter Seven
IS DAVE REALLY MEAN?

Michelle Cook and Merrill Markoe haven't been the only victims of Dave's moodiness and insecurity. In the eleven years Dave hosted *Late Night,* he developed a reputation for being mean to guests. While that obviously sat well with viewers, many of whom probably tuned in expressly to see what arrogant celebrity Dave would rake over the coals that night, it was a reputation that bewildered Dave himself, who never consciously set out to be cruel to anyone. It's just that his mouth often works faster than his head, and if he sees an opportunity for humor—even if it's at someone's expense—he takes it before thinking it through. It's the way he's always been, even back in grade school.

Part of it is Dave's innate distrust for and dislike of actors, many of whom he feels take themselves far too seriously. If a celebrity comes on and starts spouting nonsense about his or her craft or art, it drives Dave up a wall. And he'll usually respond by cutting them down a peg or two at the first opportunity.

"Oh, please, actors," he once said to interviewer Pat Hackett.

"I like it when actors go on shows like 'Entertainment Tonight' and talk about how their characters have 'grown.'

I actually heard one sitcom actress—Carson asked her what was different about her character—and she said, 'Well, this year she's getting a haircut.' And I thought, 'Yeah! Yeah! Let's tune in to that! She's going to have shorter hair? Oh, my god!' And she said it like, 'We're really starting to get this character pinned down on the hair issue.' "

"We never mean to be cruel," Dave told interviewer Charles Young.

"It always saddens me to hear someone might take it that way, but I've had this problem since third grade."

The problem Dave is referring to is his innate sarcasm. If someone says or does something stupid, a witty put-down just automatically pops into his head and out of his mouth before he knows what's happening. It's not that he consciously plots to embarrass his guests. He certainly doesn't review the list of guests scheduled to appear that night and think of great ways he can humiliate them on the air. But when he sees an opportunity for a laugh, he can't help but take it.

If that offends some people—and Dave is truly distressed if it does—it's also undoubtedly what makes his show so watchable.

"When people say, 'You hurt his feelings, you hurt her feelings'—that I really have to be careful about," he told *Rolling Stone* back in 1985.

"I don't want to be perceived as an asshole who just says, 'Line 'em up, bring 'em in, and let me make fun of them.' They spent weeks booking people on the show, and then they leave in tears and I think, 'What the fuck was that all about?' We spend two weeks getting somebody and in eight minutes they're out of here sobbing. I think, 'Yeah. Another job well done.'

"My big problem has been, and maybe always will be,

that if someone says something that I feel I can get a laugh by adding a remark to, I'll do it ninety percent of the time. And I know that gets in the way of an actual interview. And I know that can be annoying and I try to keep myself from doing it but something in the back of my mind always says, 'If you don't do something that gets a laugh here, this is going to be dull.' What I forget is that just because something's gotten a big laugh doesn't mean everyone enjoys the humor."

Though his conscience may nag at him occasionally, Dave understands that going for the jugular is often part of his charm. After all, who doesn't like to see some smug Hollywood actor or actress get knocked off his pedestal from time to time? Especially when it's done in a witty way. Dave wouldn't be as popular as he is if people thought that he was intentionally setting out to hurt people. Dave is often as upset as his guest if he discovers that the latter has left the building in tears because of some offhand remark he made.

On the other hand, he doesn't want to hold back either, just because it gets the occasional plastic surgeon-enhanced nose out of joint. That would be cheating his audience, and his audience—not Mr. or Ms. Big-Time Hollywood Guest—is his chief concern.

"I don't mean to hurt anybody's feelings," he told interviewer Richard David Story. "If I think I'm on the verge of being rude and insulting, well, 90 percent of the time I'll go ahead and be rude and insulting."

That's good news for Dave's legions of fans, who would argue that it's Dave's quick wit and sassy rejoinders that make the show a whole lot funnier than, say, genial Jay Leno.

One reason the public doesn't object to his occasional

on-air rudeness is because it's usually reserved for Hollywood hotshots.

It's Dave's philosophy that zillionaire celebrities are fair targets for his sometimes acid tongue.

When *Time* interviewer Richard Zoglin told him that some viewers found him condescending, smug, and occasionally mean, he replied:

"I suppose I am all of those things, but we never invite somebody on to demonstrate condescension—or condensation. If somebody comes on and is a bonehead and is loafing through an interview, I resent that and maybe I will then go after them. But if you come on and are polite and well-groomed and behave yourself then you've got nothing to worry about. I'm stunned at the number of people in show business who come on and don't seem to get that what we want from them is a performance, you know, tell us three stories out of your life."

And, just as Joan Rivers once defended her ribbing of the Royal Family by saying that anyone who owned England, Ireland, and Scotland should be able to take a joke, David Letterman feels that ridiculously-paid celebrities are fair game for his particular brand of humor.

"If I get accused of being mean to a guest, it's like, well, they're making two billion dollars a year . . . can't we make fun of somebody like that?" he once asked *TV Guide*.

There was the time, for example, when Dave had Don King on the show. Whereas another interviewer might have studiously ignored King's bizarre trademark bouffant, Dave began the interview with the question all of America had long wanted to pose:

"Let me ask you something. What's the deal with the hair?"

Don King took the question in stride, but other celebrities aren't so thick-skinned.

Nastassja Kinski reportedly hates Letterman because he made fun of her hair, which was inexplicably teased into a concoction that stood straight up about a foot above her head. Dave explained what happened to *Playboy:*

"Out she comes and it looks as if she had her hair wired around a nine iron. So I figured, anyone who appears like that on television must be doing it for a joke. You've got to trust your instincts and my instincts said, 'This woman has a barn owl on her head; ask her about the barn owl.'

"But the hairdo wasn't a joke and she got insulted and withdrew."

Nastassja reportedly left the show in tears, so upset about Dave mocking her hairdo in front of millions that she tried to get the show yanked.

Dave will occasionally make sport of people who aren't even guesting on the show.

He mercilessly mocks *Entertainment Tonight* host Mary Hart about her terminal perkiness.

"I do think there is some sort of a hormonal problem there that makes her that way," Letterman once said.

Hart didn't take offense; she later appeared on the show and was as perky and good-natured as ever.

Not everyone is such a good sport about being teased on national television.

Mark Hamill was reportedly offended when the show used him in one of their multiple-choice routines. The question was: "What does Mark Hamill do 400 times a day?" The choices were a) Brush his teeth B) Comb his hair C) Thank God for *Star Wars.*

Dave got a lot of laughs at Bo Derek's expense when he pulled out her high-school yearbook so he could show view-

ers her graduation photo. Dave couldn't believe his luck
when the perfect-ten beauty said she didn't recall attending
the school. That was all the opening he needed to pursue
the dumb blonde angle. After trying to get her to explain
how she could have forgotten attending high school, Letterman urged her to go for an equivalency exam so she
wouldn't wind up scraping pans for a living.

Another beautiful blonde he couldn't help taunting was
Sharon Stone. When the nervous actress stammered trying
to get out a sentence, she told Dave: "I can't put a sentence
together. Thank God I can take my clothes off, eh?"

"It's good to see somebody call a spade a spade, isn't
it?" Dave replied.

Dave, who is not nearly as mean-spirited as he sometimes
appears, later said that he went home with his stomach in
knots after learning that Sharon Stone was crying in the
Green Room.

Dave isn't the type to psychoanalyze his every behavior—he tried therapy twice and quit both times—but he
does have a theory on why he often feels compelled to tease
guests.

"I always was very insecure and still am," he told *TV
Guide*. "I envy comedians who can go out and enjoy being
in front of people. It's still something of a traumatic thing
for me. I'm generally uncomfortable around people. I'm
also a confirmed pessimist—if anything can go wrong, it
sure as hell will. Look, I'm a smart-ass and have been for
some time. I wasn't born that way; it evolves as a way of
compensating. You'd get bad grades as a kid so you'd trip
the guys who got good grades. Good-looking girls don't go
out with you so you throw eggs at their houses. Later, you
learn to do roughly the same thing with your mouth.

"I don't think we make people out to look like morons.

Believe me, I can cut a guy to shreds, whap, whap. I don't want to hurt anyone, don't need to. But, hell, if a guy bills himself as the Mattress King, you can legitimately hold him responsible, make him explain himself seriously—which can be funny as hell. It's just inane comedy. I'm a smart-ass, but I'm benign."

Cheryl Tiegs was reportedly angry after she went on the show to plug her line of Sears clothes. Dave asked her if she really shopped at Sears. She insisted she did. Dave said he didn't believe her. Tiegs got annoyed.

"It's really easy for me, in the fray of the battle, to try and make a joke out of something somebody has said or something somebody is wearing or whatever," he told reporter Stacy Jenel Smith.

"And it might be funny at the time, but later I'll think maybe it was a cheap thing to have done. I try and monitor myself, but I'm not always successful."

Then there was the time he had Marilyn Mach Vos Savant, the woman with the highest I.Q. in the world, on the show.

"You're the smartest person in the world? Well, shouldn't you be doing something important with your life if you're the smartest person in the world? Like maybe working on the Jarvik 7 or something?" Dave was referring to the artificial heart being worked on by Dr. Robert Jarvik.

Vos Savant took the teasing in stride. It fact, it seemed to attract her. When Letterman insisted that he was smarter than she was and urged her to ask him something so he could prove it, she asked flirtatiously: "What are you doing Saturday night?"

"Why, everyone knows I bowl on Saturday nights," replied Dave without missing a beat.

Letterman didn't prove he was smarter than Vos Savant

that night, but it appears he may be psychic: Six months after he sarcastically suggested that Marilyn should be doing something meaningful like working on the Jarvik 7 artificial heart, Vos Savant met Dr. Robert Jarvik and began dating him. They were married a year later.

Not all guests find Letterman's ribbing as charming as Vos Savant did.

Dave had a well-publicized blowout with Cher, who shocked the usually unflappable host by calling him an asshole right at the start of the interview. Dave obviously remains conflicted about the incident because, in past interviews, he has both said he was hurt and amused by the incident. Here's what happened: Cher came out, settled herself in the chair, and when Dave welcomed her to the show, she told him she'd been reluctant to appear.

"Why?" asked Dave innocently.

"Because I heard you're an asshole."

When Cher saw how flustered Letterman became—he never quite recovered himself for the interview and was not at all his usual glib, bantering self—she sent a note of apology.

Letterman later told *People* magazine that Cher's remark had really stung him.

"It did hurt my feelings. Cher was one of the few people I've really wanted to have on the show, and then she calls me an asshole. I felt like a total fool, especially since I say all kinds of things to people. I was sitting there thinking, 'Okay, Mr. Big Shot, can you take it as well as you can dish it out?' "

But time seems to have mellowed the memory for Dave, who recently told *TV Guide:*

"I just loved it when Cher came on the show and cursed me out. It was great. I think that the reason I'm sometimes confrontational is because I want somebody to lay me out. It doesn't hurt my feelings. It's just TV, kids."

David usually feels bad later if he finds out that he hurt someone with an offhand remark or flip retort, but one guest he has no sympathy for is Shirley MacLaine.

He recounts the incident for *Time* magazine.

"Shirley was too big a star to do a preinterview. We had no idea what she wanted to talk about. So the talent staff put together a list of four or five questions based on research material. Then she comes on the program and she brings with her an attitude, which she mentioned early on: 'I guess Cher was right.' I thought that was untoward, needless. And then, when I would ask her the questions, about her past lives or about her book or about her film—projects that she had devoted no small measure of time and effort to—she just couldn't be bothered. So I thought to myself: Why are you on this show, lady? There was not a gun at this woman's head. I have less and less patience for that kind of behavior."

Here's how their exchange went on national TV. Letterman began by asking Shirley about her past lives.

> Shirley: Why are you so interested in this?
> Dave: Because I know you're interested in it.
> Shirley: But I already said I don't think we can get into it and you keep harping on it. Maybe Cher was right, maybe you're an asshole.
> Dave: Why did you call me that?
> Shirley: I thought it was a funny remark.
> Dave: Calling me an asshole? In my own defense, you can't be upset with my asking you about this. You are very well-known for two things—your acting, of

course, and for your interest in this sort of thing. Are you really upset or are you pretending?

Shirley: You can't tell?

Dave: I've never met you.

Shirley: You've met me. You were running around these dressing rooms at NBC, trying to get me to go on your show. What do you mean I haven't met you?

Shirley then ventured that Dave was acting strangely because he had given blood before the show.

"You're a cute kid. You're nervous, you're tired, you gave a lot of blood. You don't know why the hell you're sitting with me, you don't know what I'm talking about, what this is all about, this woman who's had 2,000 past lives, who seems to be insane."

Dave responded to that by announcing that he was delighted they were running out of time and invited Shirley to share any last thoughts.

Dave: Is there anything you want to talk about?

Shirley: You're the interviewer, you tell me, you've wanted me here for three years.

Dave: And I think we'll probably wait another three.

Shirley later said she was annoyed that Dave kept harping on her past lives and wouldn't let her promote her new movie, *Madame Sousatzka*.

"I felt he had a hidden agenda and was trying to go at me. The research staff had obviously given him information on all my past lives and he had a joke on each of them. I take that seriously. I didn't want to play."

Though Dave doesn't remember the incident fondly, Shirley seems to have already put it in the past—one of her past lives, to be exact.

"Maybe we were irascible lovers in a past life," she says about that awful exchange six years ago.

If some guests get mad at what Dave says to them, others become miffed at what Dave's guests say about them. Roseanne Arnold was furious two years ago when shock-jock Howard Stern was a guest on *Late Night* and called Roseanne "a big, fat slob" and her husband Tom "the Yoko Ono of the 1990s." Howard then congratulated Dave for not booking Roseanne and Tom when they were in New York City hosting *Saturday Night Live.* Looking somewhat uncomfortable at where the discussion was going, Dave immediately quipped, "Now wait a minute. What really happened is that at the last minute we realized we were able to get Marv Albert."

The truth was that Roseanne had been invited to appear—with or without Tom—and had been unable to fit it into her schedule. She was furious at Stern, but also annoyed at Dave for not taking the time to set the record straight.

The Arnolds and Letterman have since made up, with Roseanne guesting on the show and Tom making a quick appearance.

Another celebrity who has kissed and made up with Dave is notoriously humorless *Today* show cohost Bryant Gumbel. His feud with Letterman began in 1985. Learning that Jane and Bryant were taping their show in Rockefeller Center, right beneath Dave's office window, he picked up a bullhorn and bellowed: "Attention, people of New York!"

He then called startled passersbys' attention to the discrepancy between the massive newspaper advertisements that had run hyping the *Today* show and the teeny-weeny one that promoted *Late Night.*

Then, when he had gotten everyone's attention, he yelled into the megaphone: "I'm Larry Grossman, president of NBC News . . . and I'm not wearing any pants!"

When word got back that Gumbel was peeved, Letterman did what we've come to expect of him: He continued to harangue Gumbel mercilessly on the air.

A petulant statement from the *Today* show producer just added to the sandbox-fight mentality that made Dave's action so hilarious in the first place.

"If David wants to carry out a vendetta against Bryant, then it doesn't bother us," said *Today*'s producer.

"We're not going to get sidetracked in little freak shows. We're here to beat *Good Morning America.*"

But clearly it did bother Bryant Gumbel, who finally issued his own statement on the subject.

"I've always said, 'I don't expect David to do a *mea culpa* on the air. That's never been my way.' But I would have thought that he would have been enough of a man to pick up the phone privately and say, 'Hey look, it's gotten way out of hand. I'm sorry.' That hasn't happened. And I'm not asking for it to happen. I'm really not. I guess what I'm saying is, the fact that it hasn't happened tells me a lot about the guy. Do I want to be on his program? No. Do I hate the guy? No. Do I want him on my show? Noooo."

It took four years, but Dave and Bryant have since made nice and Gumbel has even been on Dave's new CBS show. Letterman extended the peace pipe by returning to Bryant a copy of the now infamous memo Gumbel wrote, and an NBC employee leaked, in which the grouchy anchor condemned coworkers like wacky weatherman Willard Scott. Gumbel called Letterman to thank him for returning the stolen document and they called a truce. Several weeks later, to make their reconciliation official, Gumbel popped in on *Late Night with David Letterman*. To show there were no hard feelings, Gumbel even helped read "The Top Ten List," though several of the jokes were on him. The subject—Questions Asked of Prospective NBC Employees—included "Any problem carpooling with Bryant?" and "You wouldn't leak a guy's memo, would you?"

Dave can handle the occasional starlet with her nose out of joint, but even he must have been uncomfortable when he inadvertently infuriated mobster Joseph "Joe Dogs" Iannuzzi.

Iannuzzi is a former Gambino mobster turned FBI informant who was under the Federal Witness Protection Program when he wrote a book called *The Mafia Cookbook*. U.S. Marshals warned him that if he went on TV to promote his book he'd be booted out of the Federal Witness Protection Program. But when the Letterman people came knocking, the offer was just too good to refuse, so Iannuzzi ditched the marshals and boarded a plane for New York. Imagine his chagrin when he arrived in New York City and discovered that his appearance had been canceled.

"Dave thinks he's got a problem with Margaret Ray showing up in his living room," Iannuzzi barked.

"Wait until he gets home one night and finds me waiting for him."

Luckily for Dave, Joe Dogs has yet to make good on the threat, issued in October 1993.

All these incidents have made some guests afraid to either return to the show or come on at all.

Jamie Lee Curtis reportedly won't be back because she resented Dave talking about her body and asking her why she liked to get naked in her movies so much.

Joan Collins became incensed with Dave at the 1986 Emmy Awards, when she heard that Letterman had told viewers he couldn't wait to attend the Awards show and see if Joan Collins is "all she's cracked up to be." He also referred to the age-sensitive star as "Old What's-Her-Name." Word trickled out that Joan, who had the misfortune of running into her nemesis backstage, fumed every time she saw him giving her his famous gap-toothed grin. So fun-loving Dave escalated the war in 1989 by sending a page across the hall to another NBC studio where Collins was hawking her new perfume.

"I'm afraid to go over there because I know she hates us," he told the page.

"Go ask her if she'll come over here. She'll look much older in person. Say you have a friend who'd like to meet her."

Naturally, the page—accompanied by Dave's camera crew—was rudely rebuffed at Collins's dressing-room door.

"I almost got killed," the page moaned when she returned to Dave's set, much to the laughter and delight of Letterman and his audience.

"David may think it's funny, but Joan doesn't," her publicist said. "After this escapade, don't expect to see her chatting on *Late Night*."

There's something about the Emmy Awards that brings out the worst in Dave. Perhaps it's all that "Aren't-we-celebrities-great" pomp and circumstance Letterman loathes so much. In any event, a few years earlier, he had managed to infuriate the Emmy producers when he was badgered into hosting the 1986 event by NBC, who thought it would be great prime-time exposure for their late-night star.

Everyone, including Dave, lived to regret it.

"He made things extremely difficult," confided a crew member after the show. "The producers didn't really want any host because that slows the show down, but NBC insisted on Letterman. He wouldn't cooperate with the dance-and-song number they wanted to do, even though they tried to make it funny because they know he thinks those productions are ridiculous. He wouldn't tell them what his jokes were going to be in advance, or how long they would take, which made it difficult to cue commercial breaks."

There was a winner in that Emmy debacle: cohost Shelley Long. She had such a bad reputation from *Cheers* that the crew thought she'd be a real prima donna. Compared to Dave, they thought she was a dream.

Another guest Letterman won't be shooting the breeze with any time soon is actress Martha Raye, who took her thin skin all the way to a courthouse in 1987.

Raye wasn't even on the show when she got her nose out of joint. She became incensed when David joked one night that he had seen "the most terrifying commercial on television last night featuring Martha Raye, actress, condom user."

Though the remark was obviously a send-up of the seventy-eight-year-old actress's denture commercials, she insisted she had been defamed and slapped the comedian with a $10 million defamation of character lawsuit, even though Letterman aired a retraction. (Raye retorted that the retraction was done in a sarcastic and arrogant manner.) Raye's court papers said that Letterman's remark implied that Raye was sexually promiscuous, had loose morals, and had frequent sexual intercourse with people she believed to be infected with or exposed to the AIDS virus. Raye added that all of the implications are false (what a surprise!) and were made with a reckless disregard for the truth.

Sometimes even Dave realizes he's gone too far and when he does, he apologizes.

In late August of 1988, Pittsburgh Steelers owner and

NFL cofounder Art Rooney, Sr., died. The day after his death, Letterman said in his opening monologue that Rooney's death occurred during pro football's exhibition season, which "led to some confusion as to whether the death actually counts."

Even Dave's adoring studio audience thought he had gone too far on that one and they booed him. The next day, he issued an apology.

"It was not my intention to defame the memory of a fine man," he said. "You have my deepest, most heartfelt apologies."

Certain celebrities may not think Dave is funny, especially when he finds an Achilles' heel—like sixty-year-old Joan Collins's age sensitivity—and goes at it like a pitbull. But it's a brand of humor that obviously hits home with much of America.

And, in Dave's defense, some celebrities go on his show looking for a fight. Or at least that's the way Dave sees it. In 1985, Letterman told this story to *The Cleveland Plain Dealer:*

"I had a show the other night with Van Johnson. I've watched his movies all along and thought of him as a real engaging fellow on the screen, as well as being a good actor. But when we had him on, he was pretty much incorrigible. I think it was a case of him coming in thinking, 'Well, I'll show this young pup' and so on. He came out all ready to fight—and there was no fight. So it all pretty much laid there in an unpleasant heap between his chair and my desk. It was real awkward.

"When I see that sort of thing, I try to relax the person, let them know we're not out to make fun of them. But I'm real bad at getting out of a situation when it goes that far."

Dave knew he was in for a lot of premeditated shocks

when he invited Madonna on *Late Show*, in March 1993, but even Letterman seemed a bit taken aback by the Material Girl's behavior, which included uttering the f-word a dozen times, bringing her panties out for Dave to sniff (he declined), and recommending urinating in the shower as a way to combat athlete's foot.

"You used to be really kind of cool," she said at one point. "You just kiss up to everybody on the show now."

"I can suspend that for tonight," Dave replied.

"It turned kind of ugly, didn't it?" Letterman said to the audience after he finally got Madonna to leave the stage (she had stayed through her segment and the next guest's spot, displacing a grocery bagger from Iowa). "I tried to be nice to her. I'm exhausted now. What if she's here tomorrow night?"

Others are savvy enough to take Letterman's ribbing.

When Marilu Henner, one of Dave's favorite guests, appeared on his new CBS show, the then pregnant actress joked: "I had a sonogram, but I wasn't sure if I should bring it and have you make fun of my child before he was born."

Dave says he just can't help himself.

"I just see a chance to make a joke, and I make it and then . . . it's like the excuse people have when there's a domestic shooting. You know, 'I'm sorry. I lost control for a second. I'm fine now.' "

While he may joke about his reputation, it often bothers him.

In 1987 he told the Associated Press that he had seen something disturbing in the now-defunct series *The Days and Nights of Molly Dodd:*

"There was a line in the premiere episode about 'I stayed up last night and watched David Letterman humiliate someone.' And I was very sensitive about it because I'm not like that."

Letterman has also been criticized for appearing grumpy on the air, but that's something he won't apologize for. He simply doesn't believe a host should hide his or her feelings from the audience. He believes people would prefer to see an honest performance. Like everyone else, he has good days and bad days, so why, he ventures, should he pretend otherwise?

"You see so much happiness and so much phony effervescence and so much manufactured joy on television," Dave told *Washington Post* writer Tom Shales.

"In fact, this is something Jack Paar told me a long time ago: It's okay to let people know you're upset, or pretend you're upset, because then, if they're sitting at home, they say, 'Jeez, I wonder if he really is upset!' And I've always kind of felt that there was a certain amount of truth in that."

However, he doesn't mind going for the jugular if a guest isn't doing his or her part to contribute to the show. Laziness on the part of a guest is one thing that incenses Dave, a perfectionist who wants every show to be a winner.

"If some bonehead comes on and loafs through an interview, I resent that. And I go after them."

One person he went after was Grace Jones. The close-cropped singer/actress did the unthinkable and arrived late for a *Late Night* appearance, leaving Dave without his opening guest. He was furious and spent his entire monologue saying things like "Who needs Grace Jones anyway?" and telling the audience that she's always late.

Things didn't get better when Grace finally arrived. It was a case of late not being better than never.

"Why are you always late for everything?" Letterman demanded when she finally walked on stage.

Not to be intimidated by Letterman, the towering star grabbed him by the shoulders, looked into his eyes, and said: "If you had a schedule like mine, you would be late, too."

"I thought she was going to punch him in the face," Grace's agent said later.

Her agent claims that, despite her bravado on the air, she was so shaken by Letterman that she broke down in the dressing room later.

Not every celebrity is easily thrown. For example, Don King, unlike Nastassja Kinski, didn't take offense when Dave demanded an explanation for that hair of his.

"You have to parry with him," King told *People* magazine. "But if you get into a repartee game, he's gonna win."

Another celebrity who doesn't find Dave's guest chair too hot to sit in is actress Christine Lahti. She says that the secret to handling Dave is to insult yourself first and put yourself down so much that there's nothing left for Dave to do but to build you back up.

Jane Pauley, Dave's old pal from Indiana, is philosophical about her appearances.

"I know I'm going to be embarrassed within an inch of my life."

Another guest who knows how to play Dave's game is Cybill Shepherd. When Dave discovered that Shepherd, who was booked to appear on his show later in the week, had sent to the *Late Night* studio the dress she planned to wear, he decided to turn it into a running gag. Every night the viewers were treated to the vision of Cybill's dress on a mannequin. When Cybill finally appeared on the show, she walked out in a towel. She couldn't wear the dress, she explained, after everyone had seen it already.

Dave has also been criticized for mocking the man (or

woman) on the street in his famous remotes. It's one thing, people say, to make fun of the rich and famous. It's another thing to barge into a doughnut shop and make the clerk look foolish by asking him or her questions like how many doughnuts a person should eat each day. As the camera crew filed into tiny shops and began filming away, befuddled salespeople would blurt out foolish things like, "three dozen." It was very funny, but at the expense of the doughnut shop workers.

Dave explained what happened to writer Charles M. Young in a 1983 interview:

"The premise was simply: doughnut. It just turned out that most of the shops were run by recent immigrants. We really had no idea beforehand, and we decided afterwards to make an effort in the future to find people who speak English. Who would have thought all the doughnuts in New York were made by people from Serbia?"

Merrill Markoe defended the segment.

"We're not talking to these people about their worth as human beings or their hopes for their children," she said.

"We only ask about inane things. The burden of being a jerk is on us because we're stupid enough to ask about doughnuts. It's just a different way of looking at American culture."

And people forget that Dave can also be quite touching and reverent. On January 28, 1986, the day the *Challenger* space shuttle blew up, killing all the astronauts as well as the first civilian-in-space—teacher and married mother of two Christa McAuliffe—he used his monologue time to speak movingly about the disaster and say how much he regretted having to do his show on such a tragic day.

"It's never been my intention to cause ill will among the

fraternity and sorority of celebrities," Dave told writer Jennet Conant.

"I think some people may feel that they're not being treated with enough respect or that their work is diminished through some flip attitude on my part. But I'm a wiseass and a smart-ass and I always have been."

Orson Bean once summed up Dave's unique humor this way:

"He's an acquired taste like Scotch Whiskey. I worked with him when he replaced Johnny Carson one night and he seemed like a cold fish to me. And now I think he's a genius."

Of course, what the audience doesn't always see is that Dave can be extremely gracious to guests, too. He once leaned over during a commercial break and told then-overweight actress Ricki Lake, "You know, you're very pretty."

Though Dave has made an effort to be nicer to guests on his new CBS show, the folks who prefer mean-spirited Dave needn't worry.

"I've gotten better as an interviewer, but I'm still kind of like the kickstand, and the guest is the bicycle. If there's someone on and I'm not interested, heh, well. . . ."

Part Three
The Perils of Success

Chapter Eight
DAVE'S PRIVATE DEMONS

David Letterman may come across to viewers and celebrity guests as arrogant and self-assured, but nothing could be further from the truth. Those who know David best say he is the most insecure person in the world, shocked at his own success, convinced that it could all be taken away from him at any time. He is a classic sufferer of the Imposter Syndrome, believing he has somehow tricked people into thinking he's talented and that someday, when the truth leaks out, his gig will be up.

Privacy-freak Dave rarely lets down his guard in interviews, but he once let slip to *Interview* magazine's Pat Hackett that his insecurity has its roots in childhood.

"I have a crude theory that I'm sure is not true, but I base it on the people I was hanging around with night after night (at comedy clubs in the late seventies). I think it's either people who did not get enough attention as kids or kids who got way too much who go into comedy."

So did you get too much attention or too little, the interviewer asked, not really expecting Dave to answer.

"I got too little. I clearly got too little. Comedians, by and large, are not fun people to hang around with. They're dejected and depressed and sullen and nasty and backbiting and jealous and I'm right in there, I'm included. You don't want to spend any time with me, either. But they all have that one desire in common—to draw laughter out of people. You want to show that girl in high school who wouldn't give you the time of day, 'Look what I can do in front of 200 people. I can get them to laugh! You wouldn't go out with me back then, and I was getting D's in Shop, but. . . .' And I think that's probably the motivation."

Amazingly, Dave then admitted to Hackett that he had attempted therapy—twice. Dave's fans will be pleased to know that he failed therapy. It's hard to imagine the wise-cracking, intensely private talk-show host lying on a couch in a psychiatrist's office, recalling his dreams from the night before and revealing his innermost thoughts and secrets. Not surprisingly, Dave found that he was unable to be open enough with a therapist to make the visits worthwhile. He jokes that he was unable to be honest in therapy because he wanted to make a good impression, but the truth is that David is not a man who goes in for self-examination: not of his abilities as a talk-show host; not of his worth as a human being. Thank you very much, but he'd rather stay messed up. It's worked for him so far.

"There were two periods in my life when I went to see a therapist and it came down to the fact that I would have to make massive changes in my personality. And I was reluctant to make those changes, so I said, 'Nah, I'm done here. I'm fine now.' So I'm just as screwed up now as I was then."

It's not surprising that Dave quit counseling. In his professional life, he's tenacious. From the time he declared his communications major at Ball State University, every move he has made has been motivated by the desire to be a major player in the broadcasting field.

His personal life is another story altogether. At work, he'll review the videotapes of his show over and over, searching for areas that could stand improvement. There's no such soul searching in his personal life. There just isn't time.

When the going gets rough in Dave's personal life, he'd rather get going than stop and explore the reasons. When his marriage to Michelle Cook was disintegrating and she begged him to work things out, he asked for a divorce. When things started to get uncomfortable with Merrill, he called it quits. Since career is the number one motivating force in his life, he simply can't—won't—take the time to work on his personal life. And if his personal life suffers for it, well, then that's just part of the price you pay to be at the top. He can live with that.

Part of Dave's aloofness with people, his tendency to keep all but a very few friends totally at bay, has its roots in his childhood. Starting in high school, when Dave found himself shunned by the cool cliques, rejected by the girls he desired, he adopted an attitude of indifference. At the time, it was just a stance he took to maintain his dignity, to show the other kids at school that he didn't want to be a part of their world anyway. But as he became an adult, he never shed his armor of apathy. To this day, he remains distant from all but a very few close friends—most of whom are, not surprisingly, work associates.

Even those relationships tend to be somewhat superficial. Dave will take in a ball game with one of his writers, but he won't accept a dinner invitation to his house.

Young David was rejected by the cool kids in high school and now it's payback time. These days, Dave is the one doing the shunning. He seems to keep his distance especially from what is the adult version of the cool cliques: celebrities.

When *People* magazine asked stars who had been on *Late Night* many times and seemed to have a personal relationship with Dave—celebrities like Teri Garr and Sandra Bernhard—if they were indeed friends of the enigmatic talk-show host, they all said the same thing: We wish. We'd love to have a personal relationship with him. We'd love to be one of Dave's cool friends. In fact, *People* magazine, if you can relay that message to Dave in your article, that would be great.

They all believed Dave truly liked them, but admitted that they had had no personal contact with him outside of appearing on his show. Without exception, he had made no overtures to any one of them in any capacity besides inviting them to be a guest on his show. Much to their regret.

Even *Late Night* bandleader Paul Shaffer, who's known and worked with Dave for over a dozen years, has only the most minimal contact with him outside the studio. When *Time* magazine interviewer Richard Zoglin asked Dave back in 1989 if Paul Shaffer was as good a friend as he appeared to be from watching the show, Dave replied:

"I have a great deal of respect for Paul and if he decided to quit the show, I don't know that I would continue without him. We're close; we chat every day before the show and after the show. We've been to dinner many times, and he's been to my house many times. I like him, and I think he's the best at what he does. But we're not best friends. I think it would be odd for me and Paul to be best friends away from the show and then have any kind of acceptable relationship on the show."

And then, the inevitable joke: "By the way, this is Paul's last night. I caught him using my comb, so we had to let him go."

It's interesting that Dave noted that working with one's

best friend would be an untenable situation, considering the fact that he'd worked with his live-in lover, Merrill, for ten years. Perhaps that's where Dave learned his lesson about not mixing business with pleasure. Working and living with Merrill, discussing the show twenty-four hours a day, was one of the things that doomed their relationship.

It wasn't too surprising that he eventually broke his new rule about personal relationships at the office when he began dating current girlfriend Regina Lasko, a former *Late Night* staffer. Where else would Dave possibly meet women? He's not going to meet them at the many star-studded events that he gets invited to, because Dave refuses to attend them. Dave has never been part of the Hollywood or New York party scene, preferring to go directly home at night. Unless it's a gala honoring someone he admires and respects, like Johnny Carson or race-car driver Nigel Mansell, he'd rather go home. He hates being out in public, and can barely stand to eat in restaurants because of all the attendant fuss his presence causes. He does his charity work quietly, preferring to write a check than participate in public spectacles like telethons and walkathons.

In 1986, he was beside himself because NBC had coerced him into cohosting that year's Emmy Awards with *Cheers* star Shelley Long. He wanted no part of it.

"The way I look at it," he confided to *New York Times* reporter Glenn Collins a few months before the ceremony, "they have till mid-September to find someone else for the Emmy deal. I'm especially afraid that they'll want me to sing and dance in a large group of people."

They did, Dave refused, and the show—from Dave's point of view and the point of view of the Emmy producers who had to work with him—was a disaster. Dave never had to host the Emmys again.

Though he gets ten weeks vacation, Dave doesn't travel often because he hates to be too far away from work. Basically, Dave remains the loner he was in high school. Now that he could be part of the in crowd—now that he is actively sought out by starlets and professional athletes—it's his turn to do the shunning. Whether it's payback or a defense mechanism that is so deeply rooted it's impossible to shake, only Dave knows.

It's amazing that a man as cynical as Letterman would have even attempted therapy, and absolutely understandable why it failed. If Dave won't share himself with, and open up to, his closest friends, why would he spill his guts to a complete stranger, albeit one with counseling credentials? The answer is, he couldn't.

Letterman acknowledges that the reason he failed therapy—as opposed to therapy failing him—is that he withheld his feelings from his therapist. He couldn't bear to drag his deepest, darkest secrets out for a therapist to scrutinize. Worse, he didn't want to be made to examine them himself. The little he did tell the therapist about himself, he now says, wasn't very truthful. Eventually, the exercise seemed futile.

"It's like Sunday school," he once said about therapy. "You want 'em to think the best of you."

It's a shame that many viewers—who maybe tuned in on one occasion and caught David raking some guest over the coals—now and forever believe that Letterman is an arrogant ass. Nothing could be further from the truth. If anything, David is still the shy young boy who longed to hang out with the popular athletes and the pretty girls. He's finally in their league, finally made it onto the A party list, but he still can't—and perhaps never will—believe he belongs there.

Moreover, he doesn't really want to belong. He perhaps distrusts celebrities so much because they're just adult versions of the stuck-up cheerleaders and football players who rejected him as a youth. Or, as Dave likes to say, winners of the genetic crapshoot. There's nothing Dave hates more than an actress who sits haughtily on his stage, talking about her craft, when Letterman, the studio audience, and the home viewers know darn well that she wouldn't be sitting where she is were it not that she was blessed with high cheekbones, perfect teeth, and an elegant upturned nose.

For all his loathing of pretentious actors and shallow actresses, Dave does occasionally have on a guest that he deeply admires. That's when cocky, mean-spirited Letterman disappears, replaced by geeky, goofy Dave. For every guest Dave has sassed into stunned silence, there's a guest that he's been shy and awkward with. He still gets a bit tongue-tied around truly stunning women like the occasional model he has on his show and, being a sports nut, he's positively deferential around guests he admires like athletes who are at the top of their games. He acted like a thrilled teenager when Bruce Springsteen appeared on his last *Late Night* show, and has always treated his personal heroes, like Johnny Carson and race-car driver Nigel Mansell, with the greatest respect. When such luminaries are on, David Letterman acts exactly the way any of us would if we suddenly found ourselves face-to-face with someone we admired: He gushes, he fawns, he stammers.

Dave doesn't really understand why he has this reputation for meanness and arrogance. Well, he does understand that it comes from his razor-sharp wit, which, he's willing to admit, has been used to slash a dull or combative guest from time to time. But what he doesn't get is how a man as shy, humble, and down-to-earth as Dave has always been could be saddled with such a stinging reputation. After all, Dave is—and always has been—the first to say that he can't understand how he got where he is and spends every day wondering when (not *if*, but *when*) it's all going to come to an end.

Dave is hardly arrogant, if arrogant is defined as someone who thinks he's better or more special than everyone else. If anything, he's the world's most insecure pessimist.

During his third year as host of *Late Night*, for example, Dave was taken aside by the NBC network brass and congratulated on his amazing twenty-five percent jump in ratings. His response?

"I don't know what the hell happened. We're not doing anything different on the show. Maybe we've just worn people down. They just say, 'Oh, alright, oh, God, we'll watch your damned show.'"

And then, the disclaimer: "The ratings'll probably just go back down again."

He rarely watches his own show when it airs at night because he finds it so painful to watch his performance. All he can see are the flaws, never the successes. And they loom much larger to Dave than they really are. When he points out mistakes he's made on the show and the person he's with claims not to see them, he thinks he's being humored.

"I've heard that I have a cool personality, which is a contrast to how I feel most of the time," he once told *Chicago Tribune Magazine* writer Larry Kart.

"I can sit at home and watch myself host the show and turn to the person who is watching with me and say: 'This is where it happened. This is where the s.o.b. collapsed and we were lucky to get out with our lives.' And they'll say,

'You're kidding me—what are you talking about?' And I'll think, Oh, yeah . . . you can't tell."

Dave has never learned how to take compliments gracefully. Just as he has an overwhelming need to go for the jugular if a guest puts his neck on the cutting board during a show, Dave can't bring himself to just say, "Thank you." He always has to find a way to question, disparage, or diminish any praise that comes his way.

He didn't consider it a compliment, for example, when he was told in the early eighties that he had developed quite a rabid following.

"They used to call me a cult favorite," he said back in 1986. "I thought that meant 'nobody's watching.' "

Dave is philosophical about his pessimistic nature, which he doesn't necessarily consider a bad thing. His theory is that if you expect to fail, you're better off because then you're not as devastated when it happens.

"Reality dictates that you're probably better off being insecure," he once told United Press International.

"That way, you won't be surprised when it (cancellation) happens, although the other school is that you know it's going to happen so relax and enjoy it along the way. I have not been able to do that."

To say that Dave has had trouble enjoying the ride to success is an understatement. When he was working at small stations in Indiana, he fretted that he'd never make it to the big markets, meaning Los Angeles, New York, and Chicago. Once he went to Los Angeles, he was terrified that he was going to make a fool of himself doing stand-up and have to return to Indiana, broke and humiliated. When he got his morning show and it was canceled so abruptly, he feared he'd never work in the business again, even though NBC immediately signed him to a lucrative holding package so as not to lose their promising star. When he got *Late Night,* he spent the first three years worrying about being pulled off the air, and the next several years wondering how in the world he was going to manage to keep his ratings strong day after day, year after year. And when he lost *The Tonight Show,* it all just confirmed his worst fears about himself. He really wasn't good enough. Oh, sure, he could entertain prisoners, insomniacs, and college kids at the sleepy 12:30 A.M. time slot, but no one trusted his talent enough to put him on at 11:30 P.M. No one thought him worthy of taking over for Johnny Carson. He had suspected that he was worthless all along; now he had the proof. Even when all the major networks were fighting over him in the wake of the *Tonight Show* debacle, he never really believed they were battling over him, David Letterman. He just thought that Creative Artist Agency superagent Mike Ovitz had managed to pull the wool over everyone's eyes and convince the network big boys—whom Letterman didn't think were terribly bright anyway—that Dave was worth a small fortune. What a joke, Dave thought. No wonder Mike Ovitz has the reputation he does as being the mother of all agents. Just look at what he was pulling out of his hat for old Dave Letterman of Indiana.

And finally, when he landed his $14 million per year, three-year contract with CBS—which should have given him some idea that he had something special—he was the most terrified of all. There were those fleeting moments of satisfaction, to be sure, like when Dave got to stick it to NBC and tell them he was leaving. Or when he held his CBS press conference and basked in the glory of his $42 million deal. But once the reporters and photographers left and Dave was alone to ponder the move, that old familiar feeling, terror, struck deep to his very core again. This is a fine mess I'm in now, Dave thought. What if the much-ballyhooed $14 million a year show doesn't fly? What if I can't play to Peoria an hour earlier? What if Jay Leno does prove that he was the better man for the job, after all of Dave's bellyaching about how the position rightfully belonged to him? The humiliation of it all was too great to think about.

"Dave is terribly modest about his work," says Connie Chung. "He will not bask in the glory of his comedy."

A small window into the way David Letterman's mind works can be found in an interview he gave where he discussed the creation of *Late Night*. He worked and worked and worked toward finding a winning formula for the difficult 12:30 A.M. time slot until finally something clicked and people began watching. Only Dave was now clueless as to what it was that he had done to make people watch the show.

"In the beginning you try everything and you don't know which button to push to get the thing off the ground. And suddenly, when you get a little momentum, you're not sure which one of those buttons caused it."

The worst thing for Dave is not failure, it's success. Because his pessimistic nature tells him that staying on top is impossible to sustain, and the ride back down won't be so pretty. Considering the following words from a mid-eighties interview, one can only imagine how absolutely terrified Dave is feeling now that his *Late Show* is king of the 11:30 P.M. time slot.

"I can remember a few years ago when things started really improving for us. I remember having this amazing sense of dread: 'Aw, jeez, now that people are watching, what are we going to do?' The other thing, maybe from a more practical position, is it's hard to keep coming up with great new ideas."

If Dave has a love/hate relationship with his own show, it's an ambivalence he shares about the medium in general.

"I have two feelings about television," he told *New York Post* reporter James Endrst.

"I think television stinks, and I think it's supposed to stink. I don't think we want it to be good. There are exceptions, of course, but by and large, I don't think we want it to be so good that people spend any more time watching it. I think it's just about the way it ought to be."

It seems Dave was listening back home in Indiana when his parents used to tell the young boy to turn off the television, get off the couch, and get outside to play. He may earn his living from the medium, but he recognizes that too many Americans—particularly children—spend far too many hours plopped in front of the boob tube.

For all his smart-ass ways on the air, Dave is also notoriously shy. It's really such a shame; now that the geeky guy who couldn't get a date in high school is in demand, he's too introverted to take advantage of it. Now that the cool people are ready to accept him—indeed, they're tripping over themselves to get his attention and gain his acceptance—he wants no part of their world.

"I have no patience for people who come on a show, who are in show business and sit there and expect to be paid tribute," he once said.

One of Dave's frequent guests is Dr. Ruth Westheimer. Dave may not have stuck with his real therapist, but Dr. Ruth thinks she knows what makes the enigmatic talk-show host tick. When Dr. Ruth appears on the show, she doesn't see the intimidating, smart-mouthed host that celebrities fear; she sees the shy, straitlaced boy from Indiana who attended church every Sunday.

"He stumbles every time he has to say the word orgasm," Ruth once joked to *People* magazine. "But he's getting better."

Dave didn't deny it. He could never be a shock-jock like Howard Stern, lining babes up on the show to ask them about their bra cup size. Though he loves to have Stern on his show, doing that kind of schtick.

"Dr. Ruth Westheimer does embarrass me with all her talk of clitorises and penises," a beet-red Dave once said.

Teri Garr, who has been on *Late Night* so often, has perhaps the most telling anecdote about Dave and just how insecure he is.

"It's weird," she told writer Jennet Conant, who profiled David Letterman for *GQ* magazine.

"I'll be on the show, and he'll push a note right under my face. And it'll say 'I HATE MYSELF.' So I'll say, 'No, no, Dave, you're wonderful.' And he'll take it back and underline 'I HATE MYSELF' twice and push it back. What's that about?"

Garr—who, despite what viewers might think, insists she's never had anything even approaching a personal relationship with the talk-show host—has a theory about Dave.

"Dave's a regular, middle-class ordinary guy who doesn't like it when you spill Coca-Cola on his new carpet. Now he's been thrown into this incredible thing, and he doesn't want to become Elvis. To go on and do a show every night the way he does, you have to say to yourself, I am pretty fucking great. He doesn't want to admit that about himself."

Dave's shyness manifests itself in other ways. He has said publicly that he still gets nervous performing before a live audience, would never want to go back to the terrifying field of stand-up, and is generally uncomfortable around people. In fact, he has said on more than one occasion that it's his discomfort with guests that sometimes brings out the worst in him. He simply doesn't know how to be Joe Cordial during an interview. Heck, he says he doesn't really know how to interview. So he tries to banter with guests in an informal way which sometimes leads to unfortunate slips of the tongue. Later, if he hears that he's truly hurt someone's feelings, he's full of remorse.

Dave may not have a lot of friends, but the friends he has he's had for years. He remains friendly with a few comics from his stand-up days, like comedian Jeff Altman, and he's close to a handful of staffers who have been with him for years. He's extremely close to former *Tonight Show* producer Peter Lassally, whom he hired to produce *Late Night* when Johnny Carson retired, but Lassally is more a father figure to him than a pal. He's friendly with Johnny Carson, but since Johnny is also notoriously private and the men live on opposite coasts, they only see each other occasionally.

Dave is a real man's man who has only a few female friends or work associates (he once insisted that *GQ* send a man to interview him, but relented when they insisted on sending writer Jennet Conant), but one of the people he does count as a close personal friend is his secretary Laurie Diamond, a former Broadway dancer who has been with him for a dozen years. He affectionately calls Laurie "Rose" and occasionally drags her onstage or sends the camera panning her way as she watches the show from the sidelines.

Other than that small group and his girlfriend Regina, very few people claim to know him well, or venture to call him a friend.

People remain so convinced that frequent *Late Night* guest Teri Garr was once Dave's girlfriend that an interviewer once asked if she'd like to marry Letterman. Her response was incredulity.

"He's never even asked me out for a cup of coffee!"

Comedienne Sandra Bernhard made the same complaint to *Penthouse* magazine when the bawdy bisexual was asked if she'd ever had an affair with Dave, on whom she likes to plant a long-lingering kiss when she first goes on stage.

"I swear to God, I wish, I fantasize, but it's never happened," said Sandra. "I've never even had dinner with David."

Bandleader Paul Shaffer is about the only *Late Night* staffer who has had the rare honor of having dinner at Dave's house. And a rare honor it is. Dave is notorious for his unwillingness to socialize.

In his book *The Late Shift* author Bill Carter recounts an incident in which a business associate of Dave's was throwing a dinner party for Marty Klein, who was then Letterman's agent. When the associate's wife called to invite Dave, he declined, saying, "You know I never go out. I stay home and I just watch baseball games. I never go out. I never leave my house. I just pick up a pizza. How could you think I would leave my house to go to someone else's?"

When Dave does dine out, he usually chooses modest restaurants near his Connecticut home rather than Manhattan hot spots where he might be bothered by tourists. But even quaint country inns have their hazards for the publicity-shy host.

A bartender at a popular New Canaan, Connecticut, restaurant recalls how David had been a regular, first with Merrill and then with current flame Regina, until a new waitress asked him for an autograph.

"He used to eat here a couple of times a week and, because we knew he liked his privacy, we took pains not to bother him. Then one day he came in and there was a new waitress. She ran over and asked for his autograph. He complied, but he didn't come back for about a year."

He's particularly guarded about his relationship with Regina. Says a neighbor: "You see him jogging and you see her jogging. But you never see them jogging together."

If it's the paparazzi Dave is trying to defeat, the trick has worked: He has never been photographed with his love of the past five years. A tabloid managed to snap a picture of Regina jogging alone near Dave's home in Connecticut, however. Regina is perfect for Dave because she's the type of average-looking woman who sort of fades into the background. Shopkeepers and restaurateurs who have seen Regina can't seem to describe her, other than to say she's very plain-looking. This is probably less an indictment of poor Regina than an observation about Dave. Out of all the young beauties he has to choose from—and he has his pick of plenty—he chooses to be in a monogamous relationship with a woman who, while not homely, certainly doesn't turn anyone's head when she walks down the street.

It's obvious, however, that Regina is someone special in Dave's life, because he's a frequent customer at a local jewelry shop in New Canaan, where he's bought several $70,000 necklaces for his sweetheart.

"Either she really loved the first one he got her, or he's completely unimaginative," says a source, "because the necklaces are all identical, just the jewel differs. He's bought her one with a diamond, one with a ruby, and one with an emerald."

Perhaps Dave's relationship with Regina is working out because they don't work together anymore. (Though the couple began dating when she was a *Late Night* staffer, she now works as a production manager on *Saturday Night Live*.)

Another touching part of Dave's personality that one would not assume from watching him on the show is how protective he is of his ladyfriends. Whereas poor Alison Stern has to listen to her husband, Howard, tell the world daily about his desire to screw whatever stripper bimbo or struggling starlet he happens to have in his radio studio that morning, David Letterman is absolutely circumspect about not holding his girlfriends up to ridicule, or giving them anything to worry about when it comes to his fidelity.

When he first started dating Regina, he told *USA Today:* "I am dating a woman, yes. I don't want to talk about it, because even if you say something good about the person, you have hell to pay when you get home. They say what the hell is this? . . ." He still feels bad about having revealed her name in an interview with *Rolling Stone* magazine because "people started following her family around."

Whether it was planned or coincidence, it was probably a smart move on Regina's part to leave *Late Night* when things started heating up between her and her boss. The last thing Regina wants is for her relationship with Dave to fall into the same destructive pattern of all-work-and-no-play that ultimately killed Dave and Merrill's ten-year romance. Having the kind of close working relationship that Merrill and Dave did is probably not healthy for any couple, but it's an especially difficult situation when David Letterman is in the equation.

Dave, even his closest friends and admirers agree, is hell to be around before and after the show. He starts to relax about an hour before air time, but in the several hours before that he's a nervous wreck, rejecting joke after joke, skit after skit, guest after guest, until he's driven all his writers and bookers mad. His postmortems are legendary. After each and every show, he sits in his office and watches the tape, beating himself up over mistakes, real and imagined. It doesn't matter how much the audience howled or how much the staff assured him that it was a great show: Dave knows he could have done better.

Merrill recalls the tension of those times all too well.

"He's very self-critical," Merrill told *TV Guide*. "He goes nuts after a show if he sees himself stammer for a second on the tape.

"He's incredibly insecure and very self-torturing. He doesn't ever reward himself for a job well done. He always feels that he screwed up. In fact, in all the years I knew him, I never once heard him say he thought something went pretty well. The most he ever gives himself is remarks like, 'Well, I guess that stuck to the tape.' Or, 'No one got killed today.' "

Dave may not have been feeling very funny when he came up with that line about the show's ability to adhere to the videotape, but it did serve one purpose: CBS turned it into a hilarious promotional spot when they were advertising Dave's new *Late Show* last summer.

"Sometimes we did shows that were so bad they didn't stick to the videotape," confided Dave in the TV ads. "Well, you can just imagine . . . then we're screwed."

Speaking of those ads, CBS—pleased as a peacock to have stolen Letterman from their neighboring network—incessantly ran the astonishing eighty promotional spots Dave taped in the weeks before *Late Show*'s August 1993 debut, much to the embarrassment of their painfully shy host. It was just one more example of how Dave shuns his celebrity.

"They ran promotional announcements two or three times

a minute, it seemed like," Dave later complained to Barbara Walters. "After a point it started to embarrass and sicken me."

The man who refuses to watch his own show at night was enormously relieved when the show finally debuted on August 30, and he no longer had to see himself on television dozens of times a day.

Chapter Nine
THE WOMAN WHO WON'T GO AWAY

Like any other celebrity, Dave certainly has good reasons to fear and abhor notoriety. It's not just the inconvenience of having autograph-seekers shove paper in your face wherever you go, or the embarrassment of having complete strangers stare at you as you attempt to twirl spaghetti with some finesse in a restaurant, or the annoyance of having your every public utterance repeated, printed, and dissected by the masses. It's the very real danger of having some loony admirer cross the line between infatuation and obsession . . . and perhaps even move toward violence.

Margaret Ray of Crawford, Colorado, was the woman who crossed that line.

It all began in the spring of 1988 when Margaret, a short, small-boned, thirty-six-year-old brunette with a history of mental problems, arrived in Greenwich, Connecticut, to visit her mother, bringing her three-year-old son Alexander along with her. Greenwich is not too far from New Canaan, Connecticut, where David Letterman has a house. More often than not, David just spends weekends at his Connecticut home, preferring the convenience of staying in his Manhattan loft on weeknights.

In May of 1988, Dave was in California on an extended visit. He was staying with estranged love Merrill at her home in Malibu because the Writers' Strike had shut down work on his show in New York. At some point in time—nobody knows precisely when the obsession began—Margaret had come to believe a fantasy that she was David Letterman's wife and that her son, Alexander, was Letterman's son, David, Jr. So she made her way to Dave's modest three-bedroom home in New Canaan, Connecticut. Discovering that David was not at home, she forced a window open and let herself and her toddler in. It was amazingly easy to break into Dave's house. Because he hates pretension of any kind, Dave lives in a house that sits not too far from the street. No gate or fence encloses it. There are no NO TRESPASSING signs or threats of dogs on the premises. The house is totally accessible by simply walking up a stone path from the street pavement to the front door.

Disappointed that Dave was away, Margaret nevertheless made herself right at home. She peered into his kitchen cabinets and helped herself to whatever she could find, fixing meals for herself and Alex in the pleasant, spacious kitchen. She snooped inside closets, desks, and dresser drawers. She made herself and little Alex comfortable in one of the guest bedrooms and made herself useful cleaning the house. She eventually came upon the car keys to Dave's $70,000 Porsche and began to take herself and Alexander out for spins around the neighborhood. She probably could have gone on this way for weeks had she not made the mistake of driving to New York City (perhaps to see what her "husband" was up to and why he had not yet returned home). When she approached the Lincoln Tunnel that connects New Jersey to New York, however, she found herself unable to come up with the $3 toll. Undaunted, she calmly explained to the toll booth collector that there was no need for alarm, that her famous husband would be happy to make arrangements to pay the fee.

"I'm Mrs. David Letterman and this is David, Jr.," she told the skeptical toll collector. "Don't you think David Letterman is good for the toll?"

Yes, he did believe Letterman was good for the three bucks. But everyone in New York knew that Dave was single. And Margaret couldn't produce any identification that proved she was Mrs. David Letterman. So he called the police, who tracked down Letterman at Merrill's house in Malibu.

An astonished Dave told cops, "It is my car, she's not my wife, and she does not have permission to drive the car."

Margaret was promptly escorted to police headquarters.

Until Margaret Ray entered his life, Dave had never been harassed by a fan. In all his years on television, he had only had one frightening incident. A man once managed to get onto the set in the middle of the *Late Night* taping. He sat down next to Dave and said, "I want to talk to you." Letterman froze, the producer called a halt to taping, and security guards were hurried onto the stage to remove the intruder. It was the only time *Late Night* has ever been stopped in the middle of taping.

When police arrived at Dave's house after arresting Margaret, they discovered that Margaret had been busy while she played her demented game of pretending to be Mrs. David Letterman. She had rearranged some furniture, shifted around some rugs, repositioned his plants, and used his typewriter to, she later told cops, write some comedy material for his show. (Maybe she was pretending to be Merrill.)

Back in Malibu, bighearted Dave declined to press charges. The police urged him to file a complaint. They told him there was more to the story than this one break-in. They had discovered that, several months earlier, Margaret had been spotted around NBC headquarters in New York running up charges as Mrs. David Letterman. They reminded him that stalkers often start out as lovesick puppies, but they could turn on a dime into deadly pitbulls.

Dave still refused to press charges. The woman was obviously sick. She needed help, not prison. And she had a small child. He didn't know what he could do for her, but he didn't think the crime warranted jail time. No, he just couldn't bring himself to press charges.

Reluctantly, the cops released Ray with a stern warning to stay away from David Letterman. Apparently, the warning wasn't stern enough. Just five days later, Margaret was nabbed climbing into Dave's window. This time, the Connecticut police were tipped off by a local cabbie who had driven her there from the train station. The taxi driver told police that he thought her actions were odd when she came up short of the $7 carfare.

"She asked me to wait. Then she walked up to a window and crawled through into the house. A few minutes later, she came back out through the front door and offered me $2 in pennies (guess she found Dave's piggy bank).

He notified the police, who arrived at the house in time to find Margaret lounging in the living room, sipping grape juice, eating canned pineapple slices, and cutting pictures and stories out of magazines. She was also writing what she said were scripts for Letterman's show.

"She appeared comfortable," said the policeman. "She had been eating in there."

This time, Ray had the mental wherewithal to drop the

"Mrs. David Letterman" alibi. She tried to convince Connecticut authorities that Letterman was paying her to take care of the house while he was in Los Angeles.

"I am Mr. David Letterman's housekeeper, and he has hired me to keep his house up while he's away," she told police.

When they didn't buy her story and told her she'd have to come with them, she implored them to let her stay long enough to straighten up the house.

"Dave wouldn't want to come home to anything but a clean house," she told them.

Police convinced Dave that he should press charges this time, for his sake as well as hers. In the meantime, little Alex was placed in the custody of his maternal grandmother.

Ray was held in the local jail until June, when a judge found her incompetent to stand trial. He ordered that she be examined by psychiatric doctors.

"The defendant is found not competent," ruled Judge James Bingham. "She is able to understand the charges against her, but she is unable to assist in her own defense."

She was admitted to a state mental hospital, where she remained until her release in October 1988. She went back to Colorado for a few months, but returned in February to attend a custody hearing regarding her son Alex, who was still living with her mother in Greenwich, Connecticut.

The temptation of being so near Dave's home in New Canaan, Connecticut, must have been too much to resist, because Ray was promptly picked up when a neighbor noticed her on Dave's lawn. By the time cops arrived, she had once again managed to break into the house and was found in the foyer. She was held for two days and released on a written promise that she would appear on criminal trespass and possession of marijuana charges the following week. Before that court date could roll around, cops had picked her up again. Acting on a tip, the cops had once again found her in David's living room. Because she was going through Letterman's belongings and had stuffed some of his personal items into her coat pockets, burglary was added to the charges. One of the items she took was Dave's watch, which she said she was using to time herself as she mopped and dusted the house.

"We're on a first-name basis now," joked a local cop.

She told the police she had been hoping to pay Letterman "a surprise visit."

Margaret didn't seem to mind being back at the Connecticut women's prison for yet more psychiatric testing.

"I have a fondness for this institution," said Ray.

She then added, with an astounding lack of self-awareness: "This place gave me a great deal of maturity."

By this time, Dave started making use of the well-publicized insanity on his show. One night viewers were treated to a panoramic view of his living room.

"Just checking on the house," he quipped.

Another night he called his home and feigned relief when no one answered.

"No answer. That's a good sign," he said.

Meanwhile, Margaret was making zany remarks to the press.

"It's nobody's business," she replied when pressed about her obsession with Dave, whom she described as "the dominant figure in my life."

"When are people going to get hip to the fact that this is a grand-slam scam?"

Inside the courtroom, Ray pleaded with the judge to let her make a statement. Her lawyer, obviously cognizant of her deranged state of mind, refused to let her speak. She did manage to complain to the judge that she wanted to confess, but her attorney wouldn't let her.

"I wanted to plead guilty and was not given credibility on that stance," she said sadly.

Once again, she was ordered to undergo psychiatric treatment at Fairfield Hills Hospital in Connecticut. She was soon released on probation.

Four months later, in August 1989, she was nabbed at Letterman's house again, for the fifth time. This time, authorities threw the book at her, ordering her to prison for nine months.

Softhearted Dave continued to feel sorry for her.

"She is suffering from some kind of mental imbalance," he said. "It's a situation that lends itself to people making funny remarks but when you understand what it is, there's nothing really funny about it. She has a real problem and it didn't really affect me that much. It was really just a matter of trespassing."

Ray served seven months of her nine months sentence, getting out of jail on March 16, 1990. Three days later, Margaret made her sixth appearance at Dave's house. This time, the comedian was home. Margaret burst in upon the shocked comic while he was relaxing in his living room. Usually cool Dave ran for a phone, called the cops, then hid in his own house until police arrived to pick her up.

"This is getting so ridiculous that I think we're just going to buy her a house next door to him and move her in," joked a local.

The latest drama had actually begun several hours before Ray waltzed into Dave's living room. Letterman had noticed a broken window on the first floor of his home and called police. They found Ray wandering around his yard and ordered her to leave and not return. But return she did, breaking right into his house.

The usually glib comic declined to comment on the latest scare, but had his lawyer issue a statement.

"Our only hope is that there will be some type of psychiatric treatment so she can resume a meaningful and law-abiding life."

This time around, publicity-shy Letterman was forced to testify because he had been home during the break-in.

Asked if he knew Margaret Ray, Dave told the court: "When she broke into my home, that is the first time I discovered she was on this planet."

He described how Ray was almost absurdly cooperative.

"I told her I had called the police and she said she'd wait for them downstairs."

In May 1990, Ray was sentenced to a year in prison, but wound up back in Fairfield Hills Hospital again for psychiatric care.

When Letterman left the courthouse, he would only say that "These are very difficult times."

Eleven months later, Letterman became a bit alarmed to learn that Ray had escaped the mental hospital, leaving a note saying that she had returned to Colorado and would not bother the talk-show host again.

"She promised not to fool around with David Letterman, not to bother him again," said Fairfield Hills Hospital supervisor Wayne Prescott.

The Colorado authorities questioned her and apparently believed her.

"There's no reason at all to believe that she will bother Mr. Letterman again," said Fred McKee, undersheriff in the Delta County Sheriff's Department in Crawford, Colorado.

"My understanding is that that phase of her life is over."

Nevertheless, Sgt. Chuck Bartling of the Delta County Sheriff's office promised to watch her.

"We'll be keeping an eye on her place," he said.

Cops in Dave's hometown just laughed.

"We know where she's headed. She's headed to Dave's."

The Connecticut cops were ultimately right. Margaret managed to behave herself for almost a year, but in March of 1992 she reappeared in Letterman's town. An alert cabbie refused to drive her from the train station to Dave's house, phoning police instead.

"She was very vague as to where she wanted to go," said cab driver Brian Zito. "Then finally she said, 'Do you know where Letterman's house is? Well, that's where I want to go. He's expecting me. I have papers to drop off.' A red flag went right up, I told her I wouldn't take her and I picked up the phone to call the cops. She walked right out. Apparently, she hitchhiked over there."

Since she hadn't actually made it to Letterman's house to trespass, they couldn't arrest her. So they simply put her on a train headed back to New York City.

Two weeks later, a cop spotted her walking near Dave's home. Again, because she wasn't actually on the property or in his home, she was let go with a warning.

"Her movements aren't restricted and we have no reason to restrict her," explained Sgt. Nicholas Warren.

"If she were to enter his property, we would take appropriate action."

Again, Letterman proved what a big heart he has. Upon learning that Ray was back in the area, he instructed local cops to simply shoo her away, not arrest or prosecute her.

By May, however, cops had had enough. When neighbors called police to say Ray was wandering in Letterman's garden, they picked her up and charged her with trespassing.

Ray had managed to get into the house again, this time leaving two cookies and a nearly empty bottle of Jack Daniels in the foyer as proof of her visit.

Though Margaret's visits were becoming more frequent, Dave continued to feel sorry for her. He told *Rolling Stone* magazine that he felt so bad that once he even gave her time to get away before the police arrived.

"She was on the property and wanted a glass of water and I went in to get her one—well, first I said, 'Finish raking the yard then I'll get your damn water.' So I went inside and called the police. But then I thought, 'She's never threatened me, it's not like I have children that she's terrorizing, it's not like I'm finding dead raccoons in my disposal.' I just felt like 'Wait a minute, this is lopsided.' So I went back out and I said, 'Margaret I've phoned the police; you better get out of here.' And she—not went nuts, she is nuts—she started shrieking and then took off and the police picked her up."

Dave may not have felt threatened, but he did admit that it was a very uncomfortable feeling the times she managed to break into his home while he was there. Once, Dave and his girlfriend Regina had just returned from vacation. It was two o'clock in the morning and it was immediately obvious that the place had been—or was being—occupied.

"There was an immediate sense of something not right," Dave told *Rolling Stone* magazine.

"Things had been moved in a way that you would never move your own belongings. The kitchen sink was full of dirty dishes. So I realized that somebody was in the house. We got out and called the police and watched—it was odd—the police going from room to room turning on lights. They finally found her asleep in bed and bounced her."

But that was only a taste of what was to come. Dave continues:

"The incident that was most frightening came a week later. We had just gone to bed. For some reason, I thought I smelled smoke, which is not a good sign. So I sat up in bed and at the end of the hallway I could determine the silhouette of the woman standing there. That scared me. It scared me for a second, and then I realized, 'Oh, I know what this is, there's no trouble.' I rolled over, and I called the New Canaan police."

Dave was finally starting to get frustrated with the entire affair, but he was damned if he knew what to do about it. He had consulted with his lawyers about getting her psychiatric help—he was willing to pay for it himself—but he found that if Margaret didn't want help—was too ill to understand that she needed help—his offers of financial help would do precious little good.

The counseling she had been receiving during her enforced lockups, when she was found incompetent to stand trial, obviously hadn't helped either. But since she hadn't killed anyone—yet, the cops reminded him—there was only so long that the mental hospital could hold her against her will.

In other words, for a woman like Margaret Ray, whose family clearly didn't know how to help her, either, the system simply didn't work.

Letterman was finally starting to become a bit spooked by the whole sick affair. In the beginning, he thought Margaret was just something of a pest, and a sympathetic figure at that because of her obvious mental illness. But after all the publicity surrounding actress Rebecca Schaeffer's death in 1990 at the hands of an obsessed fan, even Dave had to wonder if Margaret could turn on him and get violent.

"The thing is, she's insane," he told *The Stamford Advocate*. "And you don't want to do anything to make it worse than it is. It's been five years now and I've tried a lot of things and none of them has worked."

At her court date in May 1992, when Margaret was being arraigned on trespassing charges surrounding her seventh unauthorized appearance at David Letterman's house, she sounded, for the first time, like she could be turning on Dave. Gone was the woman who had, a few years earlier, meekly asked police if she could clean up Dave's house before she went to jail so he wouldn't be mad. The Margaret who showed up at this hearing was loud and defiant. And full of hatred for David Letterman. Worse, her fantasies were getting more deranged.

"He knew I was coming!" she shouted to reporters on the county courthouse steps. "AND HE JUST STOOD ME UP!"

Experts predict that most stalkers will eventually turn on the object of their obsession once they feel they've been rejected.

"Initially, the stalker idealizes the person being pursued," says psychologist Reid Meloy, author of *Violent Attachments*.

"But when a stalker is rebuffed, that attitude can flip."

With Dave finally agreeing to press charges, perhaps Margaret was beginning to wonder if the object of her romantic obsession was really worth her devotion. That's the situation you don't want on your hands with someone who is suffering from the mental condition now recognized as erotomania, an unhealthy romantic interest in someone who returns none of your feelings. Because once the erotomaniac feels the situation is hopeless, he or she will give up in the most final way of all: destroying the object of their affection.

It's happened many times before. Actress Theresa Saldana was brutally slashed by a man who was incensed that she would not return his love. Because a passerby came to her help, she survived the brutal attack—just barely.

Around the same time the nation was caught up in Sharon Tate's murder at the hands of Charles Manson and his followers, it almost went unnoticed when The Lennon Sisters' father was gunned down on a golf course by a lunatic who had convinced himself that Peggy Lennon would be his wife—if only her father weren't standing in the way. Years later, John Lennon would be killed outside his Manhattan apartment building by deranged fan Mark David Chapman. The list goes on and on.

In an interview with *Washington Post* columnist Tom Shales, Letterman clearly feels sympathy for the woman who has haunted him since 1988.

"There are nothing but misconceptions about this woman. This woman has, in my assessment, been failed by the judicial system, failed by the state psychiatric system— if in fact there is one—failed by her family and failed by her friends. She is a woman who spends her days in deep confusion."

Dave says Ray has written to him every day for the past six years, though he declines to reveal what she writes, only remarking that when she's on her medication they are quite lucid and when she's off it they're nothing more than meaningless scrawls.

Amazingly, Dave remains convinced that Margaret won't turn on him, the way so many stalkers do when the object of their love fantasy rejects them.

"There was a time when I felt frustrated and annoyed by

it. But I never really felt I was the victim—this woman is the victim. She's had a very sad life. She's got like six or eight kids and is estranged from them all. We gave her many, many benefits of the doubt. Finally, she went to jail for about a year and got out last fall. I don't think we'll hear from her again."

Dave was a bit too optimistic in that February 1993 interview. The following July, she was arrested after police found her sleeping near the tennis court on Letterman's property.

Dave describes the incident to Tom Shales:

"This last time I was out of the country for a week and the security system was on and Margaret hopped over the fence and was camped out on my tennis court. The pool guy said Margaret was bumming cigarettes off him."

When Dave returned home, he discovered a note from Margaret that said, "I'm camped out in your tennis court." At first he thought it was an old note. But just to be safe, he called the police.

"They came down here and we found she had been camped on my court for three days and doing her laundry in the swimming pool. At that point, the police advised me to invoke the stalker law and I said, 'It doesn't apply. This woman is no more to me than a nuisance. She's not a threat.' "

Letterman said he and his lawyers have tried to think of a way to help Margaret, but have come up empty-handed.

"I'm just befuddled and perplexed. Not because she's doing anything to me, but this woman needs so much help and so much attention and has not received anything."

Chapter Ten

THE BATTLE FOR
THE TONIGHT SHOW

As insecure and pessimistic as David was in his day-to-day work life, he eventually came to believe that he would inherit *The Tonight Show*. Indeed, after laboring tirelessly and devotedly at the difficult 12:30 A.M. spot for NBC, generating enormous profits in a time slot that no other network could fill successfully, he came to believe that he was owed *The Tonight Show*.

Despite his apparent insecurity—Dave's postmortems, where he would rake himself over the coals for any little part of the show where he felt he could have done better, were by now legendary—Dave knew in his heart he was doing a good show. And he had always been ambitious. He had no desire to continue to labor in his obscure time slot forever, entertaining, as he liked to say, prisoners and college students. Hell, he was even getting too old for the time slot. And his natural pessimism told him he couldn't hold that audience forever. When he began *Late Night* in 1981, he was a cocky thirty-four-year-old, young enough to attract college students and twenty-somethings who, despite working a full day, had the wherewithal to stay up into the wee hours of the morning watching his show. But Dave had aged in the ten years he'd been at the helm of *Late Night* and so had his audience. Thirtysomething households with two jobs and screaming babies were not as likely to be able to keep up with old Dave, much as they'd like to. Despite some NBC executives' misgivings about Dave's ability to tailor his wacky, late-night humor for the more mainstream 11:30 P.M. audience that was used to sophisticated Johnny Carson, Dave knew he could do it. He wanted to do it. There was only so long, after all, that a man rapidly approaching his fifties could keep jumping into vats of onion dip. Or want to, for that matter.

But there was another reason Dave desperately wanted Johnny's job: his childhood dream. Johnny Carson was his idol. Of course, it's easy to idealize someone who is merely a character to you on your television screen. But Dave had gone to Hollywood and New York and made a name for himself on late-night television. He'd met his hero, Johnny Carson, had dined with him, had played tennis at Johnny's Malibu home. They'd become friends. His childhood hero had not let him down. If anything, getting to know the great man had only intensified Dave's desire to be his heir.

It hadn't always been that way. Dave always wanted *The Tonight Show,* but he hadn't always felt he deserved it. Dave had Johnny Carson on such a pedestal that he couldn't imagine anyone deserving the King's chair, never mind a geeky guy from Indiana like himself. In the early years of *Late Night,* when Dave's show was picking up speed and rumors were already rife that Carson was tiring of his show and looking to step down, reporters would ask Dave if he wanted Johnny's show. He always said no. Absolutely not. He was happy at his 12:30 A.M. slot. He could do a more offbeat show in that hour. Step into Johnny's shoes? No way. America would mourn Johnny forever. They would never stand for a replacement. Anyone stupid enough to take the job would fail miserably. Let some other sap take the fall. He'd stay right where he was, thank you very much.

In his first five years at *Late Night,* Dave truly felt that way. He was terrified enough doing his own show every night. He was anxious enough trying to hang onto his own viewers. He had enough stress in his life trying to top his own famous stunts, gags, and remotes, trying to keep his own material from becoming wearisome and childish.

In the late eighties, however, Dave's attitude started to change. *Late Night* was doing well and Dave had started to calm down, as much as a hyper individual like Letterman can ever relax. Now when he heard rumors that Johnny was tiring of his job and thinking of quitting, it made perfect sense to him that he take the spot. Somebody was going to get it, after all. And replacing Johnny didn't necessarily have to be the disaster he used to imagine it would be for any comedian trying to step into the legend's shoes.

Let's say he got the spot. First of all, he'd automatically inherit much of Carson's audience, for whom *The Tonight Show,* as much as Johnny Carson, had become something of a bedtime ritual. Plus, he'd have his core audience of loyal viewers who would no doubt follow him to the earlier time slot. Though he used to discount his "cult" following as a euphemism for small (and possibly insane), he knew that the word also meant devoted. Rabid. Loyal. Hell, the fans who had cut their teeth on him when they were still in college would probably welcome the chance to see the show an hour earlier and get to bed at a decent hour.

So at some point in the late eighties, Dave decided he very much wanted to replace Johnny Carson when he stepped down. It only made sense. He had the successful show following Johnny; it was only right that he be given first shot to move up and let another bright young whippersnapper come along and wreak fresh new havoc in the late-night hours.

But even though Dave had flip-flopped on wanting the job, he still refused to say so in public, for the simple reason that he thought it would be impolite. Disrespectful. Unbecoming. Boorish. David admired Johnny too much to let it appear that he was lusting after his job. That might make Johnny think that Dave was suggesting Carson was getting a little long in the tooth for his old show, that it was high time he stepped down. No matter how often Dave was asked, he refused to go on record as saying that he wanted to take over *The Tonight Show* when Johnny retired. He would rather leave the impression that he had no interest in his hero's job than risk having Johnny think that he was salivating at the prospect of putting Carson out to pasture. He thought it would be the height of audacity to speak publicly about desiring a job that was currently filled—especially since Johnny had given no clear sign that he was ready to retire.

In an interview with *Rolling Stone*, Dave later explained why he didn't actively campaign for Johnny's job.

"Who am I to be sidling up to him and saying, 'Oh, by the way, Johnny, when you step down—and we're not saying you're close, you understand—let's grease it for me to step in.' Who could be that presumptuous? Because in essence what I would be saying was, 'John, the clock is ticking, it's time to go.'"

So the well-brought-up young man with the solid Midwestern values always answered the sensitive question with a polite shake of his head and a sincere statement about how he hoped Johnny would go on forever.

"I think ultimately I would be happy just to be considered," he once said, sounding much more like a beauty pageant contestant or Oscar contender than sassy David Letterman.

David was totally sincere when he later told interviewers that he had declined to campaign for Johnny's job out of respect for Carson. But there was good sense in what he did, too. Though David was not into Hollywood politicking—he was probably the only multimillion-dollar celebrity who still retained a lawyer from his hometown in Indiana—he was smart enough to know how to play the game. There were good reasons not to offend Johnny Carson by appearing to be lobbying for his job before he had even announced his retirement. Everyone, after all, had seen what had happened in 1987 with Joan Rivers. After being given the great honor of being named Johnny Carson's permanent guest host—a career track that put her in the lead of the pack hoping to inherit Carson's job when he retired—Joan betrayed her benefactor by going behind his back to accept a competing talk show from Fox-TV.

Letterman immediately recognized what a major tactical error Joan had committed.

"I think one thing you can't do in show business is burn bridges behind you," Dave said at the time.

"Show business is such an odd, quirky thing that you can be sued for several million dollars one day and then the next day the same company hires you to go work for them."

Dave sympathized with Joan, but said her mistake was that she hadn't been upfront with Johnny.

"I don't think anyone begrudges her making a move for success on her own terms. I just think she handled it in a graceless fashion."

Still, he sympathized with her.

"It's really a difficult thing to start a new television show

David Letterman on The Tonight Show. When Dave first appeared on the show as a stand-up comic in November, 1978 he scored such a hit with the audience that Johnny extended the rare invitation for him to sit down for a few minutes after his routine. (*Courtesy of Suzie Bleeden/Globe Photos, Inc.*)

When Dave hosted The Tonight Show in the late seventies and early eighties, he often brought his Comedy Store pal Jay Leno aboard as a guest. (*Courtesy of Globe Photos, Inc.*)

David was just 34 years old when he launched Late Night with David Letterman on February 1, 1982. (*Courtesy of UPI/Bettmann.*)

Dave's tacky, wacky debut of Late Night with David Letterman in 1982 included his introduction by the NBC Peacock Girls, whom Dave said had "come home to molt." (*Courtesy of AP/Wide World Photos, Inc.*)

David's favorite female guest is actress Teri Garr, who has been on his show more times than any other woman. Dave once convinced Teri to take a shower on the air. (*Courtesy of Photofest.*)

Maryjane B. Kasian's poodle Benji proved he could stand on two legs on Late Night's popular segment, Stupid Pet Tricks. Kasian later slapped Letterman with a lawsuit for joking that she had surgically altered her dog so he could stand upright. (*Courtesy of Photofest.*)

Dave chats with Late Night regular Larry "Bud" Melman. When Letterman moved to CBS, NBC claimed stake to the character, so now the bald, bespectacled actor appears on Late Show as himself, Calvert DeForest. *(Courtesy of Photofest.)*

Johnny Carson showed up at his protege's show one night to present him with a gift from Ed McMahon: A million-dollar check from the Publishers Clearing House. *(Courtesy of Globe Photos, Inc.)*

Fellow hoosier Jane Pauley is a frequent guest on Letterman's show, having known (and been taunted by) Dave since their early broadcasting days back in Indiana. (*Courtesy of Bill Bastone/Star File.*)

This pig's Stupid Trick is gaining weight. Owner Bob Corbett showed off his prize-winning, 1,205 lb. boar and told Dave that "Hog Chief" was going for the world weight record. (*Courtesy of AP/Wide World Photos, Inc.*)

In an early Late Night episode, Dave took his camera crew on a tour of Manhattan doughnut shops to answer such weighty questions as, "How many doughnuts should the average person eat each day?" (*Courtesy of Photofest.*)

Sonny and Cher chose Late Night with David Letterman as their reunion forum. Though they said in advance that they wouldn't sing, Dave cajoled them into a moving rendition of their hit, "I Got You Babe." (*Courtesy of Photofest.*)

David and bandleader Paul Shaffer have been together since Late Night debuted on February 1, 1982.   (*Courtesy of Globe Photos, Inc.*)

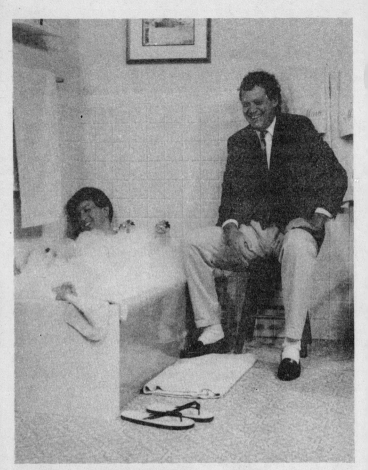

Convincing Teri Garr to take a shower on his show was not Dave's only cleanliness coup; here he gets sportscaster Marv Albert to share a few thoughts with Dave as he enjoys a bubble bath. *(Courtesy of Globe Photos, Inc.)*

A cigar-chomping Dave accepts his Emmy Award at the 1985 ceremony. The following year, he hosted the affair. (*Courtesy of Vinnie Zuffante/Star File.*)

Dave relaxing in his old NBC office in his favorite attire: jeans, t-shirt, and sneakers. Letterman only wears contact lenses when he's taping his show. (*Courtesy of Globe Photos, Inc.*)

In the ten years he hosted Late Night with David Letterman, Dave has flung himself against Velcro walls and lowered himself into vats of yogurt dip. Here, he dons a suit of sponges and climbs into a lifesized container of water. (*Courtesy of AP/Wide World Photos, Inc.*)

Dave challenges speedster Nigel Mansell to a race on Connecticut's Merritt Parkway while presenting him with Auto Racing Driver of the Year Award. Dave has gotten so many speeding tickets on the Merritt that he once had his license suspended. (*Courtesy of AP/Wide World Photos, Inc.*)

Sandra Bernhard helps Dave celebrate his 1,000 show by bringing on a surprise guest—pal Madonna. Sandra and the Material Girl have since had a falling out and no longer speak. (*Courtesy of AP/Wide World Photos, Inc.*)

Dave admits that interviewing isn't his forte, especially when he has to play host to a champ like Oprah Winfrey. (*Courtesy of NBC/Globe Photos, Inc.*)

The first time Cher appeared on David's show, she shocked the Late Night host by saying she'd heard he was an "asshole." Dave later said that the remark had hurt his feelings. (*Courtesy of Globe Photos, Inc.*)

CBS president Laurence Tisch is clearly pleased with his latest acquisition as David Letterman holds a press conference in January, 1993 to announce that he will be moving from NBC to CBS. *(Courtesy of AP/Wide World Photos, Inc.)*

Grace Jones is one of many celebrities who have had on-air run-ins with Dave. Letterman was annoyed because Jones, his first guest, had arrived a half hour into taping. *(Courtesy of Geoff Butler/LGI.)*

Workers ready the landmark Ed Sullivan Theater on Broadway for the arrival of Dave's new Late Show with David Letterman. A billboard in the background boasts of Jay Leno's popularity as Tonight Show host. (*Courtesy of AP/Wide World Photos, Inc.*)

Dave thanked the dozens of construction workers who had done a rush renovation of the Ed Sullivan Theater by inviting them to take a bow on his first show. (*Courtesy of AP/Wide World Photos, Inc.*)

An early guest on Dave's Late Show was Vice President Al Gore, who was the subject of that night's Top Ten list. One of the items revealed that Gore's Secret Service code name is "Buttafuoco." (*Courtesy of Photofest.*)

When David Letterman was signing off at NBC, he said he'd be honored to appear on Late Night with its new host, Conan O'Brien. The visit occurred on February 2, 1994. (*Courtesy of AP/Wide World Photos, Inc.*)

David Letterman rarely attends media events, but he was delighted to be part of the Plaza Hotel dinner honoring his mentor, Johnny Carson. (*Courtesy of Brett Lee/Star File.*)

from scratch. I was really lucky because NBC kept us on the air when we were struggling, and they kept us on two or three years into it when another organization might not have kept us on. Joan was dealing with television stations across the country which were not perhaps prime broadcasting outlets. If you're on a channel in a city that nobody watches twenty-three hours a day, there's no reason to believe that for one hour a day they're going to turn over and watch you."

Johnny was not so understanding. In fact, to this day, he has not forgiven her. No one was surprised when Johnny didn't offer his condolences when her show bombed badly and was canceled rather quickly. But many eyebrows were raised when Johnny didn't even relent and write Joan a nice sympathy note after her husband, Edgar Rosenberg, killed himself shortly after the cancellation. It seemed to most people that such a tragedy deserved a bit of softening on the part of the hard-hearted host. Especially when, years later, Joan extended an olive branch by writing Johnny a lovely letter of condolence when his son was killed in a freak accident.

But Johnny was adamant: Cross me once and there will be no forgiveness. It was a lesson a lot of Hollywood types paid attention to. And it was certainly a lesson not lost on David Letterman.

Letterman's refusal to lust publicly after Carson's job changed, however, in February of 1991. Someone leaked a story to the newspapers that NBC wanted to dump Johnny Carson. The article, carried in every major paper in the nation and based on an anonymous source, said that the *Tonight Show* ratings were just so-so, Johnny wasn't on top of his game anymore, and the network would just love to see him retire so they could hand the baton over to his permanent guest host, amiable comedian Jay Leno. Though at the time it was a mystery who leaked the story, it was later revealed that Jay's aggressive manager, Helen Kushnick, had planted the item. Jay Leno, a gentleman like Letterman, knew his agent was pushy, but he had no idea of the machinations she was capable of. It did cross his mind that Helen had planted the item, especially since that was the buzz around Hollywood. He knew how much Kushnick wanted her client to win *The Tonight Show*. Sometimes Jay thought Helen wanted it more than he did. But when he confronted her with the gossip, she swore up and down that she had nothing to do with the news plant. She knew Jay, a straight shooter with a strong sense of right and wrong, would fire her on the spot if he knew the truth. So she followed the old defense saw of Deny, Deny, Deny until Jay had no choice but to take her word for it. Knowing Johnny was hearing the same gossip he was, he called him and assured him that his camp had nothing to do with the leak. Johnny knew Jay well enough to know that Jay wasn't responsible, but he was fairly certain Helen was the source of the story.

Though he didn't let on to the public, Johnny was furious. He was even more livid when NBC issued a rather weak denial of the story. The statement they issued basically denied that Johnny was being pushed out but said nothing about hoping he would stay. Johnny, of course, fully expected NBC to gush on about how the story was complete nonsense and they hoped he'd remain at the helm of *The Tonight Show* forever. When that didn't happen, he felt he had been humiliated. The writing was clearly on the wall. He now knew there was a germ of truth to the story, that NBC was looking to infuse *The Tonight Show* with fresh blood, hoping to get that all-important younger audience that advertisers love so much. If the truth be known, Johnny had been getting a bit tired of doing the show. He wasn't adverse to the idea of retiring—it had been twenty-nine years, after all—he just wanted to go out in his own sweet time, on his terms. And he certainly didn't want the public to get the perception that he was being pushed out. He deserved better than that.

Besides, he had had his own retirement date in mind already. Since he began his show in October 1962, stepping down thirty years later would make for perfect symmetry. But Carson couldn't get over the way NBC had treated him in not issuing a stronger denial. And the fact that the story had been planted in the first place meant the sharks were starting to circle. If they wanted him out so badly, he decided, he'd be damned if he was going to stay. So on May 23, 1991, he announced that he would be stepping down one year from then, on May 22, 1992, to be exact.

The scramble for Johnny's job was on. There were really only two serious contenders: Jay Leno and David Letterman. Unlike Dave, Jay had been glad-handing and politicking for *The Tonight Show* ever since he landed the permanent guest-host spot. Also unlike Dave, he had made it a point to nurture both personal and professional relationships with the head honchos at NBC, namely Warren Littlefield, president of NBC Entertainment; Robert Wright, president of NBC; and John Agoglia, head of NBC productions.

Dave, on the other hand, had a terrible relationship with NBC. His association with the NBC brass had steadily declined over the years he'd labored at *Late Night*—especially since General Electric bought RCA and NBC. Dave felt GE stressed bottom-line finances over quality television.

It wasn't that Dave didn't know how to play the schmooz-

ing game that Jay—who was honestly a nice person—
played so handily. Dave just didn't want any part of it. He
abhorred office politics. He hated celebrities who had zil-
lions of handlers. He loathed the idea of agents, managers,
publicists. He still had the same manager—Jack Rollins—
who had signed him on back in the late seventies when he
was an up-and-coming comic, and he retained his old attorney from Indiana.

Dave honestly didn't believe he had to play the schmooz-
ing game to get *The Tonight Show.* With his solid, Midwestern ethics, Dave honestly believed that Johnny's job, quite
simply, would go to the best man, irrespective of behind-
the-scenes politicking. It wasn't a popularity contest, after
all. Dave's and Jay's respective popularity with the public
counted, to be sure. But it didn't make sense to Dave that
the NBC brass would hand over a plum position like Johnny
Carson's job on the basis of which candidate they liked
better. He assumed they'd pick the best man for the job,
and in his heart he felt that he was that man.

Moreover, he felt the network had tacitly promised him
the job. His show was owned, after all, by Johnny Carson's
company.

"It seemed to Dave that the logical progression for his
career would be to get the earlier time slot," said ex-girl-
friend Merrill.

Unfortunately for Dave, he was wrong. Very wrong.
That's not the way the Hollywood machine worked. Jobs
did occasionally go to lesser talents who lobbied for them.
Conversely, plum positions were sometimes held from talents whom the executives considered churlish and uncoop-
erative. And that's exactly where Dave's problem with NBC
rested. It was a personality conflict.

Dave perceived GE-owned NBC as a stingy organization

that nickel and dimed him at every turn, trying to cut corners wherever they could even if it was to the detriment of his show.

NBC perceived Dave as a chronic complainer who was never satisfied with anything they gave him, a man who was too good to schmooze his bosses now and again, if only to humor them.

While Jay was making friends with every NBC hotshot in Hollywood, Dave was whining about having to host the Emmy Awards as a favor for NBC.

Dave described his strained relationship with the peacock network in an interview with *Los Angeles Times* writer Rick Du Brow:

"I'll take responsibility for all of that. I think that we felt for a long, long time like we were laboring in kind of anonymity. And I allowed myself to generate some resentments—most of them petty, by the way. And I think it was an area we just weren't actively nurturing."

One of Dave's major battles with NBC involved their plan to make him share his studio with *The Maury Povich Show*. In other words, Maury Povich's crew would tape in the morning and then clear out, and then Dave's could come in in the afternoon and take over. Dave thought the idea totally unworkable, amazingly cheap, and downright insulting. In Dave's eyes, penny-pinching GE was looking to save a few dollars at his expense, and at the expense of his show. Dave had nothing against Maury personally; in fact, Maury's wife Connie Chung was one of his favorite guests. From Dave's point of view, it was just a totally unworkable proposition, and he fought NBC on it tooth and nail.

"I think I would have to take responsibility for the deterioration of the relationship. At times we'd go years without trouble. The kind of thing that sort of upset me—and

I guess I overreacted to it—was when they wanted to rent out our studio during the day to Maury Povich.

"I just thought: No, this isn't right. And it's not right not because I'm Dave Letterman—it's not right because that's not how you run a television show. You don't slam another production in there and inconvenience everybody—because television, night in and night out, is a dogfight and you need every little advantage you can muster."

Dave says he and NBC never understood each other. In fighting them on the Maury Povich idea, he knew he was just being professional, making sure that his show could continue to operate to the best of its ability, which would not be the case if his staff was running around putting things back in order after the Povich show pulled out.

NBC, who had never understood their deeply private employee, assumed Dave was pulling a star trip. It just showed how very little they knew about the shy guy from Indiana who was sweating bullets each and every day, trying to do the best show possible for their network. Dave knew he was misunderstood, but didn't know how to rectify NBC's perception of him after all those years. And, until *The Tonight Show* was in the balance, most of the time he just didn't care.

"I felt like, 'This is an ideological disagreement. These people don't understand that it's not ego. It's not because I think I'm Mr. Big Shot. It's because it doesn't make any sense. It's a mistake.' And I believe that's when I sort of gradually got the feeling like my time there was limited, that I was ultimately expendable."

Dave's studio didn't go to Maury, but the entire ugly proceedings left a bitter taste both in his mouth and over at NBC headquarters.

It wasn't the first time the network had angered Dave.

He had long been annoyed with the penny-ante way NBC ran their operations, including a series of nit-picking, cost-cutting procedures that had been imposed on his staff, cuts he derisively called "nickel-and-dime" stuff. He blamed General Electric and pinpointed his disillusionment with NBC to the year 1985, the year GE bought RCA and NBC.

"Money is the most important thing to GE," he told the *Los Angeles Times.*

"They can run their company any way that they want but GE sort of infringed on us. Before, the network left us alone. Then we got into some situations under GE that never came up before."

"It was almost like this," Letterman once said. "Dave, when you're done with your ties, would you mind if we take them and rent them out to restaurants where you have to wear a coat and tie? We can make a little money that way."

The cost-cutting measures particularly infuriated Dave because GE had gone behind his back to sell his *Late Night* reruns to cable's Arts & Entertainment network.

"Contractually, they're supposed to consult me on this and to my knowledge, I had never been consulted," Letterman complained to *Washington Post* columnist Tom Shales.

"It was presented to me as a done deal."

Even worse in Dave's mind, it was a bad deal. It wasn't just that his cut was so small, it was that GE, in his mind, had gotten a lot less for the reruns than they were worth. Dave had wanted to hold onto them longer and then sell them for a much higher price when the market for hour-long syndicated shows grew stronger.

"A & E got thousands of hours of television for just pennies a serving. My position was, 'Let's find a way to reprogram these things the way they did the old "Saturday

Night Live" shows and sell them off in half-hour form.' But in their eagerness to show people they were finding ways to make money, they were settling for a much worse deal than they should have."

Letterman was also uncomfortable with the whole idea of *Late Night* being in reruns. He didn't want his old shows airing incessantly; he figured they would diminish the value of the show. GE went ahead and made the deal anyway, knowing it was a quick way to pick up some cash. Letterman fumed. In the end, no one was really a winner. To appease Dave, who was, after all, supposed to have some sort of rights over the material as consultant, they agreed to let him pick the shows that would be aired and spend a great deal of money editing them.

NBC later tried to make amends by offering Letterman forty percent of the revenue. They also shortened the contract from five years to three. But, as in all their dealings with Dave, it was a case of too little, too late. And it was an ominous foreboding of what was yet to come.

As usual in his dealings with GE/NBC, nobody was happy.

So when the rumor mill began saying that Jay Leno was a shoo-in for Johnny's job, Dave didn't know what he could do to stop it. It wasn't like he could get on the phone to one of his golf or tennis buddies at NBC and say, "Hey, pal, what's the deal?" Dave basically had no personal relationships with his bosses at NBC. It wasn't even so much a case of his disliking them; he just didn't have any feelings for them one way or another, and was not the type of guy to have the boss over to dinner on a regular basis because it was the politically correct thing to do.

His mentor, however, did have people he could call on Dave's behalf. *Tonight Show* producer Peter Lassally had taken a liking to Dave ever since he first booked him to appear on *The Tonight Show* back in 1978. Though Jay Leno had worked hard to get all the NBC and *Tonight Show* executives on his side in what he knew would eventually be a battle for Johnny's job, he could never win over Peter Lassally because of Peter's deep affection for David, whom he considered a son.

So shortly after Johnny announced his retirement and the rumor mill started working overtime that the smart money was on Jay Leno to get the job, Lassally called Dave. The date was June 3, 1991. Peter told Letterman that Jay was about to get the job Dave had dreamed of for so long, and he wanted to know what the hell Dave intended to do about it. Letterman fell silent.

Author Bill Carter recounts their exchange in his book *The Late Shift*.

"Dave, don't you want *The Tonight Show?*" Peter asked incredulously.

"Well of course I want it!" said Letterman, surprised at the question.

"Well, what are you going to do about it? You can't just want it; you have to do something about it."

Peter then explained the realities of show biz to Dave, who had managed to keep himself amazingly isolated from network politics. Contrary to what he had believed all along, Dave wasn't going to get the job just because he deserved it. His only hope of getting it was to campaign for it, like Jay had been doing behind the scenes for the past few years. And time was running out. Peter convinced Dave that he had to do what he had spent his career avoiding: come right out and say, loudly and clearly, "I want Johnny's job." And he was going to have to forget his distrust and distaste of entertainment lawyers and managers.

First, Lassally convinced Dave to quickly hire a good entertainment lawyer who could arrange a meeting with NBC brass.

Time was of the essence; Lassally knew an announcement was soon going to be made that Jay Leno had the job. Lassally convinced Jake Bloom, one of the premier entertainment lawyers in Hollywood, to represent Dave in a meeting with NBC the following day.

Carter describes that fateful meeting, which included Warren Littlefield, president of NBC entertainment, and John Agoglia, who was president of NBC productions.

"Littlefield stepped up to the task at hand. He started off the conversation they were all expecting to hear: The network had analyzed the late-night situation. They knew the day was coming when Johnny would step down. For the last several years they had watched Jay Leno grow into the role as guest host. Obviously NBC had every reason to be proud of what Dave had accomplished on the *Late Night* show. But the choice had to be made. And they all felt Jay had proved he could succeed with the 11:30 audience. And so, Warren said, summing it up in the form of a pronouncement, they had decided to name Jay Leno the new host of *The Tonight Show.*

"That was Letterman's cue. In a strong but even tone, he started to speak: 'Well, I'm sure that Jay will do a great job. But I must tell you, we've been here for ten years. We're a unit of forty people; we know how to do this show. The next best thing for everyone would have been if we could have done *The Tonight Show.* That's always what we wanted to do; that's what we've had in the back of our minds. This is a real disappointment. But if this is your decision, you can contact my lawyer, Jake Bloom.' Then Letterman stood up from his chair, looked directly at Littlefield and Agoglia, and said: 'Gentlemen, this is completely unacceptable. I want you to release me from my contract.' "

The next day, June 5, 1991, the announcement was made: Jay Leno was getting *The Tonight Show* when Johnny retired in a year.

Dave was devastated. Everything he had worked for, longed for, dreamed of since he was a young boy in Indianapolis—it was gone. He later said it broke his heart to see a newspaper advertisement heralding Jay Leno as the next host of *The Tonight Show.* He went into a lengthy depression. He later told CBS morning anchor Harry Smith about those dark days after the decision was made.

"There was a time about a year ago when NBC chose Jay Leno for *The Tonight Show* when it seemed to me that I was superfluous. I really felt that maybe my time had come to step out of network television."

Though Johnny Carson stayed out of the battle for his job and has never publicly said which candidate he privately backed, he clearly wanted his protégé Dave to get the spot. Unfortunately, NBC hadn't given him a vote in the matter. If Letterman was brokenhearted about losing *The Tonight Show,* Carson was heartsick for him.

Dave had initially felt good about the way he had strode confidently out of the NBC meeting. He was pleased that he had let them know that losing *The Tonight Show* was unacceptable and therefore he wanted out of his contract.

Until someone leaked the whole ugly mess to the press. Naturally, the dailies had a field day with the story of how Letterman told NBC to shove it. The stories that ran did not convey Letterman's calm at the meeting; they concentrated on his fury, making it sound like Dave stormed out of the meeting yelling and screaming. Dave was mortified.

The worst thing that can happen to a shy, insecure person like Letterman is to be embarrassed. Now he felt humiliated. He had not only lost *The Tonight Show,* but the world now knew he was being a big baby about it.

Only that's not what people really thought. Many television experts thought NBC was making a big mistake in giving *The Tonight Show* to Leno over Letterman. Letterman's legions of devoted viewers wanted the chance to see him replace the legend and start his show at the more reasonable hour of 11:30 P.M.

When Carson felt Letterman had had sufficient time to calm down, he invited him on his show. He knew Dave well enough to know that Letterman would be feeling embarrassed about all the fuss surrounding his loss and the subsequent threats he had made to the network. Carson not only wanted to make a show of solidarity with Dave, he wanted to give Letterman a chance to clear the air about his feelings over losing *The Tonight Show* to Jay Leno.

Letterman's appearance on *The Tonight Show* that August 30, 1991, was highly publicized, as were Dave's bad feelings about losing out to Jay Leno. Johnny capitalized on the latter by suggesting to the audience that Letterman might attempt a coup to capture the *Tonight* job.

"When we come back from commercial break," he told viewers, "if David Letterman is sitting at this desk and says he took over because I was too ill to go on, don't believe him."

After bringing Dave out to thunderous applause, Johnny began the interview in an uncharacteristically salty way: "Just how pissed-off are you?"

"You keep using language like that, you'll be out of a job," replied Letterman, without missing a beat.

Then Dave turned serious.

"Would I like to have this show? I would."

As was always the case with Dave, the sentimental moment was quickly over.

"From what I know about you," Dave continued, "a guy can make a pretty good living doing this show."

"There were rumors you were going to bomb NBC," Carson said.

"I hate waiting in line," Letterman replied.

Embarrassed by the way the press had been portraying him as a sore loser and a hothead, Letterman tried his own damage control, assuring Johnny: "I'm not angry at NBC about this. I'm not angry at Jay Leno about this. I'm not angry at you or *The Tonight Show* about this. Now if the network had come to me and said, 'Dave, we want you to have this show,' then a week later they said, 'Dave, we don't want you to have this show,' then you could be angry about it. But I have a show and NBC can do whatever it wants to with this show."

Dave was only partially honest on that appearance. He wasn't mad at Jay Leno. Jay, after all, was the one who had helped him hone his comedic skills when he was a struggling comedian in Hollywood. He owed a lot to Jay.

He certainly had no reason to be mad at Johnny Carson. Had the decision been left to Carson, Letterman would have had the job, and Dave knew it.

But he lied when he said he wasn't angry with NBC. He most certainly was. Naturally, it was persistent Barbara Walters who got him to fess up on one of her interview shows a few months later.

Dave told Barbara that he wasn't angry or bitter; he was disappointed because "it's a great job; who wouldn't want to have that job?"

He conceded, however, that the incident served to alienate him further from his own network.

"It was yet another circumstance in my relationship with the network that I was discouraged by. After you have four or five things that are tough that you have to fight through, that you have to keep screaming, 'What about this? You said you were going to do this and you didn't do this?' Or 'What about this? You didn't tell us you were going to do this and then you did it?'—You go through four or five of those things and you realize, well, you know, maybe there's something wrong here."

Viewers may not have known what he was talking about, but industry insiders immediately recognized the references to his many struggles with NBC: their refusal to pay for his car phone; the battle over NBC's ludicrous suggestion that he share his studio with *The Maury Povich Show*; the insult of being left out of the negotiations to sell his reruns to the Arts & Entertainment cable station; his annoyance over NBC's reluctance to tape one of his anniversary specials at Radio City Music Hall (too costly); their hesitation to air it on Thursday, their strongest night of programming. (NBC eventually relented on the last two issues, but not until they had fought long and hard with Dave and his staff.)

He also had always resented NBC's interference with his show. They routinely asked him not to capitalize on incidents they thought would be too hot in Dave's irreverent hands. For example, after Sinéad O'Connor's shocking appearance on *Saturday Night Live,* in which she outraged many Christians by tearing up a picture of the Pope after urging the audience to "Fight the real enemy," the network brass instructed Dave not to joke about the incident on his show.

Yes, Letterman was sick and tired of his seemingly endless battles with the NBC brass. On the other hand, he was comfortable at NBC. He wasn't a man who liked too many changes. He loved being at NBC headquarters in Rockefeller Center, where he could play off the news shows like *Today* and *NBC Nightly News*. And, most importantly, he'd be thrilled to stay at NBC if it meant getting *The Tonight Show*.

Now that was never going to happen. Staying at NBC seemed pointless without that brass ring in front of him, inheriting *The Tonight Show*. He'd spent his whole life working toward one goal, and now that goal was lost. Worst of all, he was rapidly losing his enthusiasm for doing his own show. Before he had always been driven to keep *Late Night* on top, driven not just by his personal standards of excellence but so that NBC would realize that he was the natural person to assume control of *The Tonight Show*. He had pushed himself even when *Late Night* had at times become routine and boring for him. And now, from Dave's point of view, it had all been for naught. He was desolate.

Chapter Eleven
DAVE & JANE

While Dave was pondering how he'd been screwed by NBC, he recalled another low point in his relationship with the network, another sign that maybe the peacock station wasn't as talent-friendly as the other networks.

Oh, Dave had had his own share of battles with the network, some petty, some of great import. But he was really incensed in 1989, when he—and the rest of the nation—watched in amazement at what the network did to Dave's old friend from Indiana, Jane Pauley.

Dave and Jane went back many years. In the very early seventies, both were still living in their home state, trying to build their broadcasting careers. Dave was doing whatever television work he could get his hands on—kids' shows, the weather, farm shows—so he could put together a resumé that would get him out of Indiana and into a bigger marketplace. Jane was doing the same thing, only she was taking a more traditional reporter/anchor route on a local television station.

It didn't take long for young Jane to win the hearts of the people of Indianapolis. She was pretty, smart, as fresh-faced as an Ivory soap girl with a spotless personal reputation to match.

By the time David Letterman landed his own afternoon drive radio call-in show, Jane was a big name in Indiana. He made good use of that by teasing the good-natured newswoman on a regular basis. He also liked to make Jane the butt of his pranks, like telling his listeners that she had gotten married when she wasn't even engaged to anyone.

When Dave landed *Late Night with David Letterman,* which was broadcast in New York, he was delighted to find that his friend Jane had made it to the big time, too. NBC had shown their confidence in the young woman by giving her co-anchoring duties on their two-hour morning news show, *Today.*

For a dozen years Jane, like Dave, labored long and hard for NBC. She resented it but didn't object when her co-anchor, Bryant Gumbel, got all the plum interview assignments with important people like politicians while the "women's" interviews with cookbook authors and health experts were relegated to her. She didn't create a fuss that Bryant was making a lot more money. She didn't raise a stink that Bryant was considered, and treated like, the main anchor while she toiled as some sort of pretty sidekick. This was the late seventies and early eighties, after all, and Women's Lib had yet to fully hit its stride. If you were a young woman like Jane with a great assignment like the *Today* show, you just didn't complain too much. There were a million beauty contest winners and journalism majors dying to step into your shoes. Jane couldn't see what she had to gain by creating a fuss. Everyone, she thought modestly, is expendable. It was clear the network believed that grumpy, arrogant Bryant Gumbel was the real brains behind the operation, the real success of the show. Jane was always believed to be window dressing, primarily. She was pretty enough that male viewers enjoyed watching her and wholesome enough not to alienate women viewers.

Clearly, NBC underestimated smart Jane Pauley a lot. (Just the way they would later underestimate the popularity of David Letterman with late-night viewers, in both cases with disastrous financial results for the network.) So when Jane began to get a little shopworn around the edges, when the innocent young Ivory girl got married (to political cartoonist Garry Trudeau) and began having children (three, including twins), NBC began to think that Jane might have served her purpose. Never mind that the ratings were solid, that the *Today* show was leading the pack of morning news shows, consistently winning its time slot. Never mind that Bryant Gumbel wasn't getting any younger, either, and was putting on some weight besides. The brains at NBC decided that they'd fix what wasn't broken, that they'd do a little tinkering with their already successful morning show and see if they could improve ratings even more.

Why not bring in Deborah Norville, the cool, beautiful blonde who was so popular reading the news in the wee hours of the morning before *Today* came on at 7:00 A.M.? She wouldn't replace Jane, exactly. Everybody would just shove over a bit on the *Today* show couch and make room for gorgeous Deborah. The thinking was that Deborah would attract a whole new group of viewers to the ones who already tuned in to Jane and Bryant.

The thinking was wrong. As NBC soon discovered, the public loved Jane Pauley. After watching her for a dozen years, living through her marriage and the birth of her babies, people felt like they knew Jane. They felt she was a friend. Unlike other personalities, Jane really did seem to be, in real life, the nice, wholesome person she appeared to be on the screen. There wasn't—had never been—a whiff of scandal surrounding that one. She was clean as a whistle. And that's what people wanted when they were in their bathrobes, stealing gulps of coffee, and getting ready for their busy day ahead. They wanted a friend, not some glamour puss who made them feel ugly when they opened their sleep-encrusted eyes and peered into the morning mirror.

Jane was outraged, too, but what could she do? NBC kept assuring her that they weren't trying to push her off the couch, they just wanted her to share her spot. Modest Jane had always been so cooperative and unpretentious. Surely she wouldn't mind sharing the spotlight with another female. This wasn't *Dynasty,* after all, where starlets fought for air time with aging actresses. This was a news show. It just made good sense to give the show a facelift now and again.

Jane didn't know what to think—or do. She loved her job, and she was being assured she wasn't being eased out. But she felt humiliated. Maybe she had made a mistake in not fighting those small battles all along, like demanding parity with Bryant Gumbel in pay and job duties. Look at where her compliance and complacency had gotten her. She was being treated badly and she knew it. The papers were filled with news stories and editorials about what an awful thing it was that NBC was doing to Jane Pauley. She was beginning to realize that, for her own pride, she was going to have to do something. She couldn't continue on the show when the nation was acknowledging each day that she was being made a fool of. So she finally made the painful decision to quit the job she loved so much. She simply felt she had no other choice. It was a matter of pride.

What was happening a few floors away from his own studio at NBC headquarters in Rockefeller Center certainly didn't escape David Letterman's notice. (It hardly could have escaped a hermit's notice; like the Late-Night Wars would later, the Pauley-Norville soap opera was played out in the papers on an almost daily basis.)

He was furious at the way his friend, a fine, decent person like Jane Pauley, was being treated by their network. To David, it was just one more example of how NBC did not respect or appreciate their talent. Worse, it was a clear demonstration of just how stupid the network could be. How could they have so underestimated Jane's appeal to audiences? Her show had held the top spot for years. Why in the world would women—who make up the primary morning news show audience—want to see a woman who looked like she could be a fashion model replace a working mother like themselves who had become their pseudo-friend? How could NBC not know that women, who were fighting so hard for respect in the workplace, would take offense at a network that would put a woman out to pasture just because she'd hit her forties? Especially when they weren't replacing her older male co-anchor with a handsome young stud. In short, what in the world were the male executives in charge of NBC News thinking? Were they thinking at all?

Naturally, Dave responded by doing what he does best: He made his feelings known via his *Late Night* show. Deborah Norville jokes started popping up in his opening monologue. *Late Night* would flash her picture accompanied by the theme music from the movie *Jaws*.

Later, Dave worried when word got back to him that Deborah was upset at all the ribbing. (See, Dave is much more sensitive than people realize.)

"I don't know if she's mad at me or not," he told a reporter. "It seems like there's always somebody upset with us at the *Today* show. Hey, Morty (addressing his producer, Robert Morton), is Deborah mad at us?"

He later had Deborah on his show. He treated her with kid gloves throughout the interview, as if to prove that he had nothing against her personally.

Which he didn't. It was NBC he was angry with, as was the rest of the nation, on Jane Pauley's behalf. He explained his feelings later:

"I think Jane has always been underrated," David told *USA Today* reporter Jefferson Graham shortly after she left *Today.*

"There's more to Jane than people have had the opportunity to know. Jane handled the situation with a great deal of poise. I don't know if I were in that situation if I would have been able to muster that kind of poise myself."

The backlash was immediate. Deborah Norville, really just an innocent pawn in NBC's losing game, was treated by viewers like the beautiful young mistress who had replaced the All-American wife. Ratings nose-dived as viewers switched stations, demonstrating their displeasure at the way their old morning pal Jane Pauley had been treated. Joan Lunden was the winner of the Early-Morning Wars, as most viewers switched to her show, *Good Morning America,* on ABC. Five years later, NBC had yet to recover their top spot, even after they removed the Other Woman and replaced her with a new version of young Jane Pauley: terminally perky Katie Couric. The *Today* show occasionally wins their time period, and Katie has certainly raised ratings from the disastrous Norville reign. But the public obviously found that they liked *Good Morning America* well enough when they defiantly changed channels as a sign of support for Jane. And once viewers move on that way, it's very difficult to woo them back home.

Even though the Norville experiment hit NBC where it hurt most—in their pocketbook—they failed to learn anything from that expensive lesson. Just two years later, they would underestimate and take for granted another network talent: David Letterman. The results would be just as financially ruinous.

Chapter Twelve
THE RUSH TO SIGN DAVE

On May 22, 1992, Dave and the rest of the country watched Johnny Carson sign off for good. Jay Leno would be taking over on Monday. It was one of the saddest days of David Letterman's life, not just because he wasn't going to be the man replacing Johnny, but because he was Carson's biggest fan. He later said he couldn't sleep that night and that a depression settled over him that took weeks to shake.

No longer excited about staying at NBC doing *Late Night*, Dave had become increasingly unhappy. He'd always counted on work to keep him going. His job was what he lived for. He was beginning to wonder if he should have done things differently, if maybe he had spent too much of his time and energy on his career, to the detriment of his personal life. His marriage had failed because of his career; so had his decade-long relationship with Merrill Markoe. After spending all his energy on getting to the top and staying there, he simply had nothing left over at the end of the day to give to a lover. And now, in his mind, he had precious little to show for it. Having been rejected by NBC in favor of Jay Leno, Dave felt his career was over.

Dave's good friend and mentor, Peter Lassally, knew oth-

erwise. Peter had been in constant touch with Dave those
first few months after it was announced in June 1991, that
The Tonight Show was being given to Jay Leno. Peter knew
how dejected his old friend was. It broke Peter's heart; over
the years, Dave had become like a son to him. Peter couldn't
let Dave go on like this, believing his career was over. He
knew Dave well enough to know that someone had to step
in and save Dave from himself. He convinced David that
all was not lost; he had a million prospects. It was something everyone seemed to realize except Letterman himself.

Lassally knew what he was talking about. Knowing Letterman was angry and disappointed at losing *The Tonight
Show,* the other networks were chomping at the bit to sign
him on to go up against pleasant but boring Jay. But Dave
would have to get himself a good agent. Peter admired the
way Dave had loyally stuck, through his rise in show business, with both his lawyer from Indiana and the agent who
first signed him as a young comic in Los Angeles, Jack
Rollins. But enough was enough. For the kind of sensitive,
high-stakes negotiations in which he was about to enter, he
needed a Hollywood agent who was a master at wheeling
and dealing. So why not go for the Rolls-Royce of agents:
Mike Ovitz of the powerful Creative Artists Agency in Los
Angeles.

Ovitz is the man every major player in Hollywood and
New York wants on his side. He is an unmatched dealmaker,
with the skill to negotiate the absolute best deals for his
clients. Dave being Dave, he scoffed at the notion that Ovitz
would even agree to take a meeting with him, let alone
agree to represent him. Much to Letterman's surprise, Ovitz
salivated at the idea of representing David Letterman. They
met in Los Angeles in late fall of 1991, and the meeting
went spectacularly. Ovitz told Dave that he was delighted

to take him on as a client. He told Letterman that he had been treated shabbily by NBC, and it was time to review his other options. And, he assured a skeptical David, there were going to be a lot of options. Losing *The Tonight Show* didn't make Letterman the loser, it made NBC the loser. In time, they would see that. Meanwhile, Dave needed to get the ball rolling and explore his other options. Even though he still had a year and a half on his NBC contract, which expired in April 1993, it was time to start looking around, time to start putting out some feelers. Technically, no negotiating could take place until February 1993—that was in Dave's contract with NBC—but Ovitz thought he could make some inquiries without overstepping the bounds of Dave's contract. Dave could save his anger; Mike would take care of everything. After all, it was Ovitz's job to get even for his clients so they didn't have to get angry. If Dave did not yet realize his worth—and his self-esteem was at an all-time low because of what had happened at the meeting with the NBC brass—Ovitz the expert knew that ABC and CBS would scramble for the opportunity to put Letterman up against Leno.

Ovitz immediately began feeling out offers from competing networks. It wasn't difficult; some had expressed interest in Letterman the minute it was announced that Leno had won *The Tonight Show.*

The results of Ovitz's feelers were more than encouraging; they were amazing. Even old pessimist Dave had to be impressed by the eagerness with which the other networks began aggressively courting him.

By October of 1992, NBC realized they were going to have a fight on their hands to keep Letterman. They needed two things: to buy some time to repair their relationship with their unhappy star and to offer Dave a gesture of goodwill that would keep the lines of communication open. So they told Dave that they'd release him from the part of his contract that prohibited him from actively negotiating with other networks in exchange for a three-month extension on his present contract.

Dave agreed, and the battle to sign David Letterman began.

The offers were exciting. Knowing Dave wanted the 11:30 P.M. time slot almost as much as he wanted the honor of replacing Johnny Carson, Fox enticed him with an 11:00 P.M. time slot. To get his attention, they sent him a batting cage for his birthday, knowing that Letterman is a huge baseball fan.

CBS had Dave's friend Connie Chung make a videotape imploring Dave to move to her network. At the end of the tape, she swore that, if Dave signed on with CBS, she would agree to cry out "Oh Dave! Oh Dave!" while having sex with her husband Maury Povich for a full year. The tape was played up a great deal in the press as a cute ploy to get Dave's attention—after all, he'd been fawning over Connie on his show for years—but *Late Shift* author Bill Carter says the tape embarrassed and annoyed Letterman, who didn't even stick around long enough to watch the part about Connie's promise to scream out his name in bed.

Connie later appeared on Dave's show to try to convince him to move over to CBS.

"Sometimes you just have to leave home," said Chung.

She then asked the audience to vote on what network they thought he should move to by applauding for each station so she could measure their response. That little bit was edited out by *Late Night*'s producers, who didn't think it would amuse NBC.

ABC was not going to be left out of the action. Like

Fox-TV, they decided to capitalize on Dave's well-known love for sports by inviting him to stop by their broadcasting booth to enjoy "Monday Night Football."

Dave happily took them up on that offer. It didn't hurt to have NBC watch their star smiling out from the ABC telecast booth, looking happy and comfortable.

Frank Gifford tried to get a scoop by prodding Dave to announce that he was going to ABC.

"Wanna make some news, Dave? Are you coming over here?"

Later that week, Dave told viewers that he had gone on "Monday Night Football" because he'd always wanted to read the announcement about ABC's rights to the football telecast. Then he rolled a tape of himself actually reading the disclaimer at the game, while Shaffer played "The Battle Hymn of the Republic" on his harmonica.

NBC knew it had to woo Dave, too, but their job was much more difficult. They had meetings with Dave, explaining once again that they didn't choose Jay because they thought he was better, they simply wanted to continue their unbeatable one-two punch of *The Tonight Show* followed by *Late Night,* and the easiest way to do that was to keep Dave on at 12:30 A.M. Nothing personal, you understand, they told Dave over and over. It was just a smart business decision. Jay, after all, had already won acceptance in Johnny Carson's seat in the several years he'd been the permanent guest host. The 11:30 P.M. crowd was comfortable with Jay, just as the 12:30 A.M. crowd really loved Letterman. From their viewpoint, it would be silly to mess things up by giving Dave the earlier spot and have no one to replace him at *Late Night.* Flip-flopping Jay and Dave had been considered and discounted. It wasn't that they were so worried that Dave couldn't hold Carson's crowd; the concern was that easygoing, affable Jay would be too sleepy in the late spot, when you needed a hyper host like Letterman. As much as they tried to stroke Dave's ego, it clearly wasn't working. All Dave wanted—all he'd *ever* wanted—was *The Tonight Show.* If they couldn't give him that, he felt they really had nothing else to talk about.

Failing miserably at their attempts at serious negotiations, NBC began to get into the spirit of silliness that had been started by the other networks. One Friday afternoon at Rockefeller Center, home of NBC, dozens of staffers could be seen sporting signs begging Dave to stay.

"Dave & CBS—NOT!" read one. "Dave, Don't Go," pleaded another. "Dave, Stay Home," begged a third.

Some offers were less silly than others. There was a rumor that NBC had offered Letterman, who keeps a fleet of serious racing cars in Santa Monica, a $100,000 Mercedes with the vanity license plate: 4GETCBS.

At one point, the push to get Dave seemed to be backfiring. For everyone. The network brass at ABC and CBS obviously didn't understand Dave any better than NBC did. Dave hated being in the spotlight. He hated being fussed over. The worst part of his job was that it made him a public figure, someone who was recognized and pestered every time he tried to do something as simple as purchase cigars. Though initially flattered, he was beginning to despise and detest the attention being lavished on him and eventually made a public plea that it stop.

"I was flattered in the very beginning, but now I'm tired of it, I'm embarrassed by it, and I wish it would all go away," Letterman told *USA Today* reporter Jefferson Graham in a November 1992 interview.

"I wish there would be a resolution. I'm tired of being in the newspaper connected to this. It's been a year and a half already. If I'm tired of it, people reading it, watching it, and hearing about it on the radio must be sick of it. Frankly, I'm sorry I was ever born."

He told *Washington Post* pal Tom Shales that he was trying to ignore all the hoopla.

"I find that I've been paying less attention to these stories than everybody else has. I'm showing up for work every day and having a great time."

He added that he was somewhat perplexed by all the fuss being made over his career.

"I'm continually surprised this is of interest to anybody. If you apply it to any other walk of life, nobody would pay ten minutes' attention to it."

One person who was bound and determined not to leave David Letterman alone was CBS president Howard Stringer. Ever since Dave had announced he was open to offers, Stringer had been pursuing him relentlessly, sending him amusing notes and pictures, sharing with Dave his primo seats at the U.S. Open (those sports bribes again), assuring Dave that CBS was the kinder, gentler network he was looking for. Stringer was also in constant contact with Dave's agent, Mike Ovitz. If Letterman walked, Stringer was going to make damned sure that the only path he took was the one that led directly to CBS.

It certainly made NBC sit up and take notice. Warren Littlefield, president of NBC entertainment, began trying to mend fences with Dave, offering him anything he thought might catch his fancy and make him stay—anything, that is, but Jay Leno's job. He offered him prime-time specials. Dave looked bored. He offered Dave a weekly prime-time sitcom; Dave declined.

"If you were going to do a half hour of prime-time television, you would have to do it as well as Jerry Seinfeld does it," Letterman later said. "I couldn't do it that well, so why waste my time?"

Okay, then, how about a prime-time variety show? Letterman nixed that notion, too.

"I would not be interested enough in that format to do what it took to make it work," he said.

NBC began to realize that Dave didn't particularly want to do a new show; Dave wanted an earlier time slot for his own show. At one point, there was even talk of giving Dave the 10:00 P.M. time slot for *Late Night,* a completely unorthodox move.

Littlefield knew Dave disliked him and blamed him for giving *The Tonight Show* to Jay. At one point, to lighten up the negotiations, he sent Dave a life-sized stand-up replica of himself with a bull's-eye.

Despite all the public fawning and all the fabulous offers pouring in from the other networks, Dave still seemed unhappy. Peter Lassally, who had resigned as producer of *The Tonight Show* after Johnny left in order to become *Late Night*'s producer, finally got Dave to tell him what he really wanted. He wanted to stay at NBC. And he still wanted *The Tonight Show.*

Peter urged David to make his feelings perfectly clear to his agent, Mike Ovitz. So Dave was finally forthright with Mike. He told Ovitz he didn't care about the fabulous offers from ABC, CBS, and Fox. He didn't care about the money being thrown his way. He didn't want to do a sitcom. He didn't want to do prime-time comedy specials. What he still wanted—what he had wanted from the start—was *The Tonight Show.* Taking over for Johnny Carson had been his childhood dream. Still was. If there was any way Ovitz could pull off a minor miracle and still get him *The Tonight*

Show—and if anyone could it was Hollywood powerhouse Ovitz—that's what he wanted.

He had had his problems with NBC in the past, he told Ovitz, but he could right them. He assured Ovitz that if Mike got NBC to offer him *The Tonight Show,* he wouldn't let pride stand in the way. He wouldn't reject it because the offer had come so late. The bottom line was, this was his childhood dream. This was why he had moved to Los Angeles so many years ago. This is what he'd been working toward, honing his interviewing skills for, all those years. He knew he had a reputation for being mean to guests. He could change that. He knew that some people thought his humor too offbeat, too sophomoric, not mainstream enough for the 11:30 P.M. audience. He could change that, too. He was willing to tailor the show. He didn't *want* to simply do *Late Night* at 11:30. He wanted to do Johnny Carson's show. And he could do it. He just needed the chance.

Though Warren Littlefield had pretty much given up on trying to appease David Letterman by this point, NBC president Bob Wright had not. He wasn't at all sure that they had made the right decision in handing the job to Jay. Especially if it meant losing Letterman. Dave made a lot of money for NBC in his impossibly late time slot. No matter what they put up against Letterman at that hour, no other network had been able to touch him. No, Wright did not want to lose Letterman. He just wasn't sure yet how they were going to manage to keep him.

Leno, who was as adept at networking as Letterman was good at alienating people, was being kept aware by his confidants that his job at *The Tonight Show* was no longer secure. He didn't like that one bit. If Dave had thought he had been treated badly by NBC, Jay had news for him: This was even worse. At least Dave had never been so much as

offered *The Tonight Show.* Jay had been given the job outright and he had, so far, been doing a good job, managing
to maintain Carson's ratings. To hear that his job wasn't
secure because NBC wasn't so sure that keeping Jay was
worth losing Dave, well, that just wasn't right. Leno, in
many ways, was similar to Dave. He had been raised in a
stable, middle-class, two-parent household and had grown
up believing that if you did the right thing and kept your
nose clean, you'd be rewarded. Just as Dave had presumed
that he would get *The Tonight Show* based on merit, Jay
believed that he would keep the job based on the same
principle. He had earned it. What NBC was putting him
through now just wasn't right. Oh, there wasn't anything
concrete. NBC hadn't come out and said that Jay's job was
not safe, either privately or publicly. But the rumors were
around, had even been printed in the paper, and NBC hadn't
exactly issued any strong denials. The painful truth was that
NBC was mulling over his future. And, like David Letterman almost two years before him, he was hurt and angry.

So Jay decided it was time to stop being Mr. Nice Guy.
If they wanted to play games, he'd make some maneuvers,
too. To make sure NBC knew he wasn't sitting around twid-
dling his thumbs while they decided his fate, he rang the
press and told them that he'd march right over to CBS if
NBC took *The Tonight Show* away from him and gave it to
Dave.

NBC was left in a terrible position. Employee relations
had never been their strong suit, to be sure, but this was
unprecedented: They'd managed to make both their late-
show stars mad.

In an interview with *The New York Times,* Jay, who was
no longer keeping quiet, described how he felt about all the

speculation that he might be booted out of Johnny's chair in favor of Dave.

"Am I crazy? I feel like a guy who has bought a car from somebody, painted it, fixed it up and made it look nice, and then the guy comes back and says he promised to sell it to his brother-in-law."

But Leno's antics really got into high gear, relates Bill Carter in his book *The Late Shift,* when one of his network informants told him that an emergency conference call had been arranged among the top NBC brass to discuss the Leno-Letterman situation. The meeting was set for January 6, 1993, and involved Letterman nemesis Warren Littlefield, NBC president Bob Wright, John Agoglia, head of NBC productions, NBC Sports president Dick Ebersol, and a half-dozen other NBC big shots.

Leno was sick and tired of waiting to hear bits and pieces of gossip and hearsay from his confidants. So he decided to do something drastic and very uncharacteristic: He decided to eavesdrop on the call that would decide his future. So after his show that afternoon, he hid in a room near Littlefield's office that contained a phone that would connect him to the conference call. He was all set. Now all he had to do was pick it up and listen when the meeting began. He'd soon know who were his supporters, and who were his enemies.

The executives didn't come to a decision that night on who would get *The Tonight Show.* President Bob Wright just wanted to hear everyone's opinion before he took his next meeting with Mike Ovitz. But the meeting was helpful to Jay in that it let him know exactly who was on his side and who wasn't. Not surprisingly, Warren Littlefield and John Agoglia, the two executives who had had the most run-ins with Letterman, strongly backed Jay Leno. Dick

Ebersol, who helped to create *Saturday Night Live,* just as fiercely fought for Letterman. It turned out Dave had been naive back in the spring of 1991, when he learned that Johnny was stepping down and just assumed he'd get the position because he was the most worthy candidate. The discussion seemed to come down to a personality contest: The people who had had run-ins with Letterman, or who had heard tales of his general disagreeability, backed Jay. Even when the Letterman camp got some of them to concede that Letterman was the superior talent, the Jay supporters still championed Leno, arguing that he deserved to keep his job because he had been loyal. All Dave ever does, they argued, is taunt GE and NBC.

NBC president Bob Wright had a lot to think about. His goal was to keep both Jay and Dave, but he was beginning to realize that was impossible. Dave was most likely going to walk if he didn't get *The Tonight Show,* and Jay was most certainly going to leave the network if he was booted out of his job.

After mulling over all the pros and cons, NBC arrived at a decision. They didn't want to lose Dave. So they called Mike Ovitz and gave him their final offer. It was January 8, 1993.

Ovitz called Dave and told him the words he'd been waiting to hear all his life: He could have his beloved *Tonight Show.* Letterman was breathless; Ovitz warned him not to get too excited and to listen carefully. There was a hitch, and it was a major one: He couldn't have it until Jay's contract expired in May of 1994.

Dave's other option, Ovitz said, was to take the CBS offer, which was a three-year, $14-million-a-year contract for Dave to produce a late-night show to compete with *The Tonight Show.*

The money was incredible, a substantial boost from the $7 million a year NBC was paying him. CBS's very generous package also gave Dave ownership of his own show and the right to produce a second late-night program at 12:30.

CBS also promised Letterman a $50-million penalty payment if his show was not aired at 11:30 P.M.

Ovitz recommended that he take the CBS offer. There were risks with taking over *The Tonight Show,* he told Dave. He might lose some of his popularity if it looked like he was stealing *The Tonight Show* from his old pal Jay, a guy he had known since their days as young comics at the Comedy Store in Los Angeles, a guy whom Dave himself had often credited with helping him perfect his comedy skills.

Ovitz reminded Dave of what had happened in 1989, when Dave's old pal Jane Pauley was pushed to the corner of the *Today* show couch to make room for Deborah Norville. Pauley, humiliated, saw no option other than to quit. Loyal Pauley viewers took out their anger by switching stations. Deborah, an innocent victim, was asked to leave the couch, too. NBC's morning show has yet to recover from that debacle. The show has only rarely been able to regain the first-place ratings it enjoyed during the Pauley years.

Besides, argued Ovitz, NBC had treated both Leno and Letterman shabbily. Why would he want to stay at that network? He'd never been comfortable there.

But, once again, everyone was underestimating Dave's dream to inherit *The Tonight Show.*

New York Times reporter Bill Carter tells what transpired next.

"I can't make this decision," Dave told Ovitz. "It's every race driver's dream to drive a Ferrari. You're asking me to give that up. I appreciate what you're saying and I understand. But I just can't make this decision. I need to see how my stomach is going to feel in a few days."

Letterman spent those few days consulting with his small circle of intimates. Actually, he spent a lot of the time listening to friends say he should go to CBS while he countered that it was his lifelong dream to inherit *The Tonight Show.*

He had long talks with Peter Lassally, the man who had fought so hard to get him *The Tonight Show.* Dave couldn't understand why Peter was now telling him to forget it. But Peter had hoped to get the show for him outright. That hadn't happened; Jay had the job. And Peter thought that Dave taking the job away from Jay would prove a disastrous career move, one from which he might never recover.

Lassally reminded Dave that the public's opinion could turn on a dime. He already had a bit of an image problem concerning his treatment of guests. Did he really want *The Tonight Show* if it meant taking it away from his friend?

Only one person urged Dave to follow his heart. Dave's girlfriend, Regina Lasko, had lived with Dave during the entire ordeal. She knew how much *The Tonight Show* meant to him. She told him to forget what everyone was telling him to do and to make his decision based on what he wanted to do. If he wanted *The Tonight Show,* he should take it.

Having spoken with the most important person in his personal life, he decided to discuss his options with the man who had most influenced his professional life: Johnny Carson.

Lassally had been urging Carson to talk to Letterman, whom he knew was having an agonizing time wrestling with his decision. Carson was resisting. As much as Johnny liked Dave—and, if the truth be told, Johnny would have preferred to see Dave as his successor—Carson didn't want to get involved. It just wasn't his style.

Unfortunately, it wasn't Letterman's style to call Carson, either. Finally, it was Peter Lassally who got these two standoffish guys together. Peter first called Carson and begged him to call Dave. Having worked with Carson for twenty years, Lassally obviously knew, without Carson saying it, that Johnny would advise Letterman to leave NBC. Otherwise he wouldn't be pushing the conversation. Carson again pleaded to be left out of it, but finally he relented: He wouldn't call Dave, but if Dave wanted to call him, he'd be willing to discuss the matter with him. Lassally then called Dave and urged him to call his idol and get Johnny's take on the whole messy matter.

Bill Carter relays that conversation:

"You have to do what's best for your career," counseled Carson.

"What would you do if you were in this situation, Johnny?" beseeched Letterman.

"I'd probably walk. I'm not telling you to do that, David. But if you're asking me what I'd do if I had been treated like that, I would probably walk."

Carson's advice wasn't surprising. He himself felt he had been treated badly by NBC. When Jay's former agent, Helen Kushnick, had planted the item about NBC wanting Carson to step down, it wasn't entirely untrue and Carson knew it. So there was no love lost between him and the peacock network either.

In an early 1994 interview with *Los Angeles Times* reporter Rick Du Brow, Dave recalls the offer.

"Toward the end of my time at NBC, they came up with a plan whereby I would stay at NBC at 12:30 and then in

May of 1994 I would take over *The Tonight Show*. And I considered it for a while. And occasionally we laugh about it because if I had done that, Conan O'Brien would still be a writer, I would still be doing 12:30 and we would still be waiting to do our show in May. And that's just completely ludicrous now. I can't even imagine why I would consider that for half a second.

"I did feel that when Jay got *The Tonight Show,* for me that was really when my relationship with the network ended because I felt emotionally and in a real visceral sense that this doesn't make any sense—that you have Jay Leno and then you have me. What's the point? You're duplicating programming. I think Jay Leno and Conan O'Brien make perfect sense. But not me."

NBC has denied that they ever offered to give Letterman *The Tonight Show* when Jay's contract expired. But Letterman confirms that they did.

He tells Du Brow: "I remember the day we were talking to Michael Ovitz and he said, 'You have two offers. One is NBC: Take over *The Tonight Show* in May of 1994. Or you go in the next three months, six months, to CBS and start your own show.' Ovitz said, 'We strongly suggest that you take the CBS offer.'

"I think we were all hoping there was a slight chance we could go to Burbank and start doing *The Tonight Show.* But Peter Lassally, who had been working long and hard to get *The Tonight Show* after it had been given to Jay, and Morton (*Late Night* producer Robert Morton) said, 'No, you can't take *The Tonight Show* under these circumstances.' So I wrestled with it for two or three days and then I finally realized you have to take this chance.

"I mean, too much had happened. It would have been so unpleasant. It would have appeared that Jay would have been ousted from his job. And you know, he wanted that job as much or more than I did. If we had taken that deal, it would have been very unpleasant, very messy.

"I absolutely wanted *The Tonight Show*. But I realized that I didn't get what I wanted so I have to make the best of what I have. And it wasn't until maybe a week or two into the new show that I realized that what I had maybe was the best thing after all for me. So it kind of dawned on me gradually."

Dave made his announcement that he was jumping ship to CBS at a press conference on January 14, 1993. Finally, after almost two years of inner turmoil and public struggles, he was relaxed and happy. Puffing on his trademark cigar, Dave told the packed press room that he had decided to leave NBC because losing the 11:30 P.M. time slot had been "the biggest disappointment of my professional career," adding, "Money and financial consideration have never been a primary motivating force."

As was to be expected from the new king of late-night comedy, the press conference, held at CBS's New York City headquarters, was full of jokes.

Letterman set the tone by leading off his speech with the declaration, "The first thing I want to say is that I never dated Amy Fisher. I fixed her car, I helped her with her homework, but I never laid a hand on Amy Fisher."

When asked if GE had any business running a network, Letterman adeptly dodged the question—everyone knows his true feelings on the subject anyway—with a joke: "I don't know about that, but have you seen their toasters?"

Of his $14 million a year contract, he quipped: "This deal certainly would have put a smile on Jack Benny's face—even in the condition he's in now."

Letterman went on to say that what he'll miss most about

the peacock network are "the back rubs from Irving R. Levine," referring to the bald, bespectacled chief economics correspondent for NBC News.

Asked if he had a new name for the show yet, Letterman quipped: "We will try to get the name Buttafuoco into it."

After answering a question from a *TV Guide* reporter, he joked: "When you're done, I've got a problem with my subscription."

When a *People* reporter asked whether he would button his double-breasted jackets on the CBS show, he replied: "Ladies and gentlemen, this is why *People* magazine is the greatest journalistic institution in the world today! Thank God somebody has the guts to come up here and ask the tough questions!"

When another reporter said Maury Povich told him Letterman "had the hots" for his wife, newscaster Connie Chung, Dave replied: "I think more appropriately, the question ought to be, 'Does Maury have the hots for his wife?' Isn't that the issue at stake here?"

When one reporter asked Dave if he thought audiences would find him too radical for the 11:30 P.M. time slot, he answered: "I see myself almost every hour of the day and I seem fine to me."

Regarding his $14 million salary, he said: "Most of it's gone. I spent most of it on a speedboat, so now I'm busted," adding that he certainly is not "worth that kind of dough."

The advantage to the humongous salary, he said, was that if audiences didn't take to him, he could just go out and "buy a new audience."

That night, Letterman showed off his Top Ten reasons for jumping ship, which included: Heads CBS, Tails CBS; I've stolen as many GE bulbs as I can fit in the garage; tired of being sexually harassed by Bryant; and, finally realized that not only were they never going to make me an anchorman, but that technically speaking, this isn't even a news show.

Across the country, Jay Leno was equally irreverent at his news conference, a bit of an oddity since Jay was announcing not that he'd been hired, but that he hadn't been axed.

"I have the job," said Leno, the perpetual good guy who seems to have lost a bit of his innocence during the late-night wars. Leno, a motorcycle buff, roared into his press conference on a red Harley.

"Bill Clinton said we'd be living in an age of lowered expectations. What we're celebrating here is the fact that I already have a job, that I haven't been fired."

And he couldn't resist adding the snide comment, "Welcome to NBC. NBC stands for 'never believe your contract.' "

Asked if he felt secure in his job, he replied: "In the way Saddam Hussein feels secure."

Ever the trouper, however, Leno insisted that he wasn't angry.

"I don't feel bitter. Not for this kind of money," he remarked.

Leno makes about $8 million a year to Letterman's $14 million, which has been the subject of spoofing on *The Larry Sanders Show,* cable's satire of late-night television. In one episode, Larry (Garry Shandling) was looking to renegotiate his contract in light of Letterman's phenomenal salary. When he didn't get anywhere, he consoled himself with the thought that, "at least I'm not being taken like Jay Leno."

Leno also made reference to the dramatic conclusion of what the media had dubbed the Late-Night Wars on his show that night. When the audience didn't laugh at one of his jokes, he cracked: "I don't care if you laugh. I got the job."

Johnny Carson later made his feelings known.

"David is a good friend of mine and I believe he will do extremely well with his new show," said Johnny.

"NBC made a big mistake letting him go to CBS. I think the network is going to regret it."

Dave's last show at NBC was bittersweet. The wisecracking at NBC's expense had ended; Dave truly seemed sad to be leaving.

"I hope in some small way we've made them proud," he said.

Yes, NBC had screwed up royally where David Letterman was concerned. Snippy remarks about GE and NBC aside, Dave had loved his home at Rockefeller Center. Dave was a guy who liked to know where he was going to hang his hat every day. A stand-up kind of guy, he got comfortable in a place and remained loyal to it. It would have taken so little to have kept him. NBC needn't necessarily have given him *The Tonight Show* to make him stay. It would have helped matters a great deal if, from the start, they had given their sensitive, insecure star a little more attention. Besides *The Tonight Show,* all David had ever wanted from NBC was a little respect, an occasional pat on the back. Instead, it seemed, all he ever got was cost cutting and criticism.

Dave went out in style. In 1992, the last full year *Late Night* was on the air, it won the prestigious George Foster Peabody Award "for infusing one of television's oldest and most conventional forms, the talk show, with inventiveness, freshness and vitality." It joined six Emmys that the show had collected over the years.

Dave's last show, on Friday, June 25, 1993, was almost

a tearjerker. Fans lined up for blocks, hoping they could get standby tickets to the historic farewell show.

Not surprisingly, the monologue included a few parting potshots at NBC owner, General Electric.

"If GE had a sense of humor, they'd send a guy in right now to fire me," Letterman told the delighted audience.

"For the first time since I've been here," he continued, "I've been named employee of the month."

He opened with a clip of the final *Cheers* episode, edited to show the Boston barflies fleeing the pub just as *Late Night* is coming on the air.

The subject of his final "Top Ten List" was the last-minute things he had to do before leaving NBC. It included: Untie Willard Scott; get one more cheap laugh by saying the name "Buttafuoco"; send change-of-address forms to the woman who breaks into my house; and let my plastic surgeon take a bow—this has been his show as much as mine.

He interviewed Tom Hanks, who did his impressions of Greg Allman and Elvis.

Paul Shaffer's band entertained with tunes that were appropriate for the occasion, like "The Thrill is Gone" and Aretha Franklin's "Respect," the latter being the one thing NBC never gave their late-night star.

Naturally, he ran classic clips, like Bill Murray's appearance on his first show in 1982, when the tequila-filled comedian sang, danced, and aerobicized his way through Olivia Newton-John's hit, "Let's Get Physical."

Dave was clearly tickled pink to announce that his surprise musical guest (there had been rumors for weeks that the last show would include a guest he'd spent the past ten years trying to get on) was none other than Jersey homeboy Bruce Springsteen.

"Bruce was in town for a benefit so we called him and begged him to come on," recalls *Late Night* producer Robert Morton.

"He thought about it for a day or two and said yes."

Letterman, who rarely fawns over a guest, was positively gushing after the Boss finished his musical number.

"It's a terrific thrill for me," Dave told the audience. "I can't tell you what this means to me. Hey, am I Mr. Rock 'n Roll or what?"

In his final few moments, he spoke movingly of his eleven-and-a-half year run on NBC and voiced his hope that his successor, Conan O'Brien, would invite him back someday. (Conan did and Dave was generous in his praise for the young comic, who has neither been generating much enthusiasm among viewers or garnering much support from the critics.)

"I hope in some small way NBC took pride in this program," said David. "I can't say enough about all the people here."

Letterman is basically uncomfortable with sloppy sentiment, so the moment was short-lived.

"Hey, I'd like to see you wear a tie in the new place," he kidded Paul Shaffer, before things got too maudlin.

Then he hopped aboard a white horse and rode off his stage.

Spike Feresten showed why he's one of Letterman's top ten comedy writers when he spoke with *The Boston Globe*'s Tom Mashberg before the show.

"The staff is celebrating with pizza and tequila," said Spike. "All of it is being tested for Dave. You just can't trust food being delivered anonymously in New York."

He described Letterman's mood as "sad but a little more relaxed."

"But he's stopped bathing for some reason," Feresten joked. "Although that might be because NBC has turned off the utilities. He's starting to smell like corn chips."

Asked how the *Late Night* staff would be celebrating that night, Spike replied: "The usual. A champagne reception at the studio and then off to Dave's house for hookers and bumper pool."

In the days that followed, Dave still had some lingering doubts over whether or not he had done the right thing in giving up his dream. But whenever he'd voice his misgivings, his friends would remind him that *The Tonight Show* was already lost to him; he had lost it on the night Jay Leno took over. Had he accepted NBC's offer, he wouldn't have been replacing Johnny Carson; he would have been replacing Jay Leno. His dream had died on May 23, 1991. The important thing now was that a new one was being born on August 30, 1993.

Part Four
Starting Over

Chapter Thirteen
THE BIRTH OF THE *LATE SHOW*

Now that CBS had won the Battle of the Networks to get David Letterman, the Battle of the Coasts began, with New York pulling out all the stops to keep Dave in New York City.

"We'll stay if we can find reasonable hourly parking rates," joked Dave.

With that, the rush to keep Dave in the Big Apple was on.

David Dinkins, then mayor of New York City, enjoyed a rare moment of popularity when he announced, "If Mr. Letterman wants me to do backflips on my eyebrows, I'll try that. Absolutely."

Humorist Jamie Malinowski warned Dave what would happen to him if he moved his show to Los Angeles: "In New York, after a day of stress, ordinary people find great pleasure in verbally flaying the flesh from the bones of a drugstore clerk who has failed to deduct the fifteen-cent toothpaste coupon. In L.A., a different ethos prevails. People try to convey sincerity when they say, 'Love ya, babe.' In a place where everyone has a dream or is this close to a development deal, great emphasis is placed on taking people's hopes quite seriously. Anarchy doesn't thrive in Lotus

Land; it melts away in the hot tub. Give Dave six months there and he'll be nice. Oh, there'll still be stupid pet tricks and stupid human tricks, but he'll call them The Wacky World of Animals and Folks Do the Darndest Things. He'll redo the set in Santa Fe decor, Paul will play Eagles music and the Midwesterners-on-vacation audience will look bewildered every time Dave doesn't treat some Aaron Spelling starlet like she's Meryl Streep."

Sony flashed Letterman's picture with the sentiment "We Love Dave!" on their famous Times Square Video Jumbotron. They also ran a Top Ten list of reasons Letterman should keep his show in New York, including "The only culture in Los Angeles is yogurt" and "The post office won't forward viewer mail."

Some New York City councilmen put together their own Top Ten list of reasons why Dave should choose New York over Los Angeles, including "Our roads and bridges take years to collapse—not seconds!"

When Dave joked that he would keep his show in New York City if he could find cheaper parking, then City Transportation Commissioner Lucius Riccio offered to find him a spot near the Manhattan studio of his choice.

City Councilman John Sabini held a press conference announcing a "Keep David Letterman in New York" campaign, with *Munsters* star Al Lewis (Grandpa Munster) named as the celebrity campaign chairman.

"It's important to the city's psyche that Letterman stay here," said Sabini. "National institutions shouldn't move to other cities."

Mayor Dinkins agreed.

"Letterman's show means a lot to our economy but also to our uniqueness," said mayoral spokeswoman Jennifer Kimball.

"The loss of such a high-profile show would be a blow to our prestige."

Native New Yorker and fellow comedian Jerry Seinfeld advised Letterman to stay put.

"They get so much humor out of being in New York. It's a perfect fit. I think a move would be suicide," said Seinfeld.

Once again, Dave could not believe he was the focus of so much hoopla. The bribes started to roll in, just as they had when Dave was debating between NBC, CBS, and ABC.

Knowing Dave loved to play baseball and kept a bat and a basket of baseballs in his office at all times, a city Parks Department executive promised Dave that if he stayed in New York she'd upgrade his baseball team's playing permit "to the Heckscher Ballfields in Central Park, the city's premier ballfield location."

Mayor David Dinkins decided that if bribes wouldn't work, it was time to start making some serious threats. He warned Dave that the city was willing to put him under house arrest to prevent him from leaving.

"We'll design a special bracelet for Letterman that would sound an alarm if he gets beyond the city's limits."

The odds were stacked in favor of Letterman staying in the city. David liked the West Coast well enough and would have loved to have settled into the dream job he thought awaited him in Burbank, but now that the long fight for *The Tonight Show* had ended, he wondered what would be the point, really, of pulling up stakes and moving to Los Angeles. All it would do is disrupt his staff of forty, most of whom had become hard-core New Yorkers. While they were willing to move with Dave, most didn't particularly relish the thought of leaving their comfortable, established lives to do the show in L.A. And that was a big part of Dave's decision to remain in New York City. Despite his sometimes gruff attitude on the show, Dave is a sensitive man. He was not unmindful of the fact that most of his forty-plus staff had deep roots in New York—family, friends, and real estate.

And despite his cocky attitude at the press conference, Dave was scared to death of launching a new show—as anyone would be. He wanted—needed—to have his old crew surrounding him in the new place, all stumbling and learning together. Dave is a very clubby kind of guy, and he didn't want to lose a single member of his team. There was a lot of work to be done, work that required the help of the people who had gotten him to his present, lofty position. He knew that CBS didn't expect him to simply start doing *Late Night* on a new station at a new hour. They wanted a new show. They didn't want Dave to change too much, of course; they had spent a year wooing him because they liked the brand of humor he already had established. But everyone agreed that some changes were going to have to be made for the show to succeed in the earlier, more popular time slot.

Also, NBC was being a bit of a sore loser about the whole situation. The minute Dave announced he was leaving they had begun making noises about how Dave couldn't take such *Late Night* institutions as "Stupid Pet Tricks," "The Top Ten List," and "Stupid Human Tricks." They were even fighting over his right to take a character—Larry "Bud" Melman. Actor Calvert DeForest had created the character for *Late Night*. Calvert could do as he pleased; just not as Larry "Bud" Melman on Dave's new show. Such show staples, NBC insisted, were the "intellectual property" of NBC, and the network would sue them if they tried to resurrect them on CBS's *Late Show with David Letterman*. Never mind that those kinds of skits probably wouldn't work without Dave anyway. NBC had lost Letterman and they were damned if they were also going to lose all the *Late Night* institutions that people tuned in to see each night.

Dave was belligerent when he heard that NBC was threatening him with lawsuits if he used his popular skits on CBS. He was quick to point out that he and Merrill had invented "Stupid Pet Tricks" on their failed midmorning show, a show he owned. And he said the fight over "The Top Ten List" was ridiculous because "we stole that from *USA Today.*"

"I personally don't perceive any specific changes at this time," said Letterman at a press conference.

"One of two things will happen: We'll do the stuff we want to do and that will be fine. Or we'll do the stuff we want to do and they'll sue us.

"If this comes to trial, be sure and get a seat down front."

CBS Entertainment President Jeff Sagansky also had sarcastic words for NBC.

"You know, we have invested $1 billion in baseball over the last four years, which NBC is going to get now and we feel we have a proprietary right to the nine-inning baseball game. And so we are just going to caution them: We don't mind about eight innings or a six-inning stretch, but nine innings is going to be something that we're going to take action on this year."

But as much as Dave didn't want to deal with the added hassle of moving to Los Angeles, there were some valid reasons for moving the show to the West Coast. In 1972, when Carson moved *The Tonight Show* from New York to Los Angeles, he told *The New Yorker* that it was because it would be much easier to book talent out on the West Coast. The same still held true.

"I dig New York," said Carson, using the vernacular of the time.

"It's still the center of everything. But when you have to do that show five nights a week, the talent pool gets a little thin. Of course, you have Broadway, but practically all of television has moved to the West Coast."

Letterman also had his executive producer Peter Lassally pressuring him to move to California. Lassally, the longtime *Tonight Show* producer, missed sunny L.A., earthquakes and all.

Dave didn't want to make his decision lightly. He decided to take his time and explore all his options before agreeing to anything. CBS didn't care where he went, as long as he was happy. They were bound and determined not to make the same mistakes that NBC had made with Dave. So they told him what facilities they had to offer both in New York City and Los Angeles, and invited Dave to visit both headquarters to see what he thought. Dave had already seen the CBS compound on West 57th Street in Manhattan and was not impressed. He thought it was in much too isolated a place for him to have any fun with his man-on-the-street pieces. So he took a few members of his staff to Los Angeles to check out the CBS headquarters there. Everyone was impressed. CBS had just built two new studios at its Television City complex in West Hollywood. If Dave decided to go with L.A., he'd be guaranteed one of those spanking new, state-of-the-art studios.

On the other hand, thought Dave, moving to L.A. would be moving into Jay Leno's backyard. Just when the ugly competition the press had dubbed the Late-Night Wars had finally come to an end—temporarily, anyway—with the announcement that Jay would stay and Dave would go, Letterman had no desire to turn up the heat again by competing for guests on the same coast.

Ultimately, however, he decided that he would have to go wherever he felt he had the best facilities available to do the very best show he could.

At Letterman's press conference announcing that he was moving to CBS, he expressed his desire to stay in New York, but suggested he might have to leave.

"By virtue of the fact that our staff and crew live in New York and they've grown comfortable, I would have to say that we're leaning to staying in New York. On the other hand, the ultimate decision will be what is best for the show."

One thing that disturbed Dave about staying in New York was the CBS headquarters where he was being offered a studio. At the moment, that seemed to be his only option in New York, and it was a poor one. The building was so far west on 57th Street as to practically be in the Hudson River. Pedestrian traffic was light, as there were very few shops or restaurants in the vicinity. In short, the area was a wasteland compared to Dave's old digs at bustling Rockefeller Center, located smack in the heart of midtown Manhattan. How could he retain his wacky remotes and play-with-the-public antics in such an isolated place?

In a telephone conversation with Mayor David Dinkins, in which Dinkins implored Dave to stay in New York City, Letterman voiced his concerns.

"He said you don't get the same traffic of people," said Dinkins.

"Essentially he's concerned that he have the capacity to continue the same kind of audience that has been successful for him as he moves to a different section of the city."

CBS knew Dave was in quite a quandary. He loved the state-of-the-art facilities in Los Angeles, but didn't particularly want to uproot his crew and move there. He liked the idea of staying in New York, but hated the building and neighborhood that would house his studio.

Knowing Dave's big problem with New York was the prospect of being so far west on West 57th Street, and determined to get off to a good start with their new star, CBS came up with another option for Dave. Scouting new locations for a studio that David Letterman could call his very own, they came up with the Ed Sullivan Theater. In its heyday, it had been a grand place. It had fallen into ruin over the years, but it could be renovated, and rather quickly. They presented the idea to Dave: How would he like it if they bought him the landmark Ed Sullivan Theater in the heart of Broadway?

He loved it. He loved the idea of being part of the rich history of the theater, whose stage had been graced by every major star of the past sixty years.

Once he saw the building and how dilapidated it really was, he began to get a bit nervous. He had a show to do. Everyone knew that renovations never came in on time, and Dave needed every precious moment to put together a winning show for CBS before his August 30 debut.

It was too tempting an offer to reject, however, and he told CBS to go for it. Watching the day-to-day renovations did make him a little anxious. At one juncture, when it seemed as though the work would never be completed on time, he joked that it might be easier to renovate Ed Sullivan himself.

As it turned out, he was only half-kidding.

It cost CBS $4 million to buy the legendary theater, whose stage over its sixty-six-year life had been home to

Jack Benny, Jackie Gleason, and Elvis Presley. Ed Sullivan had hosted his legendary Sunday night variety show there from 1948 to 1971. It had been the site of Cary Grant's first stage performance, W.C. Fields's last, and the Beatles' triumphant 1964 debut.

CBS had to shell out another $10 million to renovate the theater, which had been designated a city landmark in 1988. The honor, it turned out, caused more than a few headaches for the renovators. Portions of the interior had landmark status, meaning that any changes had to be approved by the city's Landmarks Preservation Committee. Then there was the small problem of time: Dave's show was set to debut in August, just six months away.

The construction crew's task was threefold: to create a state-of-the-art broadcasting facility, restore the building's original beauty, and not step on the Landmarks Preservation board's toes.

The task ahead was humongous. The building was built long before laws were passed to guarantee equal access, so bathrooms had to be made accessible to the handicapped; the acoustics had to be fixed so that audiences would not be subjected to the noisy rattle and roll of the subway trains below; the twelve-story office building that came with the theater had to be gutted and rebuilt; the old, hopelessly outdated control rooms had to be demolished and re-created; the theater had to be rewired so that it could be connected to the CBS Broadcast Center on West 57th Street; the dressing rooms, lobby, and public access areas all needed facelifts, and the elevators needed to be fixed.

Then there was the rat problem. The place was infested with them. While Dave enjoyed some spontaneity on his show, he had no desire to air an audience panic attack caused by unexpected rodents.

Dave's new digs were going to be impressive. The blueprints showed that Dave's new home-away-from-home would be a twelfth-floor corner office lined with seven windows on two sides, plus an adjoining bathroom, a full kitchen, and a spare room.

While the construction workers, contractors, and architects were scrambling to deal with the rats, the renovating, and the Landmark Preservation Committee, Dave was reminding them that he and his crew had to be in their offices by July if they were to be ready for their big debut in August.

In the meantime, New York was celebrating its victory over Los Angeles. Delighted that Dave would soon be a neighbor, the Stage Deli—whose claim to fame is their mile-high sandwiches, many of which are strange concoctions named after celebrities—promptly reinstated their Letterman special (ham, cheese, roast beef, pickles, lettuce, tomato, and mayo on white bread) and offered Dave's staff a ten percent discount on their boss's sandwich.

Not to be outdone, Il Teatro, an Italian restaurant near the Ed Sullivan Theater, featured a new dish called polenta à la Letterman for their favorite nighttime star. The polenta is shaped into ovals that are supposed to look like the CBS Eye logo. When *Late Show* debuted, the restaurant sent the dish over to Dave with a message of good luck. His thank you note hangs proudly in their window.

The stores surrounding the Ed Sullivan Theater haven't been disappointed by their newest neighbor because he's revitalized the area. He's brought a lot of pedestrian traffic (the standby ticket line to his show is a block long, so the shops along the way get lots of business just from that). People have started to hang out in local bars, hoping to get a glimpse of Dave enjoying a beer after work. (They'll have a long wait; Dave stopped drinking liquor years ago.)

"A lot of people in the neighborhood think this is the place to be," a bartender from nearby McGee's told reporter William Grimes.

"They all want to know, does he come in here, and what does he drink. He hasn't had anything to drink. But Paul Shaffer makes up for it. He drinks Remy."

A local pet store created a section of reptiles called the Letterman Lizard Lounge in honor of their new neighbor.

"This block totally changed," a local shopkeeper told Grimes.

And she doesn't just mean that business is up. Letterman has managed to attract a better class of people to the area.

"We had problems before with thieves and robbers, even schoolkids who shoplifted. That's all stopped."

CBS anchorman Dan Rather made an appearance on *Late Night* to welcome Dave to his network. Not knowing about the rat problem the Ed Sullivan Theater was having downtown, he told Dave he was wise not to move into CBS headquarters, which used to be a dairy building.

"It has rats the size of armadillos," said Dan.

"The rats in this building are programming the place," Letterman retorted, never missing an opportunity to get a dig in at his soon-to-be-former bosses.

The real reason Dan Rather was glad Dave had decided against moving into CBS headquarters was that he had no desire to become the next Bryant Gumbel. Dan, who is as humorless as Bryant, didn't wish to become the target of Dave's infamous impromptu interruptions of his neighboring studios' live broadcasts.

Ironically, when Dave's new show premiered, Letterman managed to get under Rather's skin—completely inadvertently. The word around town was that Rather was annoyed that his staff was shutting down almost entirely between 5:30 and 6:30 P.M.—to watch Dave's show being taped, which they could access as part of the CBS broadcast family.

There were the usual millions of construction delays but, amazingly, everything came together on time for Dave's *Late Show* debut.

To show his appreciation, Dave invited the entire construction crew to come into the studio and take a bow when his show debuted—on time—on August 30, 1993. After they'd all taken a bow, he told them they could get back to their real job: yelling at girls.

Dave, who hated to leave Rockefeller Center, has been enjoying his new digs immensely.

"Look at this," he told *Time* reporter Richard Zoglin when he took him on a tour of his new office.

"It's brand-new. Clean walls. New carpet. Office furniture. I used to have a paper route and now I have three floors of a theater building on Broadway in New York City. I'm the luckiest man alive."

About a month before the show premiered, Dave was uncharacteristically calm. He told a packed news conference, "Maybe I'm just dumb, but I don't find myself in a cloud of anxiety about this."

"Of course," he joked, "I'm full of gin."

Being able to focus on the new show, after all those many months of anxiety over where he was going to work, had mellowed the manic comic.

"I kind of believe that things worked out for the better," he said prophetically, shortly before his show debuted.

"I have no rancor, though I have a little remorse. I'm just six weeks away from doing this show at CBS and I couldn't be happier. I'm so happy that I have a job and such a great job."

He had been wise not to get lost in the wasteland where CBS headquarters are located: Dave has made the most of sitting smack in the center of Times Square and the theater district, one of New York City's most colorful neighborhoods.

Viewers have been treated to lots of images of old Broadway, as Dave and his team of writers scour the neighborhood daily in search of humor.

One day a hungry Dave had a slice of pizza delivered to him, on air, handed down the theater to him by a line of Rockettes. Another time he announced that he needed a cup of coffee and invited the home audience to come along with him and the camera crew as he popped outside the theater and into a local deli for a cup of joe. The delighted immigrant owner fussed and fawned; passersby stared and waved; Dave cracked jokes and made himself right at home. He's been doing that a lot in the time he's been on Broadway.

He's made instant celebrities out of many of the local shopkeepers. Rupert Jee, manager of Hello Deli, has gotten a standing ovation on the show. Customers now routinely ask him if he's going to be on the *Late Show*.

"Who knows? Maybe. You can't tell around here."

He dropped in on Keumsoon Lee, the owner of Rock America, a souvenir shop, and got a photo I.D. made.

He paid Academy Clothes owner Bart Dadon $100 to wear one of his own tacky, sequined jackets into the subway.

Shopkeepers like Dadon don't mind being the butt of Dave's jokes. After all, it's good for business.

As Dadon told *The New York Times:* "I've done five radio interviews. There's been a tremendous response. People from as far away as Honolulu and Mississippi have stopped in here. I look forward to him picking on us for years to come."

Chapter Fourteen
DAVE'S MOM

Another instant celebrity to come out of *Late Show with David Letterman* is Dave's mother, Dorothy.

Since launching *Late Show* on August 30, 1993, Dave can't seem to do anything wrong. He's surpassed both *The Tonight Show* and ABC's popular *Nightline,* and holds the top spot in his time period. His ratings continue to rise, his popularity continues to grow. Viewers love him, advertisers adore him, critics praise him. And he's achieved it all with nary a stupid pet or stupid human trick.

Late Show garnered some of its best ratings in February 1994, when Dave hired his seventysomething mother, Dorothy, to be his special *Late Show* correspondent at the 1994 Winter Olympics in Lillehammer, Norway.

Compared to her son's $14 million annual salary, Dorothy was a steal at $616 a day plus expenses "in a really nice hotel." "It's first class all the way," said a delighted Dorothy.

Dave's white-haired, sweet-looking mother immediately captured our hearts—and the most sought-after interviewees at the Winter Games. On her very first outing, she managed to corner First Lady Hillary Clinton and ask, on her son's behalf, "Is there anything you or your husband could do about the speed limit in Connecticut?" As Dave's legion of devoted fans knew, it was a reference to her son's many speeding tickets.

Next, Dorothy nabbed Ice Princess Nancy Kerrigan for an interview. Because of the Tonya Harding, knee-bashing affair, Nancy was the most sought-after interview. When Dorothy's jealous fellow journalists asked what she planned to say to the Ice Queen, Dorothy thought about it a moment and then replied that she'd just talk to America's newest icon the way she'd speak to her grandchildren.

"She could be the girl next door," Dorothy reasoned.

David, of course, was giving his mom a lot of tips on how to handle the assignment. On his instructions, she waited for downhill skiing Gold Medalist Tommy Moe at the finish line so she could present him with a canned ham from Dave.

"Dave's always giving canned hams," she explained, somewhat embarrassed.

Loath to have people think he was getting predictable, Letterman decided on a different prize for speed skating champion Bonnie Blair. When Bonnie won her fifth Gold Medal, Dorothy was waiting to present her with a fifteen-pound wheel of Jarlsberg cheese.

"She seemed real pleased with that," reported Dorothy.

She wandered around Lillehammer's shopping district, stopping non-Americans to ask them what they thought of David Letterman. Dave, who hates celebrities who take themselves too seriously, loved watching Austrians, Germans, Italians, and Swedes looking bewildered and confused at the mention of his name.

What viewers loved about good sport Dorothy, who even ate reindeer at her son's behest (she said it tasted like filet mignon), was that Dorothy remained modest throughout.

In watching and listening to Dorothy, it's easy to see

where Dave got his Midwestern values. When it was first announced that Dorothy was going to Lillehammer to report on the games for the *Late Show*, a Cincinnati company tried to capitalize on it by offering Dorothy a free fur coat to take to chilly Norway. Dorothy turned it down flat.

"I could never accept anything like that," she said. "Besides, CBS is giving us parkas."

Dorothy confided to *USA Today* reporter Katy Kelly that she was a bit taken aback by the cost of having the hotel do her laundry.

"It cost $50 for a not very big bag. I bought a Hosiery Mate in the department store back home. I'm washing my woolen socks and hanging them in that nice heated bathroom. That way I don't have to pay these high prices."

She admitted that she had been nervous appearing on TV at first, but soon conquered her fears and got into the spirit of things.

"The first few times I kind of had butterflies," she said. "Then I realized, 'I'm just talking to David.' "

CBS producer Jay Simpson told *People* magazine that Dorothy was as delightful to work with as she was to watch.

"She's just a darling person," he said. "The minute the camera goes off, she'll say to me, 'Jay, you go have something to eat now. Stay warm, Jay. Are you cold?' The lady is just a trouper. We tell her, 'Do that over' or 'Stand over here,' 'Look in the other direction,' and she doesn't flinch. Also, she beat us up the hill on the way to the opening ceremony."

Dorothy's reporting gig in Lillehammer was not the first time she had appeared on her son's show. Several years ago, Letterman decided that *Late Night* should have a "Parents Night." All the staff members were invited to bring their parents to the studio to show them what they did for a living.

Naturally, Dave brought his mom. (Dave's dad Joe died in 1974.)

Dave's love for his mother was obvious that night. He kept close by her side for the entire segment, holding her hand as he escorted her around the studio, pointing things out and asking her what she thought of it all. When his mother seemed to be taking being on camera in stride, he decided it was time for a little fun. Dave was into his bullhorn stunts at the time, frequently picking up his megaphone and yelling odd things to the pedestrians below, such as there were starving people in the building and could someone please bring up a couple of dozen hot dogs (several people did).

Deciding this would be the perfect way for his mother to try her hand at what he does for a living, he bullied Dorothy into picking up the bullhorn and bellowing out the window that Jane Pauley was being held prisoner by NBC.

Dave beamed with pride as his mother did his bidding. It's clear Dave is close to his mother. He visits her several times a year and flies her up to Connecticut for visits. When she remarried ten years ago, David was at the wedding to give her away. He also appears to have a good relationship with her new husband, Hans. When he and Merrill were still together, they took several vacations with Dorothy and Hans.

He always flies to Indianapolis to be with her on Mother's Day, and likes to call her on his show every Thanksgiving night to find out what kind of pie she served.

As with all parent-child relationships, however, Dave's connection with his mother is more complicated than it appears. Though Dave clearly enjoyed chatting with his mom each night during the Olympics, their easy banter masked the tension that has always been a part of their relationship. When Dave was growing up, Dorothy never really believed he'd be able to build a career out of his comedy. She thought the dream he was chasing was foolish, and longed for him to grow up and settle down into something more stable. Though Dorothy has obviously been proven wrong, and come to realize that her jokey son did have a special talent, Dave has never really gotten over her rejection of his dreams in those early years. He's always trying to get Dorothy's attention, to win her respect, to hear and feel her admiration. That Dave dreamed up "Parents Night" is no surprise to those who know him. It was yet another attempt by Dave to say to Dorothy, "See, Mom, I have made something of myself. What I do for a living is not a foolish waste of time. You were wrong. I was right. I am special. I do have talent. I didn't have to settle for an ordinary life in the Midwest."

As fond as Dave is of his mother, it was his father whom he felt really close to when he was growing up. Losing him at the relatively young age of twenty-seven had a big impact on Dave's life. It's no coincidence that Dave's decision to move to Los Angeles came a year after his father's death.

It was Dave's father who had filled the house in Indianapolis with laughter, his father who showered the three Letterman children with love and attention. It was his father who gave him the positive feedback he needed to keep pursuing his dream.

"It wasn't until my dad died that I realized my mother is the least demonstrative person in the world," Dave once told an interviewer.

Years later, he told *Interview* magazine's Pat Hackett that he believed people became comedians because they had either gotten too little or not enough attention at home. He said he had gotten too little.

Letterman is not a man who likes to reveal much of himself, so friends were somewhat surprised when he agreed to appear on *Donahue* in 1985. (Perhaps Dave felt he owed Phil a favor after having spent the previous month ribbing the talk-show host with his Phil Donahue Countdown Calendar, a visual reminder of the days left before Donahue moved his show from Chicago to New York.)

Though Letterman rarely gives interviews and, when he does, he's a master at evading personal questions, Phil got him to once again espouse his theory about why people become comedians. (Most likely, Donahue's crackerjack research team had found the old interview quote and decided it was an old sore that Phil could pick at.)

Dave explained his theory again, this time saying that it was children who didn't get enough love who later go for the laughs.

"I don't know if it drove them to being stand-up comedians," he said.

"I think it just sort of created for them the eternal pursuit of re-establishing similar circumstances. Of 'I need to get the love I didn't get,' or 'I need to get as much love as I always got.' "

When Donahue pressed Letterman to tell the audience which child he was, he froze up.

"I don't want to say, I don't want to say. I can't. It would . . . No. I don't know. I don't know."

In the earlier interview with Pat Hackett, Letterman had already identified himself as the child who got too little love and attention.

And the parent who didn't give Dave the nurturing he

needed was Dorothy, the adorable white-haired woman with whom we all fell in love during the Winter Olympics.

Joe was the parent who hugged and kissed the kids, told them jokes, kept the house in stitches with his pranks, and adored his wisecracking son who took after him.

That left the disciplining to Dorothy, who loved her only son as much as Joe did but worried that he was doomed to be a failure because of his cockamamie idea to go into show business.

Dorothy wouldn't support his ambitions then, and she only grudgingly accepts that Dave was right now. No matter what Dave achieves, Dorothy still sees that foolish little boy who goes off half-cocked on things he knows nothing about.

A good example was when Dave was finally offered *The Tonight Show,* if he was willing to wait until Jay's contract expired in May of 1994.

As Dave wrestled with the most important decision of his life, he turned to his mother for support.

"Mom," he told her, "they've offered me *The Tonight Show* but I'm going to go to CBS instead."

Dorothy's reply?

"I just hope you know what you're doing."

Is it any wonder Dave is insecure? Here he is, a forty-seven-year-old man who has had his own successful show on television for ten years, telling his mother that he's made the most momentous decision of his life, a decision that will bring him personal disappointment but that will net him $14 million a year. And her reply is a subtle hint that she doubts the wisdom of his actions.

Part of Dave's deep fears about failing in show business can be directly attributed to his mother, who doesn't seem to have it in her to support or encourage her only son. She wasn't impressed when he set out for L.A. to become a comedian in 1977, and she remains almost as blasé today. It's part of her charm, to be sure, and part of the reason that Dave has been able to retain his Midwestern values and reject the plasticity and pretensions of Hollywood.

But withholding her encouragement and refusing to give Dave her approval also made her son the deeply insecure person he is today. If you can't impress your mother, after all, who can you count on?

Even when Dave had made it to the big time—*People* magazine profiled him as early as 1980 as the heir apparent to Johnny Carson, and he didn't even have his own show yet—he said his Midwestern mother remained duly unimpressed.

"Mom thinks I'm a notch or two above a carnival worker," he told interviewer Bill Shaw.

It just made Dave all the more determined to get her attention, hence the Mother's Day visits, Caribbean vacations, "Parents Night" shows, gigs at the Olympics. But Dorothy is Dorothy, and it seems she'll just never be the kind of mother to hang on her son's every word or action.

Asked in Lillehammer if she and Hans watch the *Late Show,* she said they're usually asleep by then.

"We tape it," she explained, then added, rather defensively, "At least we watch."

Chapter Fifteen

THE NEW WOMAN IN DAVE'S LIFE

One positive trait that Dave inherited from his mother, Dorothy, is his total lack of pretension and the way he abhors superficiality of any kind. It's a characteristic that has carried over into his personal life. One of the many things that sets David Letterman apart from other celebrities of his stature is his relationship with women. Though David could have his pick of almost any model and starlet, he has never taken advantage of his fame to bed a new young beauty every night. Perhaps because he was raised by a strong, no-nonsense Midwestern mother and grew up between two sisters, Dave has a deep respect for women. His love life can best be described as serial monogamy: a nine-year marriage to college sweetheart Michelle Cook, a ten-year relationship with lover/collaborator Merrill Markoe, and his current romance with *Saturday Night Live* production manager Regina Lasko, whom he's been dating for the past five years, living with for the past few.

Whereas now would be the time that most $14 million men would be capitalizing on his access to beautiful women, Dave has never been superficial in his choice of companions. Like any other man, a pretty woman will turn his head. And he's been known to go gaga over more than a few Hollywood beauties who have graced his stage. But when it comes to dating and relationships, Dave is more cerebral. He doesn't need a woman to wear as an ornament on his arm; he doesn't go anywhere. He's too smart to waste his time with a beautiful woman if she has nothing especially interesting to say. Despite his decade of "Stupid Human Tricks" like donning a suit of Alka-Seltzer and jumping into a six-foot glass of water, he's too mature to want to hang around the giggly college crowd that temporarily turned his head during his marriage to Michelle. He doesn't need a woman with a flawless figure and perfect face; he wants a woman who shares his sense of humor and can accept his workaholism. He's not like the men who, when they gain some measure of success, trade in their old, wrinkled wife for a younger, firmer model. If anything, Dave's dating pattern has been the reverse: his women—no offense, Regina—have gotten less attractive as the years roll by.

When a reporter was sent to Dave's New Canaan, Connecticut, neighborhood to check out a rumor that Dave and Regina had gotten engaged, she was astounded at the descriptions of his current ladylove.

"Nothing to look at," was the constant refrain from neighbors and local shopkeepers who seemed bewildered that a man in Dave's position wouldn't have a tall blonde twentysomething beauty queen in his bed—or, better still, a series of them.

To those who know Dave, it isn't really surprising that he's with a plain Jane like Regina. Former girlfriend Merrill wrote about Dave's aversion to cosmetically-gifted women in her book *What the Dogs Have Taught Me*.

Though she didn't mention Dave by name, she clearly

evoked his memory in an essay she wrote about a short flirtation she had with mascara, lipstick, and eye shadow.

"At first I had to hide these items from my boyfriend, who was known to feel that makeup wearers were plastic and superficial. But, like most men, he was pretty naive.

" 'You look very nice this evening,' he'd say, peering at my face. 'Were you out in the sun today?' Yeah. Right, pal. That's it. I was out in the sun, and I spent so much time out there it caused my eyelashes to stick straight out, too."

Despite what his shallow neighbors in New Canaan think about Dave's fresh-scrubbed, womanly-figured girlfriend, Dave is clearly smitten with his thirtysomething love. He met Regina in the late eighties when she was working on *Late Night.* She's now a production manager on *Saturday Night Live.*

Knowing how David abhors publicity, especially about his personal life, the couple kept their relationship a secret for as long as they could. Regina, no doubt, wanted to shout it from the rooftops, but she knew she could blow the whole deal if word leaked out and people started to make a fuss. So she agreed that they'd share as little communication as possible in the office, never daring to even exchange a word if they found themselves on the same elevator. They never left the office together; Dave insisted that they meet elsewhere, someplace they weren't likely to be seen. The plan worked. He kept Regina so well-hidden the first two years they were dating that few people knew about it. In fact, Dave might have been able to keep his relationship a secret indefinitely if he hadn't had the misfortune of getting involved in a car accident with Regina while they were in St. Petersburg, Florida, attending the christening of his sister Gretchen's baby daughter. David being who he is, the accident was reported in the newspapers, which duly noted from the police report that Letterman's passenger was a woman named Regina Lasko.

They had been dating for two years.

Back in New York, the tabloids were dying to get a look at the new potential Mrs. Letterman. The problem was, no one knew what she looked like. Whereas almost every other celebrity has to attend at least the occasional black-tie function, which requires not only a tux but a date, Dave rarely ventures out in public. So careful scrutiny of past party files revealed no photo of the mysterious Ms. Lasko. Even when it was learned that she was a production manager at *Saturday Night Live,* photographers were stymied. Which staffer was she? What did she look like? When asked to describe Regina, people looked puzzled. She's medium height. Medium weight. Brown hair. What could they say? Regina was pretty much nondescript. (Regina's ability to fade into the woodwork is probably a major attraction for publicity-shy Dave.) The *Globe* tabloid finally managed to get a photo of Regina jogging near the home she shares with David in New Canaan, cruelly labeling her the "beefy *Saturday Night Live"* producer Dave is dating. She looked like, well, she's hard to describe. To be fair to Regina, any woman is going to look awful if she's snapped puffing and perspiring at the end of her ten-mile run, with her hair pulled back and a baggy jogging suit on.

Since the word was out, Dave finally fessed up that Regina was his current flame.

Naturally, Dave couldn't give a straight answer when *Rolling Stone* magazine wanted the dirty details of how the two had met.

"Her name is Regina Lasko. Of the Ohio Laskos. When I met her, she was equipment manager for the Rangers. Marv Albert introduced us one night between periods. She was leaning on the Zamboni and I knew then my life would never be the same."

Women may be jealous of Regina, but Dave insists that life with him is no bowl of Beluga.

"Do the words moody drunk mean anything to you?" asks Dave. "I'm no day at the beach, let's just say that."

Actually, Dave is very careful with the women in his life and goes out of his way not to anger them. When he was still living with Merrill, actress Cybill Shepherd teased him on the air by saying, "So Dave, I hear you have a new girlfriend." The actress recalled later that he was visibly upset during the rest of the interview, imploring her to set the record straight and insisting that she was going to have to call Merrill and explain that she was just kidding.

Dave told *Rolling Stone* that he also tiptoes around Regina's feelings. Asked if "those lingering hugs you lately give to fabulous babe guests" get him into trouble at home, Dave replied:

"You know, almost everything I do represents trouble at home. The truth of it is, as I get older, I'm actually getting away with far less. That's why if an opportunity presents itself at work, I feel like I have an obligation to exploit it."

Perhaps the reason Dave is taking advantage of more opportunities to hug luscious babes is because his bachelor days may be numbered: He let it slip to *Rolling Stone* that Regina has begun to pressure him for a wedding ring. It's not the first time commitment-shy Dave has faced this dilemma.

"I've had that kind of pressure for as long as I can remember," replied the forty-seven-year-old bachelor.

"In fact, the only one who didn't pressure me was the

woman I was actually married to. And I think she was greatly relieved when we were no longer married."

Local jewelry shops in New Canaan report that Dave has bought his ladylove lots of expensive jewelry, but no diamond ring to date. (If you haven't been buying those $70,000 necklaces for Regina, Dave, you're in trouble now.)

What may finally prompt Dave to take another walk down the aisle is his yearning for children. Lately he has admitted in interviews that he's beginning to go gaga over rug rats.

"I would love to have a kid," he told writer Jennet Conant last year.

"I've never spent much time with kids and now I do," referring to his friend Jeff Altman's baby daughter.

"It's just the cutest, sweetest, most attractive baby," gushed Dave.

"And I think, man, this would be so nice if you could get yourself a nice, big, fat baby like this."

Dave doesn't mind talking about his newfound baby lust, but he does mind talking about Regina. In fact, he refuses to discuss her anymore.

"I mentioned her name on the air once, and people started to follow her around," he explains.

There's another reason he won't talk about her on the air or in interviews anymore.

"Even if you say something good about the person, you have hell to pay when you get home. They say, what the hell is this?"

Dave told Conant that he's solved the problem by simply clamming up about the women in his life.

"I've found that the one area I'm always uncomfortable is, um, female companions. Because I've never been able to reference that area without pissing someone off. It never comes easy. You can just sort of hear the clock ticking before it comes up as a topic: 'Sooo, I understand that . . .' Well, no, it wasn't like that, I didn't mean that. So I thought for my own self-preservation I'd just skip it."

People who have spotted Dave and Regina together—and it's not easy; Dave reportedly insists on jogging separately from Regina so they can't be photographed together—say he's very attentive to her and gentle with her.

"New England Cable News/Fox 25 News at 10" anchor Heather Kahn once spotted Dave on a flight returning from the Caribbean island of St. Barthélemy. The plane was tiny, and the ride was bumpy.

"He was just so nice, a normal guy. He held his girlfriend's hand during the scary parts of the flight."

Apparently, he relented on the no-jogging-together rule while in the Caribbean because another vacationer spotted him trying to keep pace on the beach with his much faster girlfriend.

Letterman confessed to Barbara Walters last year that he'll probably marry again because he'd like to have children and, showing his Midwestern roots again, marriage "is the prudent way to do that."

When Walters asked if he'd broached the subject with his girlfriend, he laughed and replied: "I've asked her to drop the topic. I spend a great deal of time saying, 'Ah, let's talk about that later. What's for dinner?' "

As Dave gets older and his desire for children deepens, it looks more and more like Regina will be the lucky woman likely to be Letterman's bride, if only because she was the right woman at the right time in his life.

On the other hand, no one is taking bets on the wedding day. Some of his friends think Dave will remain a perpetual bachelor. After all, he used to hint that he was going to marry Merrill someday. Once he actually told a reporter that he and Merrill were engaged. When pressed on when they were actually getting hitched, Dave explained that his concept of "engaged" was that if and when he decided to marry, Merrill would be the one.

He's done the same sort of double-talk when the topics "marriage" and "Regina" are introduced in the same question. On the one hand, he told Barbara Walters (which is, in effect, telling the world) that there is someone in his life he'd like to ask to marry him. Since he's been involved with Regina since 1989, she assumed he was talking about Ms. Lasko. Barbara, delighted with this news (and scoop!), asks if he's broached the subject with his girlfriend.

Naturally, Dave does a complete turnaround and responds that he deftly changes the subject every time Regina brings up the topic of matrimony.

So Regina shouldn't put much stock in Dave's telling people that he'd like to settle down. Embracing the concept of marriage and children is one thing; actually getting married and having kids is a whole different ball game altogether. And, despite Dave's recent attraction to babies, he doesn't seem to have much use for children. He's said in the past that he can just about take care of himself; he can't imagine shouldering the responsibility of a child. When Dave is forced to think about children, it seems he mostly likes them in theory.

"I wish I already had grown children," he once said wistfully.

If Dave does decide to bite the bullet and have children in the next few years, it will probably be with Regina. A serial monogamist, Dave's previous relationships have lasted an average of nine and a half years, so logic dictates that he'll be with Regina another five years, at the very least.

And since traditionalist Dave is not apt to sire children beyond age fifty or so, the forty-seven-year-old will no doubt
have to address the children question soon.

Chapter Sixteen
A DAY IN THE LIFE

"I've never been in prison, I've never done hard time," says Dave.

"I'm the kind of guy that on a hot day, if a neighbor comes over and needs help installing a through-the-window air conditioner, I'll be there."

That's how David Letterman described himself when *TV Guide* asked him why people should tune in to his new show.

But the real David Letterman is a whole lot more complicated than that.

Dave may look relaxed on his television show; indeed, part of the appeal is the way he conveys a "Who gives a hoot" kind of attitude on the air.

But *Late Show* staffers will tell you he's anything but laid-back. Dave treats every day on his talk show as though cancellation is just around the corner.

When Dave had been doing his show for six years and found he was still as anxious as he had been on Day One, he called his mentor, *Tonight Show* producer Peter Lassally (who is now *Late Show*'s producer), for advice. He wanted to know why he was still feeling so stressed about doing the show.

"I said to Peter, 'I can't believe it doesn't seem to get any easier.' And he said, 'Well, that seems to be the way it goes. It doesn't get easier because each night you're dealing with elements that seemingly are the same yet the individual ingredients are different enough to make it tough.' "

Dave immediately understood what his mentor was saying.

"It's not like we're building a Ford Mustang each night," says Dave. "We're building a car every night, but it's a little different from night to night."

At least he no longer gets the stage fright that used to almost paralyze him when he was a stand-up comic at the Comedy Store so many years ago.

About stepping onto the stage every night, he says: "I get a tremendous feeling of excitement. When you're about to step in front of an audience of 240 people, that, in and of itself, is exciting. It's not fright, but I always feel my heart rate come up, and I start to get excited."

If he's still excited about doing his show, he's also scared: Staffers say that the more popular he gets, the more his ratings rise, the more paranoid about failing he gets. Perhaps that's not as unusual as it sounds; now the stakes are so much higher. One of the reasons Dave is successful is precisely because he has never once slacked off in the thirteen years he's been on the air. The dedication is evident in the quality of his work: His shows keep getting better, his ratings keep rising.

"My work habits are more slovenly," Dave once joked when asked how success had changed him.

"I sleep later. I steal equipment from the office. I use the company stationery for my own personal correspondence. And I try to get other people to buy me lunch."

Here's what a typical day is like for Dave:

While other talk-show hosts arrive at their studios a few hours before show time, often in a chauffeur-driven limousine, Dave either drives himself in from his home in Connecticut (he has the speeding tickets to prove it) or takes the subway (yes, the subway) from his loft in TriBeCa.

"I couldn't be a bigger proponent of the subway system," says Dave. "So far I haven't been shot at, it takes eight minutes to get to work, it's relatively clean, and I must say that on each trip there's usually just one intimidating experience, so that's not too bad."

He used to like to jog four to six miles in the morning before work, but he can't run as much since he hurt his neck in a minor car accident three years ago.

Dave always dresses comfortably in sweats or jeans, a sweatshirt, T-shirt, or football jersey, high-top sneakers, and a baseball cap. Most of the time, the T-shirts and caps that boast universities and organizations have no personal meaning for him; they were just sent in by fans.

TV Guide reporter Mark Ribowsky once asked him why he was wearing a cap that said "Auburn."

"Because it's free," said Dave. "People send in hats, sweatshirts, T-shirts—they know what a fashion plate I am. I keep every one. Love 'em."

The network, he said, owns the suits he wears on the show.

"And they're welcome to them. Sending out clothes is too complicated a thing for me anyway."

He arrives at his office at around 10:00 A.M. Well, most of the time he arrives that early. Johnny Carson once read in a magazine article that, while he strolls into his studio at around 2:00 P.M., hardworking Dave is at his desk by 10:00 A.M. So Johnny called Dave at 10:00 A.M. No answer. He called again at 10:30 A.M. Still no answer. He finally reached him at 11:30 A.M. "So, you get to work at 10:00 every morning, eh? What happened, did traffic tie you up this morning?" Dave loves telling that one.

His secretary, Laurie Diamond, has already opened the mail and is ready to discuss what needs to be addressed. Laurie has been with Dave for a decade now and truly loves her boss. She says he often makes her play catch with him as she sits on the couch in his office and they review the morning mail.

"He's just like you see on television, always playing gags," Laurie told a woman's magazine a few years back when she was interviewed as a "Secretary to the Stars."

"One time I left a grilled cheese sandwich on my desk while I went to the copy machine. When I came back, I took a bite and tasted something funny. Dave had slipped a mint into the middle of the sandwich."

Dave's penchant for playing catch in the office once got him into trouble, when a baseball he threw bounced itself right through the window and a few unlucky pedestrians below ended up with glass shards on their heads. (His new office windows at the Ed Sullivan Theater are equipped with what he jokingly calls "bulletproof glass.")

The mail and office matters taken care of, Dave meets with his team of writers, most of whom are like Dave: male, tall, well-educated, witty. (There is one woman writer on the show.)

"I'm so fortunate to have these guys," Dave says.

"I know, because I've worked with writers named Sid and Morty who wear a lot of gold and leave at noon for cocktails. These guys aren't like that. And they don't write characters because we're not a sketch show."

What they dream up for Dave are concepts. "Dave dashing to the deli during the show" doesn't sound like much of an idea, but in the hands of a consummate ad-libber like Letterman everyone knows it will be hysterical. Dave is best when he's winging it, bouncing off events and other people, and his writers know it. One of them once remarked that they could hand Dave some spoons and he'd manage to make it funny.

Next, they review the guests for that night and go over the preinterviews that have been done so he has an idea of what they'd like to talk about and what kinds of topics he can use as launching pads for his humor. Every Friday, they hold a guest meeting at which they discuss who they'd like to line up for the future. Dave has very strong ideas about who he wants on his show, and he'll routinely reject many of the staff's suggestions. He won't have a guest on solely because Mr. or Ms. Hotshot is a big star. He wants guests who are interesting, intelligent, and have something to say. Guests who come prepared to entertain, not be entertained. Since viewers primarily tune into Dave's show for comedy, he wants guests who can be funny, even if the nature of their job is not funny. Or at least someone who's willing to be a good sport about Dave's joshing.

Ideas for stunts, gags, and remotes are batted around. (The latter involves gags that are filmed outside the studio, like the time Dave arranged to have a pizza delivered to a limo on Broadway when President Clinton was in town; when the tape later rolled on the show, he told the audience that the Leader of the Free World was too hungry to wait until he got back to his hotel.) Dave is notorious for rejecting eighty percent of all suggestions. He's extremely demanding of both himself and his staff, and will never accept a mediocre idea just so the meeting can move along.

When they're not meeting with Dave, his staff of a dozen writers spend hours scouring newspapers and magazines, looking for silly items Dave can use in his monologue or absurd guests he can book. Often when they come to him with suggestions, Dave has heard of the person/incident already because he, too, reads a voluminous amount of material each day, searching for ideas.

Dave has developed a reputation for being a difficult boss because of his high-rejection rate on everything: jokes, "The Top Ten List," guests, gags. But it's Letterman's insistence on quality that has gotten the show where it is today: namely, beating the pants off Jay Leno in the 11:30 P.M. time slot he worked so hard for.

"The Top Ten List," (renamed, incidentally, *"Late Show* Top Ten," to avoid a lawsuit with NBC) which seems so effortless when it's read and checked off by Dave each night, is a perfect example of the manpower that goes into each segment of the Late Show.

Head writer Rob Burnett is in charge of the Top Ten. He and the other writers develop several subject possibilities every day and present them to Dave by 2:30 in the afternoon. Dave picks one, and the writers get to work, furiously coming up with items until they have no less than 150 possibilities. Burnett then pares the list down to about fifty, which he presents to Dave at 4:30 P.M., just one hour before show time.

"If I can get 15 or 20 approved, we'll have done our job well for the day," Burnett told *USA Today* writer Jefferson Graham.

"He's extremely demanding. But if his reject rate is high, then that's all for the better. We get better material. People don't seem to realize that besides being a performer, Dave is also a producer. If he says yes to material that's not funny, the show would be terrible."

On some days, there are Dave's famous remotes to tape.

When Dave launched the *Late Show* on CBS in August, he had a stockpile of funny skits that he and his staff had taped during the summer months while they were waiting for the Ed Sullivan Theater to be readied.

One of the funnier ones involved Dave and his camera crew going to an obscure neighborhood in New Jersey, knocking on doors randomly, and asking people if they were going to watch his new show. One woman apologized sheepishly and told Dave she had no idea who he was.

"Regis Philbin," he replied.

Dave got a special kick out of that, since, unlike most celebrities, he loves the idea that there are people who don't recognize him.

Another early remote involved Dave driving around Manhattan using his brand-new car phone to call one of those all-news stations that invite listeners to report traffic problems. The skit was probably a bit of an inside joke as well: one of the many petty arguments Dave had had with NBC in general, and money man John Agoglia in particular, was over NBC's refusal to pay for his car phone.

In any event, as Dave drove around babbling about his new phone, he was also calling the radio station every other minute to warn them that there might be a tie-up ahead . . . but he couldn't really be sure. He'd report ridiculous things like a double-parked truck slowing things down on 79th Street and Amsterdam Avenue, when what the station was looking for was more to the tune of five-car pileups on the West Side Highway.

Finally, they begged him to stop calling. So he drove around some more and discovered a truck that had one of those "How's My Driving?" bumper stickers that invites the public to report the driver to his company if he's driving recklessly. Dave had a field day with that one, telling the perplexed company operator that her driver was doing things like accelerating.

"I'm not sure I know what you mean, sir."

"Well, the light had turned green," said Dave.

Dave then told the frustrated operator that he'd follow the suspicious driver for a while, but he couldn't stick with him all day.

Rehearsal begins around 2:00 P.M., with Dave practicing his monologue.

Owing perhaps to the overdose of testosterone in the studio, there's a lot of goofing around in the studio, like oyster-eating contests and impromptu races.

Dave's favorite part of the day, he says, is the half hour before taping.

"I get excited about having a studio full of people. Doing silly stuff, just trying to get laughs."

At 5:30 P.M. the show begins, played out before a live audience that sends away for tickets up to a year in advance. (There's also a standby line for no-shows.)

The theater is kept at a chilly fifty-eight degrees at Dave's insistence; he thinks it keeps the audience alert.

Dave likes taping in the late afternoon. He once said he'd never want to perform à la *Saturday Night Live*.

"In New York at that time of night you'd get people trying to get warm," he says. "Or looking for a place to reload their weapons."

After his opening monologue, which he prefers to think of simply as "jokes" (he thinks it would be the height of audacity to call his opening a monologue because that's what the great man, Johnny Carson, called his), he takes his place at the desk and chairs arrangement he calls home base. If you've ever wondered why Dave appears to be peering down at his guests, it's not just because Letterman is

6'2" tall; it's because Dave's seat is slightly higher than his guests.

Depending on how the show is going, Dave may or may not talk to a guest during the commercial break. Sometimes he'll dash over to the production people to make sure everything is going smoothly. Other times he'll doodle at his desk, oftentimes writing notes to the guest beside him, like the now infamous "I hate myself" note he pushed in front of Teri Garr during one break. Another guest recalls him shoving a note at her that said "Do you believe I get paid for this?"

When the show is wrapped, Dave does his famous post-mortem in his office, which he calls "Home of the Hits." His old office at NBC had a ceiling filled with pencils because Dave had perfected the art of throwing them up and having them stick to the tiles.

The new one is a bit more sedate since it's spanking new, but it retains the athletic paraphernalia that sports-nut Dave had in his old office: baseball bats, a football, a basket of baseballs, a lacrosse stick.

Dave loves professional baseball. He once said that his favorite part of the game is when some drunken fan comes along, leans over, and interferes with the ball play.

"That's what I'd like to see more of. I don't know how you facilitate more of that, but I'd like to see more of that."

He insists on watching the tape of the show immediately so he can see where he failed, where he could have done better, how he can improve for next time. He's his own worst critic, rarely finding anything good to say about the show. In fact, Merrill Markoe says that, in ten years of working with him, she can't ever recall a night when he was pleased with his performance.

If he really has screwed up somewhere, he'll rewind the

tape and, somewhat masochistically, watch it over and over. At these times, the staff can sometimes hear things being thrown around his office in anger.

"He's very insecure and self-torturing," says former girlfriend Markoe.

After watching the tape and kicking himself over things he could have done differently, jokes he missed, rejoinders that would have been brilliant, he generally goes home dreading what a dork he's going to look like that night.

He never, ever watches his show when it airs. The idea of watching it while millions of viewers are seeing all his mistakes is just too excruciating.

In an interview with the *Philadelphia Inquirer* in 1985, Dave shed some light on why he works so hard, why he feels he can't let his guard down for a moment. His big fear, he said, is that someday he'll stop being funny.

"When you're very young, you find little buttons you can push that will gain you reinforcement. And for people who go into comedy and show business, they find out 'If I say something funny, I'll get all of this praise and my confidence will be built up and I'll be liked and people will seek out my comedy.'

"So you keep working it and working it and then suddenly it's like going down a snowy hill and you hit a dry spot—it's like the rug has been jerked out from under you—and all of the confidence you've built up over the years diminishes, just like that. It drains right out of you. You think, 'Holy God, maybe I'm not so damned funny after all.' "

From what his staff says, it seems to be an assessment he makes nightly, though no one can figure out why.

Even the anniversary shows he used to do every few years, which were mainly clips showing highlights of previous shows or return appearances by crowd-pleasing Stupid Pets and Stupid People, used to terrify Dave. He says he was always riddled with anxiety beforehand, certain that he was going to end up making a complete fool of himself in prime time.

One of the few things Dave doesn't fret over is his insecurity. That's because he doesn't necessarily think it's such a bad thing.

Fear is something Dave has also learned to live with. He's acknowledged many times that he's scared when ratings are down, terrified when they're up.

It seems he's yet to recover from the devastation he felt back in 1980 when his midmorning show *The David Letterman Show* was cancelled after a few short months. In a 1986 interview with David Wecker of the *Boston Herald,* he voiced his insecurities.

"I'm very comfortable with the level we've reached. I can still see myself as kind of an underdog, still scrapping, rather than being on top.

"But I tend to be pretty insecure and pretty pessimistic. And I just wonder if this particular show and I don't have a built-in obsolescence. It's all right now. But maybe in six months, people will be saying, 'We've seen that already.'

"I'm truthfully surprised we're still on the air. And I think it would be better to go out early—to go out in flames, rather than gather rust."

The reason you don't see the terror on Dave's face night after night is because he learned how to hide his emotions long ago, when he was a not-terribly popular teenager growing up in Indiana.

"Not being a real physical person, my own defense, which was actually more of an offense for me, was to never let the other person know that they'd tapped you—never let them know that they'd caused you to lose your bearings," he told *The Chicago Tribune*.

"Where I went to high school, that was the whole thing, never let them know that they'd hit a vein."

Keeping a show as offbeat and fresh as *Late Show* is indeed a formidable task, and one that Dave obviously doesn't take lightly. If he's hard on his staff, they will be the first to acknowledge that he's even harder on himself.

Small wonder then that, by the end of the day, all Dave wants to do is go home.

Dave is one of those celebrities that New Yorkers never see in restaurants and nightclubs. He went to the famous "21" club once for dinner and absolutely hated the fuss that was made over him. All Dave wants to do after the show is leave David Letterman behind and become Dave again. The minute work is over, he gets out of his suit, throws on his casual clothes, replaces his contact lenses with eyeglasses, and dashes home for a quiet dinner with Regina. They prefer to eat in the privacy of their home but since neither cooks much, they're regulars at many of the small restaurants around New Canaan, Connecticut, where the locals know not to bother them. Pasta is probably his favorite meal, followed by pizza. Neither one drinks, Dave having given up liquor long ago when he thought he might have a drinking problem.

One reason he and Regina don't venture out much is because Dave absolutely hates being approached by strangers. When he has to be in a public place, like an airplane, he'll keep the public at bay by turning up his Walkman and burying himself in paperwork.

He loves doing the most ordinary things, like buying his own groceries (though heaven help the cashier who doesn't know the price of a can of pork and beans; he'll rake her over the coals the next day on the air); packing them sensibly—the way he was taught when he was a teenage checkout clerk—and then putting everything away neatly at home.

Another mundane pleasure Dave enjoys immensely is stacking firewood outside his home. He'll occasionally tell bandleader Paul Shaffer about the great weekend he had arranging his cord of wood.

He and Regina spend most weeknights at Dave's Manhattan loft and most weekends in his Connecticut home, where they like to jog, read in companionable silence, and watch sports on TV. Dave also admits a fondness for bad movies.

No matter how he's spending his "leisure" time, however, associates say Dave is always working.

"Dave is a voracious reader," says Robert Morton, his co-executive producer.

"He goes to the movies, watches television a lot, and plays the radio all day in his office. He's a well-read, inquisitive person who's always coming in and saying, 'I just read this article, let's book this guy' or 'I just heard this band, let's get them.' "

Weekends aren't much different for the couple. They'll jog (usually separately), rent some movies, play a game of tennis on Dave's backyard court, or sit around his pool. Regina isn't spotted around town much, but perhaps that's because Dave has kept her such a well-hidden secret for the past five years. Unless she's with Dave, few people recognize her.

Dave, on the other hand, can usually be seen at some point during the weekend, either picking up the Sunday papers in town or popping into the smoke shop for the cigars he loves so much. He recently bought a new travel humidor for his beloved smokes.

One local merchant says he's very polite about his smoking.

"When he comes into my shop, he leaves his burning cigar outside on the windowsill," said one shopkeeper.

He can also be zany.

"One time he came in and remarked how hot it was in the store," says a local shopkeeper.

"So he just took off his jacket and plopped it on the floor. I said, 'Dave, that's probably an expensive coat. Don't just throw it on the floor.' He apologized profusely, picked it up and said, 'You know, I recently had malaria.' "

He's polite to his neighbors but keeps them at arm's length, which is not surprising. Since he's only had old pals like Paul Shaffer to dinner a dozen times in as many years as he's known him, and has never entertained friends like Calvert DeForest (better known as Larry "Bud" Melman) and Jay Leno, he's not apt to be inviting the neighbors to pop in for a quick bite.

He's passionate about his privacy and was more mortified than pleased when he found himself on the cover of *Newsweek* in 1986.

"I feel like a dork when I see myself," Letterman told reporter Richard David Story.

"I mean, I look like a yard man with a learning disability. People look at this and say 'Hmmmmmm, I thought they had developed a cure for that.' "

No matter how popular he gets, how much money is thrown at him, he refuses to take himself seriously. He takes his job seriously, to be sure. But he still believes that he's somewhat of a fluke. And he can't get over the fact that he's being paid so much money to do what he does.

"Martin Mull had the best line I ever heard about show business," he told *Rolling Stone* in 1985.

"He says 'Show business is like high school with money.'
And it is. And even though I have a rather large ego—anyone who goes into comedy has a bottomless ego—I still
feel more comfortable in a not fully accepted circumstance
than I do if I'm surrounded and engulfed and embraced. I
always felt better being a little on the outside in high school,
kind of lobbing in annoying things from outside the periph-
ery. It's just easier to be on the outside making fun of it.
This show is a little fortress, a little bastion, from which I
can whine about practically anything. We're just an irritant.
We're like a gnat trying to sink *The Love Boat*."

He's sensible when it comes to money (some say he's
even a bit tight) and has been investing his money in low-
risk ventures ever since he started earning good money in
the early eighties.

His one extravagance is his cars. In an airplane hangar
in Santa Monica, he keeps a fleet of foreign sports cars that
includes a $450,000 Ferrari. He particularly loves race cars;
he devours British racing magazines and attends the Indianapolis 500 every year without fail.

He loves putting the pedal to the metal in his red Dodge
Stealth, which replaced the $70,000 Porsche that stalker
Margaret Ray tried to drive through the Lincoln Tunnel and
dented along the way. (Dave was more upset about that than
the break-in.)

Over the years, the man who admits he probably had a
drinking problem when he was younger has shed his vices
one by one. He quit chain-smoking, gave up alcohol,
stopped doing drugs, and even kicked his coffee habit.

The one unhealthy pleasure he allows himself are his beloved cigars.

Dave's big fear is that he will someday begin to buy his
own PR, that he'll start to believe that he really is someone

special. He shudders at the possibility of turning into a self-satisfied star, because he absolutely abhors it in other people.

"When I think about television and show business," Letterman told writer Peter W. Kaplan in a *Rolling Stone* interview in 1988, "it grinds my stomach. I want to say to people, 'Don't you understand this is just bullshit, driven by egos, and that's all it is?' I mean, nothing makes me madder than to be sitting there, watching somebody who's just the winner of the genetic crapshoot, and there they are, big stuff on the air, a star. It just drives me crazy."

He is a principled man who won't do commercials, no matter how much money is thrown his way. And he's been sorely tested. A few years ago, a dog food company offered Letterman $3 million to do a commercial for their product. He turned them down. They came back with $5 million. He still said no. So they upped the stakes to $25 million in exchange for David's endorsements for a period of about five years.

He declined. And this, mind you, was before CBS offered him $14 million a year to do *Late Show*.

When asked why he turned the lucrative deal down, he said: "It's because I'm nuts. I need professional help. And I need it now."

He's been asked to write his autobiography, but insists he'll never do that.

"That would be egomaniacal behavior," says Dave.

When the movie people came courting, he was his old cynical self.

"Sounds to me like I'd get someone's $12 million and throw it down the toilet."

He eventually did sign a movie deal with Disney. It was another gig he didn't particularly want, but he accepted it for reasons that are classic Dave: He thought it would be something to fall back on when his show was canceled.

"My own insecurity for my position in show business is what led me to eventually take them up on their offer," he said.

In other words, since the public was apt to discover sooner or later the ugly truth—that David Letterman doesn't know what the hell he's doing and he shouldn't be on television—he figured he might as well go ahead and have a backup plan for when that inevitable day arrived.

"I'm really confident that one day I'll make a really bad movie. It will cost about $20 million and many people who appear in the film with me will never work again."

Letterman has since negotiated his way out of the deal, returning most of his signing money.

One outside venture he did get involved in was the CBS sitcom *The Building* which debuted around the same time that *Late Show* was launched. Letterman acted as an executive producer on the series, which was canceled after just a few episodes.

Asked several years ago if there was anything within his professional ability that he hadn't done, he replied:

"No. I mean, being able to have your own network television show has been for me something that I dreamed about all my life. And one day I hope to get one. I've had this job longer than any other job I've had in my life, and that's a personal point of satisfaction. It put to rest the rumors that I'm shiftless and lazy and can't hold a job."

Being a workaholic, he doesn't take many vacations, but he does like to get down to his hometown, Indianapolis, a few times, to visit his mother and just be back home.

"I enjoy the city," he told *USA Today* writer Jefferson Graham.

"It's changed a lot, and it's only gotten nicer. The complaint that we always heard from the outsiders was that it was a bit sleepy, which was fine with me. I don't mind sleepiness.

"Everytime I go back, I'll always go to Steak 'n Shake. I'll get two double cheeseburgers, some fries and a vanilla shake and be sick for two days."

Considering Dave's popularity with the public (the dog food people obviously recognized it), it's almost astounding that he has always been so doubtful about his fame, so ready to downplay his success.

"I've always been very suspicious of the success of the show," Dave said a few years back.

"I never felt it was because people like seeing me each night. That's certainly true in the case of Carson, but not me."

Perhaps Jay Leno described David Letterman best when he said, "What you see in Dave is how the average person would react if he suddenly found himself on television."

And that's precisely why we like him.

Chapter Seventeen
DAVE: GOOD & BAD

Dave recently admitted that he had a drinking problem when he was younger. His serious drinking started in high school, propelled both by a desire to be accepted, to do the things everyone else was doing, and the need to dull the pain he felt at not being accepted by his peers.

He often talks in interviews about how he felt like an outsider in high school, how he was the kind of kid who was never a part of the cool gang. The girls in town didn't particularly go for the gangly, gap-toothed joker; he wasn't enough of a scholastic achiever to fit in with the smart kids; he wasn't enough of a jock to be accepted by the true athletes. So he banded with a few other misfits and together they would watch the fun from the sidelines, making sport of the people they really wished would accept them.

It was his unhappiness in high school, more so than the usual teenage high jinks, he says, that led him to drink.

"I spent three years riding around in a 1938 Chevy with four other guys who couldn't get dates, drinking beer and eating pizza," he told *Playboy*. "That's how we spent Friday and Saturday nights."

Dave also smoked pot, but he gave that up after six months because of a terrifying experience.

"I remember one night when I smoked down a big joint and then went downstairs and ate two pints of Häagen-Dazs and went back to bed. An hour later I woke up and thought my heart had stopped. The next day, I went to a cardiologist and said, 'I think my heart stopped last night.' He said everything was fine. But that was the end of my pot experience."

His drinking didn't slow down, however. In fact, it intensified. Whereas Dave drank out of a combination of boredom and peer pressure back in Indiana, he began seriously boozing out of terror and insecurity when he risked everything to go to Los Angeles and try to make it in the terrifying world of stand-up comedy. He was spending his nights working in bars, getting up in front of total strangers, aghast at the thought of making a fool of himself. It was so easy to just go to the bar before his set and kick back a few shots. Then there was the endless stream of college girls hanging out at the Comedy Store, anxious to make the acquaintance of the entertainers. So Dave would reach for another drink at the end of his act and soon he'd be relaxed enough to shoot the breeze with anyone who popped in. It also helped to be a little high when he got home to an increasingly unhappy Michelle, a music major with a bachelor's degree in fine arts who was spending her days toiling at K mart so her husband could pursue his dream of becoming a comedian. As Dave plowed back home night after night, dead drunk, Michelle began to wonder which he was pursuing more actively, his career or groupies.

Eventually, even Dave had to admit that his drinking had gotten out of hand.

"I used to drink heavily," says Dave of those days. "I think I had a drinking problem because I was so uncomfortable unless I was dead drunk."

He recently discussed his drinking with recovering alcoholic John Larroquette.

"I remember after I stopped drinking, like the second or third day, I missed something and I couldn't think of what it was. And I said, 'Oh, yeah, it's that annoying buzz in my head. It's gone. It's like an old friend has died.' "

David no longer drinks or does drugs, but he does admit that he smokes cigars like chewing gum.

"I'll probably have to give those up someday, too," he says sadly.

He did manage to give them up for a short time.

"I was smoking way too many—10 or 15 a day, and I just thought this was insane, so I gave them up," he said in 1989.

"It was very difficult, but I think if you're smoking anything on a regular basis you're nuts."

Dave's other big compulsion is fast cars, which can't really be counted as a vice unless you consider the trouble Dave's speeding has gotten him into over the years.

If David Letterman hadn't been a comedian/talk-show host, he definitely would have been a race-car driver.

Dave's love of fast cars is well-known and his penchant for speeding became a national joke when he instructed his mother, Dorothy, in her Olympic special correspondent duties, to ask First Lady Hillary Rodham Clinton if she or her husband "could do anything about the speed limit in Connecticut."

Dave's troubles began in 1984, when he got a $35 ticket for hitting into a car that the cops said he was driving too closely behind.

Two years later, in May 1986, an alert Connecticut cop caught him using a radar detector, which is illegal in that state. He was fined $40 and sent on his way.

The following November, he was nabbed, also in Connecticut, for driving fifty-seven miles per hour in a forty-mile-per-hour speed zone.

When the cops pulled him over, they discovered that he had a California license but not a Connecticut one.

"The law says once you establish residency in a state you must get a valid operator's license," the cop patiently explained to an annoyed Dave, who refused to sign the $147 ticket. (He did pay it, however.)

By early 1989, he had racked up five speeding tickets in Connecticut and his license was suspended for thirty days. Instead of just hiring a chauffeur for the month, Dave bought a loft in trendy TriBeCa.

"I got an apartment in New York to protect my driving license," said Dave, in one of the rare times he wasn't joking.

Two years later, Dave collided into a pickup truck while in St. Petersburg with Regina. They were in town to attend the baptism of his sister Gretchen's baby daughter. The truck was driven by Raymond Musser; with him was his eight-year-old son, Justin.

Letterman suffered minor injuries, was treated at Bayfront Medical Center, and released. Regina was unharmed. Raymond Musser, however, was knocked unconscious and hurt his head and back, and Justin broke his jaw and suffered a huge cut that ran from his mouth to his ear.

This time, however, it wasn't Dave's fault. Moments before the accident, another car crash at the same intersection had knocked out the traffic lights.

Even though Letterman wasn't to blame, he later agreed to give Justin $125,000 to settle the lawsuit he and his father had filed against him.

Though he probably would have won the case in court

since the light was broken and no one was to blame, softie Dave instructed his lawyer to pay the boy the money when he learned that Justin would require expensive plastic surgery to repair a scar left by a deep cut suffered in the crash.

"The record definitively shows neither David Letterman nor Raymond Musser was at fault in the accident," said Letterman's spokesman, Kenneth Lerer.

"After learning of Justin's medical needs, Mr. Letterman contributed monies to help meet some of those needs."

In September of 1993, speedster Dave was nailed again, in New York this time (en route to Connecticut) doing seventy-eight miles per hour in a fifty-five-mile-per-hour zone.

"The only thing he asked was how fast I clocked him at, and that was the extent of our conversation," said the police officer who handed him a ticket for $275.

Dave currently drives a red Dodge Stealth that can go up to speeds of 180 miles per hour, and network brass are terrified that their late-night star is going to wrap himself around a tree someday. They've implored him to get a driver, but down-to-earth Dave refuses. It's not just that he'd feel uncomfortable climbing in and out of a limo every day; it's that he loves to drive.

He was thrilled when he got to present an ESPN ESPY auto racer of the year award to race-car driver Nigel Mansell earlier this year, and he even challenged Nigel to a race—on Connecticut's Merritt Parkway, the scene of all his speeding tickets.

"I don't think the police would like it!" Nigel joked back.

He also loves to watch race-car driving. He's never missed an Indianapolis 500 yet and says he'd love to bankroll an Indy 500 car-racing team someday.

"It's very possible one day," says Letterman.

"It's a small dream of mine. I don't know if it will ever

come to fruition, but it is the one area outside of broadcasting in which I have a professional interest."

He's already had Mansell on his show a few times and knows that Mansell is on the team co-owned by Paul Newman.

Dave may have his vices, like the rest of us, but he's also very generous with his money. He not only treats his staff well, making sure that everyone gets a bigger piece of the money when ratings are up, but is generous with charities that tug at his heart. Most people don't know this, because Dave goes about his charity work quietly. He's too shy to consider becoming a spokesperson for any particular group, but he's happy to write a check if he hears of a worthy project or person that could use his help.

Because Dave abhors being in the public eye so much, you're not apt to see him on "The Jerry Lewis Telethon" or dragging Regina to a danceathon called "Boogying for Bosnia."

His style is such that when he hears about a good cause he'll go ahead and send a check; he doesn't sit back and wait to be approached for a donation. He likes to make contributions that go straight to the source, money that he knows is earmarked for a particular purpose and will immediately do some good.

His alma mater, Ball State University in Muncie, Indiana, has been the recipient of many of Letterman's generous gestures.

In 1985, for example, he donated $24, 285 worth of video equipment. A plaque in the school's telecommunications facility notes that David dedicated the equipment "to all C students before and after me."

Professor Darrell Wible, who had David in one of his classes, explains the inscription:

"He came in one day and sort of looked at the floor, stammered around a little bit, and said, 'I want to thank you for that C. I really didn't deserve it.' "

David also started a David Letterman Scholarship, which he directed was to be awarded "irrespective of grade-point achievement or lack thereof."

David, who graduated with a C average, clearly wants to underscore that college grades are often no indication of what a person is capable of achieving in the real world.

The scholarship is awarded based on individual projects, not overall grades. In the first year, the money went to a student named Tom Gulley in recognition of his audio-video satire of a private detective show.

A few years later, when Dave was really feeling his oats, he gave Ball State University $132,000 to buy communication equipment and to establish a separate scholarship from the one he had started in 1985.

Sixty thousand dollars was used to establish a student-operated radio station (Dave spent more time hanging out at the campus radio station than attending classes when he went to Ball), and $72,000 was targeted for a three-year internship program for six telecommunications students. The program allowed the students to receive financial support and school credit for helping the faculty develop instructional videos.

Letterman also donated his shares in General Electric, NBC's parent company, to the university.

He is also quietly active in children's charities, especially when it comes to the handicapped. He sponsors a summer camp for children with cerebral palsy.

"Mr. Letterman sometimes calls the children, or writes them a letter. And they're personally written letters, too," says Kirby Gamber of United Cerebral Palsy of Central Indiana.

Dave is always happy to get involved when he hears that a person or institution in his home state or hometown needs help. When he learned that Roncalli High School in Indianapolis needed to build a wheelchair ramp, he immediately instructed his attorney to send the amount they needed. And Dave didn't even attend Roncalli.

"My understanding is that it came straight out of his pocket," said Roncalli Principal Joseph Hollowell. "His attorney dropped by and left a check."

In another unsolicited act of kindness, he made a $5,000 donation to Tom Dreesen's "Day for Darlene," a three-day festival of sports and games to raise funds to combat multiple sclerosis.

Dave has been particularly generous since landing his $14-million deal with CBS.

Shortly after the *Late Show* went on the air, he was golfing at the Bonnie Briar Country Club in Larchmont, New York. He asked his caddy how much he usually gets tipped for the day.

The caddy said $30 or $40 dollars.

Dave gave him $400.

Dave's generosity is the best kind; it's impulsive and straight from his heart. Every day fifty or so devoted fans are turned away from the Ed Sullivan Theater because there aren't enough tickets to go around. Feeling bad for those folks one day, Letterman spent $1,700 buying them tickets to the Broadway show *Miss Saigon*.

Part Five

A New Era

Chapter Eighteen
CARSON WORSHIP

David Letterman has always been generous in giving praise where praise is due. He credits his ex-wife Michelle Cook with giving him the courage to pack up and leave Indiana so he could try his hand at stand-up comedy in Los Angeles. He credits ex-love Merrill Markoe with creating much of the humor that made *Late Night* the success it was and helped make *Late Show* the contender it is today. He credits Jay Leno for showing him, when he first arrived in Los Angeles, that he was going about his comedy all wrong, and teaching him what observational humor was all about, which remains to this day the keystone of his show.

But there is no one in David Letterman's life who has influenced him more than Johnny Carson.

"Since I was a kid, all I ever wanted to be in life was Johnny Carson," he told *Time* magazine in 1993.

"I don't know of a person in comedy or television who didn't grow up with Johnny Carson as a role model. The man has been encouraging and helpful to me in ways he doesn't know I know about."

David started patterning himself in the image of Johnny Carson as early as high school. Dave thought Johnny was just about the coolest guy he'd ever seen, on television or off. If Dave couldn't be popular and adored like Johnny, he could be as unruffled and aloof as his hero. Or, at the very least, he'd give the impression that he was confident and laid-back. So when the pretty cheerleading types wouldn't date him and the jocks wouldn't invite him to toss around the football after school, cool Dave would just think of how Johnny Carson would handle the situation. Actually, Johnny would never be in this kind of situation. But if he were, it simply wouldn't bother a cool dude like Carson. And if it did, he'd never, ever let on. So that's how Dave decided he'd act. Distant. Apathetic. Untroubled. Just as Carson would sometimes glance over at the audience when a guest was being ridiculous, raise his eyebrows, and give them that knowing do-you-believe-this-guy kind of look, Dave perfected the art of standing off to the side of the action, smirking and snickering at the kids who excluded him. He found at a very early age that rejection hurt less if you could convince yourself you were too good for the group ignoring you.

Letterman once said that, for a whole generation, Carson established the model of how cool guys behaved.

"I watched Carson when I was in high school," says Dave. "He always seemed like the guy you want to emulate."

Dave never grew out of his hero worship of Johnny Carson. If anything, he idolized Carson even more when he got to college and realized that he just might have a shot at a broadcasting career, that it wasn't the farfetched idea his mother seemed to think it was.

Once he got to Hollywood, he realized he'd been right to hold Johnny Carson up as the standard to which he aspired. The ticket to success as a comedian in Los Angeles, he was told by the other comics he met, was to get to do your act at the Comedy Store, where Johnny's people were always on the lookout for new comics to come on the show and do their routine. A guest spot on Johnny Carson's show was a career maker or breaker. Dave was determined that, should he ever get to the *Tonight Show* stage, his would be the latter. He'd make sure there would be no screwups.

Dave, as we all know, was brilliant on his *Tonight Show* debut. So much so that Johnny, his hero, made the almost unprecedented move of inviting the unknown to sit beside him on the couch for a few moments. Naturally, he was invited back, and Dave's next few times were, if anything, more impressive. Johnny and producers quickly realized that this tall, skinny kid from Indiana was no fluke. He was the real thing, and he was going to be big. Carson, who has the same nose for talent that Ed Sullivan had, smelled a star. He authorized his producers to invite Dave on as a guest host.

Small wonder, then, that Dave began worshipping Johnny Carson in earnest. Years before, when Dave was growing up in Indiana, he was smart enough to know that he admired Johnny's image, not necessarily Johnny. We all like to think that, were we to someday meet our idols, they'd have all the wonderful attributes we'd ascribed to them over the years. But most of us recognize that what we are in awe of is a media image that may or may not have anything to do with reality. Sometimes, the disappointment of meeting your idol and discovering he's not the man you thought he was, is crushing.

That certainly didn't happen when David Letterman met his childhood hero, Johnny Carson. If anything, meeting his idol intensified his desire to be just like him. Johnny was charming, gracious, and encouraging to the young comic. He didn't just take a professional interest in him because he recognized that this was a guy headed for stardom; he took a personal interest in Dave's career because he found that he liked him an awful lot. The man who had few friends growing up soon found himself being welcomed into Johnny's inner circle. It was more than he had ever imagined, or dared to hope for.

He even extended to Dave the rather rare invitation to play a game of tennis at his home. In a 1993 interview, Dave told *Rolling Stone* magazine that he hesitated about taking Johnny up on his offer because he was terrified that he was going to make a fool of himself in front of his idol.

"I finally said to myself, 'This is a living legend—you're stupid if you don't screw up the courage to go.' But in my defense, how can you just go to Johnny's house? First of all, his house is like a stadium where they have the Davis Cup trials. He's got this state-of-the-art tennis surface— something NASA developed when they went to Neptune. The whole experience was unnerving. And his wife was very nice to me. But there wasn't a second I didn't fully expect to just kind of turn abruptly and destroy a $6,000 lamp or vase. I just felt, something's going to go wrong, like I'm going to kill Johnny's wife with the ball machine. 'How could you have killed his wife with the ball machine!' It's just like I'm too big, I'm too dumb, I'm too clumsy."

Playing a game of tennis with Johnny, who is twenty-one years his senior, made Dave respect Johnny even more.

"He beat me. He's very good. He can stand in one place, never break a sweat and run your pants off."

Being embraced by Johnny Carson would cause most lesser men to get something of a swelled head, but Dave's childhood anxieties ran so deep that even getting the nod of approval from the man he admired most in the world didn't calm Dave's insecurities. Dave was so successful as a guest host that rumors began circulating almost immediately through show-biz circles that Letterman was going to be Carson's successor.

Letterman recalled those heady days to *Rolling Stone* magazine in a 1985 interview.

"In California I was literally living in a one-room apartment on stilts in Laurel Canyon, and I had hosted *The Tonight Show* a couple of times and then I went away. When I got back to my house in Laurel Canyon, I had mail from people all over the country, and they had all sent clippings carrying the same wire release saying I would be the next Johnny Carson. I thought, 'Good Lord.' The week before I was having trouble getting enough money to have the clutch in my truck replaced and the next week I'm getting clippings saying I'm the next Johnny Carson. It just made me laugh. It was like finding gold in your junk drawer. It's like you find this thing and have it analyzed and then, 'No kidding? It's pure gold?' And they say, 'Yes, it is. It's worth $60 million. We don't know how it got there, but it's yours.' It just made you laugh."

It wasn't just that Dave had proven himself adept at filling Johnny's shoes; the word was, King Carson liked Dave. Though there was nothing in his contract dictating that he be consulted on who his successor would be, everyone assumed that Johnny would have a major say in the person who stepped into the role he had filled so ably for so long.

It also hadn't escaped anyone's notice that Letterman had become good friends with *Tonight Show* producer Peter Lassally. It was obvious that Lassally had taken Dave under his wing and, when the time came, would lobby for his friend to succeed Johnny.

Dave was amazed that his name was being batted around as Johnny's heir apparent. He couldn't believe anyone was putting him in the same league with Johnny Carson, his hero.

He told the *Chicago Tribune Magazine* why he looked up to Carson so much.

"First of all, I think Carson is real smart. One thing that would indicate that is that in television, which is such a fluctuating, quixotic medium, there are only a couple of people who have been on as long as he has. Dick Clark is another one—he'll die on the air and they'll cover his funeral during a cutout on the *$20 Million Pyramid*. I think it's a sign of real intelligence that you're able to take your personality and make it sustain like that.

"Secondarily, there's Carson's personality itself. He just gives the impression that he's in control. He's likable, he can be real funny, he can be serious, and because you know he's not going to misdirect you, you're willing to put up with almost anything as long as he's in charge.

"Part of his secret is that Midwestern thing. I guess you don't expect a guy from that part of the country, someone who looks like you or me, to be clever or tricky. It's a different image than the stereotype America has of comics—guys in shiny suits telling jokes about their wives being fat. A Catskills comic can deliver a barb that leaves dead and wounded all around him, while a guy from Nebraska or Indiana can do it and it's a clean cut."

Letterman didn't dare take the talk about his being the next Johnny Carson too seriously. It was 1980 and Johnny wasn't anywhere near ready to retire. A lot could happen in the coming years, Dave thought. Naturally, the old insecurities bubbled up. Surely another comic, a more talented comic, would come onto the scene and knock Dave out of contention.

By 1981, Dave didn't have time to dwell on the Carson

successor issue anyway. He'd been given his own show to do from New York, a comedy/talk show that would follow *The Tonight Show* and try to keep Johnny's momentum.

Not surprisingly, the goal he set for himself was to follow in the footsteps of Johnny Carson—to develop a show that people would automatically tune in to every night because they knew that, more often than not, it would deliver.

"What I'd like is for this show to stay on long enough to become just a pattern of American television," said Dave when he started *Late Night with David Letterman* in February 1982.

"If we're still on the air in five years, then I'll think of it as a success. The reason Carson has been on the air for 20 years is not because he does a great show every night. He has his great shows and he has his awful shows, like everybody else. But the reason *The Tonight Show* succeeds is because people like him. They don't really turn the show on to see whoever Johnny has as guests. They turn on the show to see Johnny."

In the next few years, he was too busy trying to establish an audience for *Late Night with David Letterman* to worry about whether he would or would not succeed Carson. He still flew out to Burbank once a year or so to appear on *The Tonight Show,* usually with hilarious results.

When Letterman made his first appearance on *Late Night with Conan O'Brien,* he recounted a particularly great gag that he and Johnny had played on each other.

"Johnny and I used to live in a part of Malibu called Point Dume," recalled Dave.

"I had in those days, and still do, a 1973 Chevy pickup truck that was just beat to hell. There was like a thousand dents and because of the sea air all of these dents would rust, and it really got to be quite an eyesore.

"One day I was a guest on Johnny's show and Johnny said, 'Why don't you tell me about this piece of junk you got parked in front of your house? I have to run by there every day, and it's making me sick.'

"I said, 'I don't know what you're getting to.'

"Next thing the curtains open and there in the studio is my pickup truck! He swiped it and brought it into Burbank, and it's sitting there serving as a huge embarrassment to me in front of the entire world."

It didn't take long for Dave to think of a way to exact his revenge. When *The Tonight Show* returned the truck, Dave noticed that a headlight had been shattered in transport. So he called *People's Court* Judge Wapner and asked him if he'd come on *Late Night* and hear his case against Johnny Carson.

"Judge Wapner is sitting there and Carson and I are behind podiums," remembers Dave.

"Finally, I was able to prove—and I felt very proud of this—that my truck had been damaged when Carson swiped it. I won a $30 settlement from Johnny Carson. I felt a little bit like one of his ex-wives. Get in on that gravy train."

By the mid-eighties, when Dave had managed to achieve the impossible—develop a money-making franchise in the 12:30 A.M. spot—the rumor mill started again to churn out stories that Johnny had had enough, that he was seriously thinking about retiring. The rumors weren't without merit. Carson seemed to be on his own show less and less; every time he renegotiated his contract, he'd manage to work fewer weeks.

Dave's realistic assumption in the early eighties that there would be other strong contenders for Johnny's job had, of course, come to pass. Joan Rivers was the lead contender for a while when she became permanent guest host in the mid-eighties. She blew her chances, of course, when she went behind Johnny's back and signed a deal for her own late-night show on Fox, an outing that proved disastrous. Carson never forgave her—not for daring to compete with him, but for not having the courtesy to tell him before it was a done deal.

Dave agreed with Johnny that Joan had not handled things in the most graceful way, seemingly biting the hand that had fed her all those years, but he felt sympathy for Joan when she was axed by Fox so soon after its debut. (Compared to Chevy Chase, however, Joan had enjoyed a nice long stint on Fox.)

"I was both surprised and not surprised by that. But I do think the biggest problem there was not Joan, but just the nature of that network. She was more a victim of that," said Letterman, referring to the fact that a then fledgling network like Fox couldn't hope to attract many affiliates.

Rumors began circulating that Fox would look to steal David Letterman from NBC to replace Joan Rivers. When confronted with the rumors, Dave said his answer would be "Thanks but no thanks."

"I don't think anybody could come in at this stage of that project and get better ratings than she could."

The comedian who got to replace Joan Rivers as permanent guest host was Jay Leno, the popular comic who spent most of his days on the road, playing in comedy clubs. It wasn't long before the rumors circulated that the smart money was now on easygoing Leno to succeed Carson.

But nobody was ruling out David Letterman, who had managed to reinvent the talk-show forum with great success—even though he once said he would have preferred to have just copied Johnny Carson.

"I've always been conscious of the fact that I had to

make myself different from Johnny," Letterman told *New York Daily News* writer Alan Mirabella in 1988.

"Although, hell, I wish I was him. I'd rather be him than me."

In 1989, Dave told *Time* reporter Richard Zoglin why he admired Johnny Carson so much.

"First of all, personally, if it had not been for *The Tonight Show* and Johnny Carson, I wouldn't have a car—probably wouldn't have shoes. But the real reason I look up to the guy is the longer I do this, the more respect I have for him. Show me somebody else in the history of television who has not only survived but also dominated for a quarter of a century. I think if you don't have respect for that, there's something wrong with you.

"And he still makes me laugh. In fact, I don't even watch *The Tonight Show* because how good he is makes me nervous and insecure. I look at that show and I say to myself, 'Yeah, see, you're no Johnny Carson.' "

Over the years, Letterman has credited other performers with influencing him, namely Jack Paar and Steve Allen.

"From Jack Paar I've learned that it's not a bad idea to let people see what they might interpret as actual emotions. If you're happy, genuinely happy, or if you're actually angry, it's not a bad idea to let people know that.

"From Steve Allen, I think I learned that television is a really good place to be goofy. In fact, I think that's maybe the best application of television: goofy behavior."

But Carson remains Dave's number one hero, the man who most influenced his life and his show.

"From Johnny Carson I've learned that the most important thing—regardless of the show, regardless of the guest, regardless of the material—is to establish a consistent personality so that people always know where you stand on one thing or another. You have to be consistent because they're not going to tune in night after night after night for 30 years to see the guests. With some exceptions, nobody in this country cares enough about a particular guest to make an effort to watch *The Tonight Show* every night of the week for 30 years. The reason that they do make an attempt to tune in to *The Tonight Show* every night for 30 years is because they know Johnny Carson and they're comfortable with him and they want to see his reaction. I think it's just the same as why some friends you have forever and some you only have for a short time."

Mostly out of respect for Carson, but partly because he still felt himself unworthy of the job, Letterman always dismissed reporters' queries on the Carson heir issue.

Dave's old bugaboo—insecurity—oozes out in this 1986 interview with *The New York Times*.

"I have not been offered *(The Tonight Show)* and have never talked about it with (Carson).

"In the back of my mind, if I weren't asked someday to do it, I'd feel kind of sad. Yet, doing it—that's my worst nightmare. That I'd be foolish enough to take the Carson position if offered to me, that I'd die a miserable death in that time slot, and meanwhile NBC had given my old show to someone who was quite happy in doing it."

In light of what later transpired—that NBC did eventually come to the realization that they'd made a mistake giving *The Tonight Show* to Jay Leno and offered the job to Letterman if he was willing to wait out Leno's contract—the following is prescient:

"Maybe the prudent thing would be to let some other poor bastard walk into the fray for several months and then try doing the show."

Dave's then manager, Jack Rollins, had more faith in his

client. In 1988, he told reporter Alan Mirabella that Letterman would most likely inherit *The Tonight Show*.

"I think it's a sure bet," said Rollins. "I think so. I hope so. I think that Dave can stay around for 25 years. He has a clean-cutness, that Midwestern characteristic that audiences love, plus a driving intelligence."

"Yeah, I think it might be nice to play high-stakes poker," Letterman admitted in the same interview, finally allowing, in the gentlest way possible, that he'd like to throw his hat in the ring for the Carson gig.

"But I have a feeling it's one of those things that's going to solve itself."

What an understatement that turned out to be.

The way the issue of who would take over Carson's job solved itself was that Jay Leno's manager Helen Kushnick started the ball rolling by (secretly) telling the press that Johnny was on his way out and Jay was on his way in.

Helen eventually triumphed in her battle to get Jay *The Tonight Show* over Letterman, but she didn't enjoy her victory for long: Shortly after giving Johnny's job to Jay, NBC insisted that he fire his bulldog agent when it became apparent that she was alienating everyone in Hollywood with her strong-arm tactics regarding booking guests.

Helen's underhanded antics may have gotten her client the job, but it didn't win any points with Johnny Carson. Though he knew Jay Leno was an innocent pawn in the vicious game Helen played to oust Johnny so she could secure the job for Jay, Johnny couldn't help but feel Jay was guilty by association. Johnny felt that Jay should have known what his own manager was up to, should have known what she was capable of.

Conversely, Johnny was deeply impressed with the way Dave handled the situation, refusing to be drawn into a battle over *The Tonight Show* until Johnny had had the opportunity to announce his retirement gracefully (as gracefully as one could after Kushnick planted the news story that NBC wanted Carson out).

Unfortunately for Dave, Johnny had no say over who would replace him on *The Tonight Show,* nor did he want to take sides. He liked Jay well enough—hell, everybody likes Nice Guy Jay—but he respected David more as a talent and felt he was a more well-rounded entertainer.

Though Carson never came out publicly and said that he thought David Letterman was the best man for his job, Jay Leno knew that's how Carson felt. The bad feelings between Jay and Johnny were apparent: In the weeks before Johnny signed off for good on May 22, 1992, he mentioned his successor only once.

Then came Jay's debut as *Tonight Show* host the following Monday.

It was not so much what Jay said; it was what he didn't say. In light of all the hoopla that had been made over Johnny's last show the previous Friday, Leno's silence on the matter was deafening. Amazingly, he made no mention whatsoever of Johnny Carson. When he found himself being criticized by television critics in the following weeks, Leno defended his silence surrounding Carson, saying he didn't want things to get "sloppy."

Letterman, who was deeply depressed that Carson was off the air, and utterly despondent about not getting the job, watched that first show in total amazement. Here was Jay Leno, who had just landed the best gig in television broadcasting, acting like it was just a routine day of guest-hosting. There were no thanks to the man who had made it all possible, no mention of the guy who had occupied the chair he now sat at for the previous thirty years. Astounding.

Dave later told *Rolling Stone* magazine that, had he been given *The Tonight Show,* he would have handled things differently. Very differently.

"This is not to demean what Jay accomplished, but were it I that night, it would have been handled much differently. Because you can't just turn off over one weekend the six-month period of genuine emotion and interest and care and concern. You have to address that and I would have done it. Now you could be criticized for trying to make yourself look good by kissing up to Johnny. But there was so much positive feeling about him that it would have been hard to make too big a mistake there."

He told how desperately sad he felt the day Carson called it quits.

"I can remember watching Carson's last show and being woefully depressed. I couldn't sleep. I was up the whole night—which maybe tells you more about me than I would like. I know it sounds like I'm a complete ninny, but I felt a sadness for weeks after. It was sort of like a doctor telling you, 'Well, we've looked at the X-rays and your legs are perfectly healthy but we're still going to amputate them.' You think, 'Whaaat? Why is he going?' "

Carson and Letterman had a lot in common. Both were from the Midwest (Johnny grew up in Nebraska); both were raised in middle-class families; both had held a variety of jobs in broadcasting before landing their talk shows (as opposed to Jay Leno whose resumé only includes stand-up gigs).

Just as Johnny respected David and his talent, David worshipped Carson far too much to campaign for his job behind his back. So he decided to do the polite thing, to stay above the fray and hope to win the job on pure merit. It ultimately cost him the job. But if he lost the battle for *The Tonight*

Show, he can console himself with the fact that he's won the war. His *Late Show,* which debuted August 30, 1993, is trouncing the competition, namely Jay Leno's *Tonight Show.*

But perhaps the most satisfying part is knowing that, had it been Johnny Carson's decision, David Letterman would have gotten *The Tonight Show.*

To David Letterman, that's the greatest compliment of all.

Dave says he has asked Johnny Carson to be on his new show.

"I went up to him in the most respectful way I could and said, 'It would be great—I have a new show on CBS and if you would consider coming on I would really appreciate it.' "

What did Johnny say?

"He looked at me and said, 'Get away from the car!' "

Chapter Nineteen
DAVE & JAY

Leno's behavior on his first day at the helm of *The Tonight Show* aside, David Letterman likes and respects Jay Leno. And the feeling is mutual.

The battle over Johnny Carson's job was dubbed the Late-Night Wars by the media, but the fight was always between David Letterman and NBC, never David Letterman and Jay Leno.

Dave and Jay went back a long way. When Johnny announced his impending retirement in 1991, they had been friends for fourteen years. Because they had lived on opposite coasts for the past nine, they didn't see each other terribly often. But that didn't mean they didn't consider each other good friends.

Besides, Dave doesn't socialize with much of anyone beyond the current woman in his life. That's just the way he is.

David Letterman is also fiercely loyal. He's demonstrated that with managers and lawyers over the years, and with his *Late Night* staff. His secretary, his producer, his head writer—all have been with him since the show began. He may not see these people much outside the office, but it doesn't mean he values their friendship any less. He's there for them when they need him, and he never speaks ill of anyone he considers an intimate.

What made the fight for *The Tonight Show* particularly painful for Dave was that it involved his old pal, Jay. David has never forgotten how Jay helped him out in the late seventies, when he was so green about the art of stand-up comedy. Jay wasn't just another struggling comedian who befriended Dave because they were both in the same boat; Jay was already a success. Jay made it to *The Tonight Show* in March of 1977, a year before Dave did. Jay had bookings at comedy clubs all over the country. Jay was an up-and-comer.

When they met, Jay was the top performer at the Comedy Store, the comedian all the other comics looked up to and wanted to be like. In the cutthroat world of entertainment, where there are thousands of candidates for each precious performing job, it's rare indeed to find a man like Jay, who was always willing to go out of his way to help a young comic. Jay recognized Dave's talent immediately, but he didn't see him as a threat; he saw him as someone he'd like to help succeed because he thought Dave had the talent to get to the top. And he saw David as a friend.

To this day, Dave's and Jay's comedy dovetails on occasion. Leno told *Playboy* writer Eric Pooley that they sometimes discover that they've told the same topical joke in their openings.

"David is David and I'm me. The problem is, we do have a similar sense of humor. We laugh at the same things. One night Dave and I did exactly the same joke in both our monologues: 'Next week is National Condom Week. Now there's a parade you don't want to miss.' Nobody stole it from anybody; it just happened."

Jay has a well-earned reputation of being a Good Guy,

so the fact that he befriended Dave when Letterman came to town is not so unusual; Jay basically made a pal out of everyone. What made their relationship special was that Jay and Dave saw talent in each other. They developed a mutual respect for one another when they met at the Comedy Store and that professional respect only deepened over the ensuing years. Whereas Jay liked the other comedians well enough and tried to help them all out, he didn't necessarily think they all had what it took to make it to the top. Dave did. In Dave, Jay saw a star in the making. And Dave saw another person, besides Johnny Carson, that he hoped to emulate.

When Dave launched *Late Night with David Letterman* in 1982, he didn't forget his old friend. He honestly felt— still feels to this day—that had it not been for Jay's guidance and Jay's influence, he would not have succeeded at stand-up. In other words, he wouldn't have the career he has today.

Dave invited Jay on his show early on, and Leno was an instant hit. David didn't just invite Leno on his show because he was a friend or to return a favor; Leno was one of the hottest comedians on the comedy club circuit. He was also a real boon for Dave because their friendship allowed them an easy banter during the interview portion of the show. Letterman was still somewhat uncomfortable with his interviewing skills; having Jay on made the show so easy. The virgin outing with Leno aboard was so successful that Leno became somewhat of a regular on the show, appearing every few months. All in all, he appeared on *Late Night* on more than forty occasions. Times were good for the old friends; both their careers were booming.

In 1987, *The Tonight Show* signed Jay as Johnny Carson's permanent guest host. The show had lost their guest host the year before, when Joan Rivers made the almost career-killing mistake of jumping ship to Fox-TV.

Though Johnny's permanent guest host was always thought to be a front-runner for the *Tonight Show* job when Carson retired, Letterman wasn't worried. Despite what he said in interviews about not wanting Johnny's job, he assumed the position would be offered to him when his good friend and mentor, Johnny Carson, chose to step down.

So it came as quite a shock to Dave when Jay was suddenly pulling *The Tonight Show* out from under his feet. Dave didn't blame Jay. Who in his right mind would turn down *The Tonight Show?* Business was business. It was a shame that the old friends were going to have to duke it out for the job, but it was nothing personal. It never was.

Some people point to the infrequency with which Dave and Jay see each other as proof positive that there are bitter feelings left from the so-called Late-Night Wars. Dave counters that he sees Jay now as frequently (or, more accurately, infrequently) as he's always seen his old friend. Though they consider themselves good friends, Dave and Jay never saw each other much after their early, bachelor days of hanging around the Comedy Store. First of all, they were living and working on separate coasts. Secondly, Dave rarely socializes with anyone. Thirdly, Jay had gotten married and spent most of his leisure time with his wife, Mavis.

Even when they were both living in L.A., they were never the kind of buddies who got together except in and around the comedy club.

Jay described his relationship with Dave to *Playboy* as a "professional friendship. We didn't hang out together. Dave's a jock, he likes to go to games and I don't. To me, the measure of it is whether you truly respect and like someone. David makes me laugh and was always very generous about letting me get laughs. He always let me do what it is that I do."

Jay and David's relationship survived the *Tonight Show* battle because it was never on the line in the first place.

"I was never mad at Jay," Dave told *New York Times* writer Bill Carter about eight months after losing *The Tonight Show.*

"I feel silly all of this became a sort of issue because to me it's just, everybody has problems with work. And you talk about them and you fight about them and hopefully you reach some sort of reconciliation."

Jay is philosophical about competing with his old buddy. After all, he's been competing with Dave ever since they met at the Comedy Store in 1975.

"I never worry too much about what the next guy is doing," he told writer Eric Pooley.

"When David and I and Freddie Prinze and Richard Pryor were all working the same club, if all the comics were good, then it was a good show. If we all were bad, then it stunk. It's the same now: If everybody on late-night television is good, then late-night television is good, then late-night becomes this innovative area where creative stuff is happening. It attracts attention and increases the total audience. And it makes everyone work harder to be that much funnier."

Neither man was ever angry with each other during the long drawn-out battle over *Tonight*. Both were angry with NBC.

Letterman was angry that he was never offered the job (until he threatened to leave the network and NBC made an eleventh-hour offer that would give him the job after Leno's contract expired in May 1994).

Leno was angry that, after he'd been given the job, the

network kept publicly second-guessing whether they'd made the right decision. For several months, while Letterman engaged in active negotiations with other networks, a panicked NBC refused to deny rumors that they were ready to boot Jay Leno off Carson's throne and crown Dave King of Late Night.

Jay tried to make light of it during his show (once, the phone on his desk rang. "CBS? Oh, hi, how nice of you . . . oh, you're looking for David?") but inside he was seething. NBC was now humiliating him the same way they had embarrassed Dave when they gave Jay the job.

Always the gentleman, Leno later said that he hadn't ever actually been lied to or deceived by NBC, but he did manage to get a dig in about their foot-dragging in letting him keep his job.

"Everyone acted honorably," he said. "A little indecisive."

Months later, Leno showed that he still considered Dave a pal when he backed his old buddy over his bosses regarding the fight for *Late Night*'s "intellectual property" like "Stupid Pet Tricks" and "The Top Ten List."

"It's Dave's bit," said Leno. "Let him do his bit."

Chapter Twenty
DAVE'S LAST LAUGH

David Letterman truly went through two years of hell, starting with the day Johnny Carson announced his retirement. Dave had already learned through his sources that it was a done deal that Jay Leno was going to get the job. To a performer as deeply insecure as Letterman, it confirmed his worst fears: The network he had toiled for for ten long years did not think he was good enough to replace Johnny Carson. He had begun to tire of doing the same old show at the ungodly hour of 12:30 A.M. The only thing that had kept him hanging on those last few years, tirelessly working to stay on top of his game and keep old stunts like "Stupid Pet Tricks" and "Stupid Human Tricks" fresh, was the light of *The Tonight Show* beckoning at the end of the tunnel. The day Jay got the job, Dave felt that all his hard work had been unappreciated and ignored.

If Dave had been cranky before, he became worse in those months following Carson's retirement and Jay's ascension. There were times during those dark days when he seriously considered leaving television entirely when his NBC contract ran out in April 1993. Even when Peter Lassally convinced him to hire Creative Artist Agency superagent Mike Ovitz and the offers—astounding offers—started pouring in, it did little to soothe the pain he felt over losing his childhood dream.

When, at the eleventh hour, he was offered *The Tonight Show,* it didn't really help Letterman's state of mind. In a way, it made the agony of the past eighteen months all the worse. Everyone he admired and respected was telling him not to take it, that booting his old pal Jay Leno—the man who had taught him so much when he was a struggling young comic from Indiana—would prove a death knell for his popularity.

He himself had a moral problem with taking the job from Jay. Dave was the guy who had stuck with his lawyer from Indiana and his manager from his youth. He only relented and signed on a Hollywood entertainment lawyer (Jake Bloom) and a Hollywood superagent (Creative Artist Agency honcho Mike Ovitz) when Peter Lassally told him it was his only hope of negotiating a good deal with NBC. His original agent, Jack Rollins, understood. Letterman had been such a gentleman all throughout dealings over the many years that he understood perfectly when Dave had to hire Mike Ovitz to represent him in his negotiations with NBC. They remain friends to this day, Rollins insisting that Dave hadn't replaced him with Ovitz; he decided to retire.

In a field where every day you read about old managers, publicists, and agents who crawl out of the woodwork to demand their share once a performer hits the big time, a long-standing, trouble-free relationship like the one Letterman enjoyed with Rollins is indeed rare. Dave is fiercely loyal. No matter how popular he gets, he will never become the type of star who ditches the people who helped him get where he is. You will never see Letterman embroiled in a battle with someone from his past whom Dave shafted.

No, Dave didn't want to have his dream at the expense of Jay's. Once he made the decision to give up *The Tonight*

Show forever, to forget his childhood fantasy once and for all, a calm came over him.

It was a relaxed and happier Dave those last few months at *Late Night,* more loose than anyone on the staff could ever remember seeing him. A great weight had been lifted from his shoulders. After having become restless with *Late Night* for so long, and then living under the tension of the *Tonight Show* debacle for almost two years, he was finally free to enjoy those last few months on the show. He was also energized at the idea of starting work on his new program. He couldn't wait for the new challenge of developing his 11:30 P.M. CBS show. Dave has always been a workaholic. Though he was nervous about how his humor would play at the earlier hour, to a much more mainstream crowd, he knew that he could do it. He knew that he could take the best of *Late Night*—the parts that made it special and worth staying up for—and drop the bits that wouldn't play to parents in Peoria.

He was also excited by the idea of having his show exposed to a new and bigger audience. He knew that moving up just that one hour earlier instantly doubled his audience. That prospect both terrified and thrilled him.

Of course, he was still living with his old terrors. What if he had talked himself into a $14-million-a-year fiasco? Dave is no Chevy Chase, a guy who can take a career fiasco like his Fox show in stride. When Chevy's 11:30 P.M. show was canceled after just a few weeks, he was disappointed but not devastated. He kept reminding interviewers that his contract called for him to be paid his $3 million whether the show was yanked or not. So Chevy effectively picked up a cool couple of million for a few months' work.

David Letterman can't look at things like that. His pride is on the line in every venture. His ego is at stake every night he walks onto his stage. Dave can't bear the thought of making a fool of himself, or looking like a "ninny" as he likes to say. He's one of those people who goes through life wondering what people are thinking about him and saying about him. More often than not, he's sure it's not good.

Dave takes everything personally, takes everything to heart. He's not the kind of guy who can say, "Hey, I tried it, it failed, and now I'm laughing all the way to the bank." Failing at the 11:30 P.M. hour, the slot he had fought so hard for, would be more of a public humiliation than he thought he could bear. He had convinced CBS that he had what it took to deliver a great show and a huge audience. He had promised them that; despite his distaste for it, he would go out on the campaign trail and promote the show to the network affiliates. After all that lobbying, he had gotten what he wanted—the 11:30 P.M. spot—and along with it an embarrassingly large salary. What if it all backfired and his show ended up becoming a huge financial drain on CBS? He could imagine the newspaper stories then: "Letterman: The $14-Million Loser." Or perhaps the headline would be "CBS: The $14-Million Loser." After all, they were the suckers who had agreed to shell out that obscene amount of money. This was all Mike Ovitz's fault. He played his smoke and mirrors game and convinced everyone that Dave was worth far more than he would deliver. It was going to be a disaster. More than that, this fiasco was going to be a career ender.

Dave wasn't being paranoid when he thought about the eyes of the nation being on him when he debuted his new show. His rivalry with Jay had been played out in the papers over the past eighteen months almost daily. For a man who abhorred publicity, the media frenzy had left him feeling exposed and mortified. For a private person like Dave to have his every statement and emotion trotted out on the front page and analyzed by every reporter and TV critic in the nation, the period had been pure agony. And now, here he was subjecting himself to more scrutiny. Unlike Chevy, he couldn't return to making movies. (Actually, he probably could have resurrected his Disney movie deal, but he would not have wanted to. His cameo appearance in *Cabin Boy* was a favor to buddy Chris Elliott.) In Dave's opinion, his entire career was riding on this new show, the one super-agent Mike Ovitz had somehow managed to convince people was going to be worth $14 million a year to the network, never mind the $14 million they had spent to renovate the Ed Sullivan Theater and the millions they paid in advertising the show in the weeks prior to its debut.

In a way, CBS made matters worse by running all the television ads they did in the weeks prior to the show. Rather than give Dave a calming sense that his network was behind him one hundred percent and was going to do everything in its power to help get him viewers, it made him even more panicky.

Dave wasn't overreacting when he later told Barbara Walters that the ads had begun to "sicken and embarrass" him. It was an unprecedented advertising campaign. CBS had Letterman film a record eighty ten- and twenty-second promotional spots. And the ads weren't run during obscure airtime. The first one debuted during the All-Star Game. Those expensive ads that ran incessantly in the weeks leading up to *Late Show*'s August 30 debut represented CBS's largest support of a single star or show.

Because they were written by his own staff, they were classic Dave. In one, Letterman stood in front of the CBS logo and said, "Don't you think that CBS Eye thing is kind of creepy?" In another, he tells viewers that his new show will have "colorful hand puppets and peppy musical numbers—oh, no, I'm thinking of the *CBS Evening News*." And another: "You know, if you remove the glass from your television set, you can feed me peanuts."

The funniest, however, was the one based on the Dave-bashing Letterman used to masochistically inflict on himself after the taping of every *Late Night* show. One of Dave's favorite lines, when evaluating the show, was a cynical "Well, it stuck to the videotape." So Dave's writers came up with one promo where Letterman confides to the audience that some of his previous shows have been so bad "they won't stick to the videotape. I don't have to tell you, then we're screwed."

"We all went into this with more than a little sense of dread," Letterman told *Los Angeles Times* reporter Rick Du Brow earlier this year. "I was worried about being embarrassed."

For Dave, that was a supreme understatement. He was worried about more than being embarrassed; he was concerned about being humiliated in front of the entire nation, about sinking his career in one monumentally foolish stroke.

He began to wonder what had possessed him to think that he, dorky David Letterman from hokey Indiana, had any business taking $14 million a year from CBS. He just prayed that CBS wouldn't soon be wondering the very same thing.

After much hype in the weeks before its debut, *Late Show* finally arrived on August 30, 1993.

Much to Dave's relief, it was an instant winner.

Dave set the tone that this was going to be a new, more sophisticated show by striding onto the stage in an expensive, well-cut tailored suit. (At *Late Night*, Dave was famous for his sports coats and khaki pants.) He wanted to establish right from the starting gate that he had worked hard to devise a new format for his new time slot.

This wasn't going to be *Late Night* on a new station at a new time. (Though many of his fans probably hoped that he wouldn't change a thing.)

The applause was thunderous, the audience filled with Letterman's most rabid fans. In a nice touch, Dave—always the people's candidate—had instructed his staff *NOT* to give away any tickets to his first show to CBS honchos. He wanted his fans to get a fair shake at the much-sought-after seats to this debut show.

Naturally, Dave walked onstage to a standing ovation. When the clapping finally died down, he began his monologue with some wonderful digs at his former network.

"This morning I woke up and next to me in bed is the head of a peacock."

And: "I checked with the CBS lawyers and they told me that, legally, I can still call myself 'Dave,' " a reference to the claim NBC made to *Late Night* comedy staples like "Stupid Pet Tricks."

Then *NBC Nightly News* anchor Tom Brokaw dashed onto the stage and seized two of Letterman's cue cards.

"These are the intellectual property of NBC," he said somberly.

"I never thought I'd hear the words 'intellectual property' and 'NBC' in the same sentence," Letterman quipped.

Fans had been reading for months that NBC was going to prohibit Letterman from taking *Late Night* trademarks like "Stupid Pet Tricks," "Stupid Human Tricks," and "The Top Ten List" to his new show. Letterman didn't really want the first two anyway, but he was damned if he was going to let them steal his Top Ten list, one of the most popular bits of the show.

NBC, looking like a bad sport, insisted that it would sue CBS if they dared to use any of those segments.

After settling behind the desk at his new digs, David made a big production of announcing that there would, in fact, be a *"Late Show* Top Ten," again to thunderous applause. As he prepared to read the list, Letterman confided to the audience, "This is going to cost CBS."

There was a surprise appearance by Paul Newman, who stood up in the audience and shouted, "Where the hell are the singing cats?" pretending that he really had intended to go see the long-running hit musical *Cats,* which occupied the theater across the street.

Since Bill Murray had been Dave's first guest on his first *Late Night* show, he invited the comedian back to christen his new *Late Show.* Murray acted as manic as he had eleven years earlier, at one point taking out a can of black spray paint and writing "Dave" on Letterman's desk.

It wasn't the funniest show Dave had ever put on, but it showed promise. Dave had managed to assure his old fans that lots would be the same, while promising new viewers that they were entering a new era of late-night television.

He's kept his word. He's retained all the hyperactive, interactive wackiness for which *Late Night* was famous. Maybe he can't send his cameras over to Meg-at-the-book-publishing-company anymore, but he finds new people to play with every day. One evening, he picked up his *Late Show* phone and dialed the telephone booth near the Ed Sullivan Theater, just to see who would answer. Tracy from Arizona picked up the phone and she wasn't in a very fine mood; she had waited three hours for a standby *Late Show* ticket, only to be turned away. Bingo! Dave invited her to come on in and take a seat on the stage.

He regularly invokes the memory of Ed Sullivan, going bug-eyed as he conjures up the spirit of the late, great, variety-show host.

He defiantly kept on reading his Top Ten list, and only—to avoid a lawsuit with NBC—changed the title to *"Late Show* Top Ten." And he's doing new twists with the list, one of the most popular segments of the show.

On *Late Night,* Dave simply read each item as it appeared typed on screen and checked them off one by one. Now, he's gotten more creative with the Top Ten. One night, he announced that viewers were going to be treated to "The Top Ten Nicknames Cabbies Give Passengers." Then he cut to a videotape in which cabs rolled out, one by one, with their favorite names for passengers written, graffiti-like, on the hoods of their cars.

Another night he took advantage of his guest, deep-voiced James Earl Jones, by having the actor read the "Top Ten Words That Sound Better When Pronounced by James Earl Jones."

He's had musical groups and guests like Tony Bennett sing the Top Ten.

One Top Ten list revealed names for the new show that had been rejected, like *Paul Shaffer and Butt-head.* Letterman enjoys doing his Beavis and Butt-head imitation on the new show almost as much as he liked saying, "Buttafuoco."

Because he couldn't take the actor Calvert DeForest's popular character Larry "Bud" Melman to the new show (part of NBC's, ahem, "intellectual property"), he has created zany new characters for us to love, like Donnie, the CBS Page Who Likes to Suck Up.

"The show is so fun and wonderful and that doesn't even describe it," fawned Donnie the Suck Up.

"I would say, 'funderful' really. The show is funderful. You, David Letterman, are funderful."

Audiences and celebrities alike seem eager to support Dave in his new venture. When Jay Leno first took over *The Tonight Show,* there were a lot of ugly behind-the-scenes battles for guests because his pitbull manager, Helen Kushnick, was using all kinds of pressure tactics to prevent major stars from appearing on any other talk show before they made a guest appearance with Jay. Now that Helen has been relieved of her duties (at NBC's directive), all that back-stabbing has come to an amicable end and Dave seems to be the winner. Since *Late Show* is garnering the highest ratings, guests are breaking down Dave's door to get on his show. Letterman has had no trouble attracting major leaguers like Tom Hanks, Jeremy Irons, Diane Sawyer, and Demi Moore, though he's yet to hook his fantasy guest, Johnny Carson.

The big stars aren't just appearing on David's show as guests, they're popping up in his wacky, pretaped skits.

Perhaps because deeply private Dave had relented and appeared on two of her specials, Barbara Walters agreed to be in a post-Oscar tape that was hilarious.

When Paul Shaffer asked Dave if he had watched the Oscars, he said that he'd had the privilege of attending a small Oscar-watching party that Barbara Walters had tossed in her Manhattan apartment.

That was funny enough, knowing how David abhors parties, but the tape was priceless. It began with Dave and Barbara on the couch, surrounded by about a dozen guests, watching Barbara's annual pre-Oscar interview show. There they sat, glomming down junk food like buckets of fried chicken and Big Macs as they watched Barbara interview Steven Spielberg, Elton John, and Meg Ryan. When an early TV clip of Meg Ryan crying on a soap opera appeared, the camera cut over to Dave, who was weeping uncontrollably. By the end of the Oscar telecast, Dave was asleep on Barbara's shoulders.

Dave has always liked ribbing Regis Philbin of *Live with Regis and Kathie Lee* and Philbin has become somewhat of a regular on Dave's new show, popping in with baskets of gift prizes for the audience.

Letterman then returned the favor, popping in unannounced one morning to Regis and Kathie Lee's live show.

"Sorry to interrupt this rehearsal," said Letterman. He then gave Regis a half-eaten sandwich that he said he found in a cab and presented Kathie Lee with a wilted bouquet of flowers.

"How are the twins?" he asked Kathie Lee, who never seems to stop talking about her two children (whom everyone knows are not twins).

He insisted on helping them out with their trivia contest, telling the confused contestant: "The answer is Glenn Close. Enjoy the luggage."

Finally, he handed out 8 X 10 glossies of his mother Dorothy, who made such a name for herself at the 1994 Winter Olympics.

Viewers needn't have worried that the earlier time slot would force Letterman into becoming a humorless talking head.

If anything, Dave has added more high jinks to his new show, because the Broadway district is eminently more colorful than Rockefeller Center. He's made dashing out of the studio to visit his *Late Show* neighbors a regular occurrence, establishing wacky friendships with people like Mujibar, who runs a tacky souvenir shop, and Fern, who works at the copy store.

Mujibar and his partner have been such a hit with audiences that they've appeared in *People* magazine. The two of them are always trying to crowd each other out of the picture as Dave wanders around their store, buying things like Empire State Building paperweights and Lady Liberty crowns.

Fern the copy woman has become a minor celebrity, too. Dave gets her to xerox various body parts and send the results to the show.

Dave doesn't just pester the local shopkeepers; he's barged in on a Broadway show or two also. One day he made a surprise visit to the cast of *Cats,* which plays right across the street from Dave's home at the Ed Sullivan Theater.

He's also updated the childish pranks everyone grew to love on *Late Night.* Instead of dropping beach balls and watermelons out of windows and mowing down Energizer Bunnies and Smurfs with steamrollers, he goes to nearby 53rd Street on a semi-regular basis and tries to knock things down with bowling balls. He's even gotten bowling champ Don Webber, a PBA Hall of Famer, to bowl in midtown with him.

He scored a major guest coup when he got Vice President Al Gore on the show, even though he'd tried to get Hillary Clinton. Gore, who has a reputation for being stiff, was surprisingly relaxed and funny on the show. He was a good sport about being the butt of the Top Ten, which included an item about "Buttafuoco" being Gore's Secret Service code name.

Dave has often said that all he asks of his guests is that they have a good story or three to tell, and Al Gore came prepared. He told Dave all about his personal political buga-boo—government waste—and brought along a visual to explain what he was talking about. He said that there was a rule that ashtrays that the government was considering purchasing had to pass the smash test: When hammered, they had to shatter into no more or less than a certain number of pieces. To demonstrate, he brought out an ashtray and goggles and, after making sure Dave was fitted with protective goggles as well, he proceeded to hammer a nail into the test ashtray. The audience loved it.

Political figures have been good for Dave in his new show.

He had a whole week of fun after Rudolph Giuliani was sworn in as New York City mayor in January 1994. During the swearing-in ceremony, former prosecutor Giuliani—who had run on a campaign of getting tough on crime—was unable to reign in his own chubby seven-year-old son, Andrew, who read the oath along with him, waved to the audience, leaned on his father, held up his fist in a sign of power, and generally made a pest of himself during the proceedings. Dave tried to get Andrew on *Late Show* but Giuliani and his wife, broadcaster Donna Hanover, declined. But just as Gore had subbed for Hillary, the mayor himself agreed to sit in for his son. He laughed good-naturedly as Dave made him sit through a videotape of Andrew's antics. For days afterward, a child actor who looked like Andrew would occasionally pop up behind Dave's fake window, flailing his arms for attention.

Dave was particularly pleased that he did so well with his political guests on his new show. In the early days of hosting *Late Night,* he tried having serious political figures on, and the shows bombed. Dave, naturally, took full responsibility, blaming his poor interviewing skills and ignorance of politics.

Having had disastrous shows with Bill Bradley and Daniel Patrick Moynihan showed Dave that, while such figures have a place on television, "we proved pretty certainly it was not with me."

Though he tried to get Hillary on the show when she was in New York City on business, he probably isn't eager to have her husband on the show. When Clinton was running for president, Dave told a reporter, off the record, that he didn't think philandering Bill stood a chance. Now, Dave says he's scared that Clinton is going to exact his revenge.

"I just know something terrible is going to happen, like the IRS is going to come after me," he joked.

These days, a newer, more confident Letterman was equally at ease with the vice president and New York City's mayor as he is with the national grocery sacking champion.

Dave has come a long way. And he's got the number one ratings now to prove it.

"When we premiered, David saw the crown was up for grabs and went for it," *Late Show* producer Robert Morton told *Los Angeles Times* reporter Rick Du Brow.

"NBC didn't realize that David Letterman was a franchise player. I think Jay Leno is very good but not a franchise. NBC did not think David could play at 11:30 and they misjudged it."

What an understatement. NBC has lost the domination of the 11:30 P.M. hour that they enjoyed throughout Carson's thirty years hosting *The Tonight Show,* and it's not likely they'll recover it any time soon. (Unless they can find a way of stealing Dave back.)

Dave has also kept an important promise he made to himself when he launched *Late Show.* He's managed to tame the worst of his sometimes wicked tongue without losing his edge. A master at rebuttal, he never misses an opportunity for a funny rejoinder or sarcastic zinger. But he no longer goes for the jugular.

"He's really toned down," says a former staffer. "I've seen people come on and say things, really dumb things, and I'm just waiting for him to drive a truck through them, and all he says is, 'Well, good.' "

The man he replaced way back in 1982 also has kind words for Letterman.

"He's reinvented himself," observes Tom Snyder. "He had the reputation, earned or unearned, of being mean-spirited on the old show. Now he is at ease with himself. Whatever demons he had at NBC have vanished, and he is totally in command. He displays a confidence on TV that I find awesome."

Ironically, Tom Snyder is now the lead contender for the 12:30 A.M. show that Letterman's CBS contract allows him to develop.

Letterman's executive producer Peter Lassally told reporter Rick Du Brow that Dave was determined not to do the same show he did on NBC.

"I think David has done a remarkable job," said Lassally.

"I know the obvious things to see are that he wears suits and nice clothes. But his whole attitude is completely different. He's warmer and friendlier and has more energy than ever before. He used to have the tag on him of being mean-spirited, and that tag has been destroyed."

Lassally says the kinder, gentler Dave we see on CBS is intentional on Letterman's part.

"Peter is exactly right," Letterman told Du Brow.

"And the only thing I can liken it to is, you meet a girl and you fall in love with her and now it's time to meet her parents and you want to make absolutely sure you make the best impression possible on these people.

"I think that was the kind of pressure I felt going from 12:30 to 11:30—new people you want to make an impression on. I know what my limitations are. I know the kind of mistakes I can make. And I just wanted to make absolutely certain that I could sidestep them."

One of the mistakes he wanted to avoid was being mean to guests—or giving the impression that he was mean to guests. Actually, it's a reputation Letterman has always felt was undeserved. It was mainly his inexperience as an interviewer, he's often said, that used to get him into trouble. If a guest wasn't saying much of anything, he'd get nervous and edgy. So he'd fall back on Old Reliable—his astonishing, but sometimes cruel, wit. Often that meant getting a laugh at the expense of his hapless guest.

There are sure to be viewers who will miss the old, sharp-tongued Dave. A lot of people tuned in to *Late Night* expressly because of Dave's reputation for making mincemeat out of the celebrities that every other talk-show host fawned over.

But it seems people like the new Dave. He raced past Jay Leno in those early weeks of competition—when a lot of critics dismissively attributed his ratings to the curiosity factor—and has never looked back. Dave kept his promise and, though he despised it, went out on the road and hawked his new show to CBS affiliates across the country. His labors paid off: *Late Show with David Letterman,* which started out airing in just sixty-five percent of the country, has picked up so many affiliates that it is now airing in eighty-three percent of the country. (Though he's yet to crack that old bugaboo Sioux City, Iowa. Ironically, the city that Letterman laughingly refers to as *Late Show's* "home base" for the Top Ten list is the only major city in the U.S. that does not carry the *Late Show.* Sadly for Sioux City, CBS has given up trying to woo them.)

"We're no longer auditioning in that market," says Tony Malara, president of affiliate relations at CBS.

Though *The Tonight Show* is carried in ninety-nine percent of the country, affable Jay Leno has been unable to touch Letterman's numbers. At press time, Letterman was drawing nineteen percent of available viewers to Leno's thirteen percent. *Nightline* has remained steady throughout the Late-Night Wars; it grabs fifteen percent of the 11:30 P.M. audience.

CBS is, of course, thrilled with its late-night star. It's the first time CBS has had a winner in that time slot. Letterman is earning every penny of his $14 million annual salary, having boosted CBS's earnings a whopping thirty-nine percent for the fourth quarter of 1993, compared with the same time period the year before.

The *Late Show* is delivering an unbelievable eighty-seven percent increase over the days prior to *Late Show* when CBS was running action movies in that time slot.

Though CBS obviously had far more faith in Dave's drawing power than NBC ever did, Letterman exceeded even their expectations: They told affiliates and advertisers before *Late Show* debuted that they could guarantee that Dave would deliver a 4 rating. (A ratings point is equal to 942,000 homes.) Instead, Dave is averaging a 5.9 rating, over 5.5 million viewing homes.

Letterman is loving every minute of it. For the first time in his life, he's not questioning his every move. He's faced the most important dilemma of his life—taking *The Tonight Show* away from Jay Leno or giving up his dream and going after a new one—and he made the right choice. For once,

David Letterman has no need to second-guess his decisions. Even a man as insecure as Dave has to admit that he made the right move. How could he not, with his unbelievable success staring him in the face.

The best part of David Letterman is that he'll never let this success go to his head. He's allowed it to bring out the best in him, to make him a happier, more relaxed individual. But his innate modesty and Midwestern lack of pretension will remain with him always, no matter how hot he gets. He isn't smug about proving NBC wrong. He's not going on interviews and rubbing their nose in one of their biggest financial mistakes. When asked about *Late Show's* phenomenal success, he's vintage Dave. He never expounds on his talents, but continues to express genuine surprise and delight that so many people like him. He's as nervous as ever that it could all change tomorrow, and works just as compulsively and maniacally to make sure he puts on the best show possible each and every day. But he's also allowing himself, for the first time in his life, to stop and smell the roses.

The man who rarely took a vacation popped over to Italy on his first *Late Show* break, and he couldn't say enough about things Italian on the air when he got back. Dave is finally stopping to reap the rewards of his success. You get the feeling there will be more trips in the future, a major breakthrough for a workaholic like Dave.

His happiness shows on the air, and it's contagious. It's probably yet another reason for his astonishing ratings. Whereas the old *Late Night* Dave was frequently grumpy, the Letterman that's been rejuvenated on CBS seems, finally, as pleased with his shows as his audience is.

"We've been sort of giddy ever since we went on the air," he told Du Brow.

"We just couldn't believe that all of a sudden, people were looking at this little nickel-and-dime thing that we've been doing for years and were, by and large, pleased with it. It's the most rewarding thing I've ever encountered in my life.

"It's like the underdog team that gets into the World Series and takes the first three games and you think, 'Man, we've got a shot at this thing,' and then the rest of the series they're playing over their head."

With *Late Show*, Letterman has hit the winning home run in the World Series of late-night television. And no one is more surprised than Dave.

So, as Dave used to like to say on *Late Night:* Can you feel the electricity in the air? Can you feel the excitement? Strap yourselves in. Phone the neighbors. Wake the dog and give it a beer. Because Dave's new *Late Show* is more fun than humans should be allowed to have!

Rosemarie Lennon is a reporter at *Star* magazine. Prior to her work at *Star,* she was an editor at *New Woman* magazine and *Woman* magazine. She lives in New York City.

FUN AND LOVE!

THE DUMBEST DUMB BLONDE JOKE BOOK (889, $4.50)
by Joey West
They say that blondes have more fun . . . but we can all have a hoot
with THE DUMBEST DUMB BLONDE JOKE BOOK. Here's a
hilarious collection of hundreds of dumb blonde jokes—including
dumb blonde GUY jokes—that are certain to send you over the
edge!

THE I HATE MADONNA JOKE BOOK (798, $4.50)
by Joey West
She's Hollywood's most controversial star. Her raunchy reputation's brought her fame and fortune. Now here is a sensational collection of hilarious material on America's most talked about
MATERIAL GIRL!

LOVE'S LITTLE INSTRUCTION BOOK (774, $4.99)
by Annie Pigeon
Filled from cover to cover with romantic hints—one for every day
of the year—this delightful book will liven up your life and make
you and your lover smile. Discover these amusing tips for making
your lover happy . . . tips like—ask her mother to dance—have his
car washed—take turns being irrational . . . and many, many
more!

MOM'S LITTLE INSTRUCTION BOOK (0009, $4.99)
by Annie Pigeon
Mom needs as much help as she can get, what with chaotic schedules, wedding fiascos, Barneymania and all. Now, here comes the
best mother's helper yet. Filled with funny comforting advice for
moms of all ages. What better way to show mother how very much
you love her by giving her a gift guaranteed to make her smile
everyday of the year.

*Available wherever paperbacks are sold, or order direct from the
Publisher. Send cover price plus 50¢ per copy for mailing and handling to Penguin USA, P.O. Box 999, c/o Dept. 17109, Bergen-
field, NJ 07621. Residents of New York and Tennessee must
include sales tax. DO NOT SEND CASH.*